THE
SPIRIT OF BRITAIN

THE
SPIRIT OF BRITAIN

AN ILLUSTRATED GUIDE TO LITERARY BRITAIN

EDITED AND INTRODUCED BY
SUSAN HILL

RESEARCHED AND COMPILED BY
PIERS DUDGEON

HEADLINE

First published in Great Britain in 1994 by
HEADLINE BOOK PUBLISHING

British Library Cataloguing in Publication Data
Dudgeon, Piers
  Spirit of Britain: Illustrated Guide to
  Literary Britain
  I. Title   II. Hill, Susan
941.00321

ISBN: 0–7472–1185–X

Typeset by J&L Composition, Filey, North Yorkshire
Printed by Tien Wah Press (PTE.) Limited, Singapore

HEADLINE BOOK PUBLISHING
A division of Hodder Headline PLC
338 Euston Road
London NW1 3BH

CONTENTS

INTRODUCTION

The sense of place has been of passionate importance to British writers, novelists and poets, autobiographers and chroniclers; place – a landscape – a country – a region – a village, town or city is often, to the imaginative and creative writer, far more than the sum of its physical parts, more than simply – though simple is not, perhaps, the word – a setting and backdrop to a story, the object of description.

Landscape, the physical place in which a writer is born, lives and works or even on occasions merely visits, is an inspiration, a mood, an atmosphere and even a character, but above all an influence. Where people are born and those scenes among which they pass the bulk of their lives, unless they are entirely anonymous (new towns, featureless outer suburbs) have always affected them profoundly, influenced behaviour, mood, outlook, prospects; it has always been so and always in the past been *more* so. When most people worked physically, with their bodies rather than their wits, they were literally shaped by their jobs and those jobs were an organic part of the places in which they lived: agricultural labour differed greatly even within the confines of a particular place: in Thomas Hardy's novels the daily life and work of the furze cutter on bleak, brooding Egdon Heath was very different from that of the dairy maid Tess of the D'Urbervilles in the lush sheltered vale, the business of a corn merchant not at all the same as that of a sheep shearer or a reddleman. Mountains, the sea, windswept bare flatlands, rivers and moors, fens and lakes and lochs, or slagheaps, roaring furnaces, printing works, cotton mills, blacking the factories and counting houses all had their own character and all exerted a particular influence and shaped and formed men and women and their lives, all breathed their own spirit which affected writers deeply in themselves as well as those characters about whom they wrote. They have always tried to convey places, not only in every nuance of weather, light and season but by trying to capture in words that indefinable, intangible spirit which is composed of a thousand minute fragments, sights and sounds and scents. But more, the effect of certain places is quite extraordinarily powerful and can be not only moodaltering but lifechanging. Places can calm or inspire, excite, move, oppress, even terrify: they may provoke an almost religious response, of awe, wonder and gratitude, a profound sense of humility: or they may simply delight and instill a refreshing sense of carefree joy, liberating and empowering. They may provoke thoughts of doom and claustrophobia, fear, so that every step taken is made in trepidation, and a glance over the shoulder is instinctive and self-protective. The same places may inspire different moods and thoughts in a short space of time in the same writer. The diarist, Francis Kilvert, describing an autumn day looking out over the mountains can write 'the sky a cloudless deep wonderful blue and the mountains so light blue as to be almost white. The slight mist of an early autumn afternoon hanging over the gorgeous landscape.' On another September day he sees the countryside as something a little more imposing. 'As I sit writing in my bedroom and looking from the window at the glorious morning spread upon the mountains the Wye valley is filled full of mist from side to side. Out of the great white fog sea rises an island ridge of trees above Wye cliff and one great solitary fir stands up alone like an isolated rock and stems the tide of the rolling mist. The sun has risen cloudless and the fog sea gleams brilliant and dazzling, and shining like silver.' But on a June day he climbs Cader Idris. And what he sees and feels are very differently described. 'Cader Idris is the stoniest, dreariest, most desolate mountain I was ever on. We came now to the edge of a vast gulf or chasm or basin almost entirely surrounded by black precipices rising from the waters of a small black tarn which lay in the bottom of the basin. Then we stumbled and struggled on again over rough tracts and wildernesses of slate and basalt. The sun was shining on the hills below, but the mist crawled down and wrapped us as if in a shroud blotting out everything. The mists and clouds began to sweep by us in white thin ghostly sheets as if some great dread Presences and Powers were going past and we could only see the skirts of their white garments.'

If it pleases, delights and satisfies us to revel in the emotional, spiritual, imaginative and even physical reactions to a sense of place and its atmosphere and spirit, we want to immerse ourselves in them in all their variety repeatedly, visiting real landscapes to be overawed or entertained, interested and refreshed. For climbing the fells or looking out over a great dark brooding loch, taking a coracle out at dawn onto the watery fens, striding out across the flat, open, deserted beaches or exploring the nooks, crannies and crevices

The Blackmore Vale of Thomas Hardy's Tess of the D'Urbervilles.

of the old parts of cities where the past presses in upon us and crowds the brain for all these activities there is no substitute. Absorbing a sense of place, a landscape, a city, through the imaginative literature is a quite other activity and not a second best. Sitting in an armchair we are transported to places and move among characters, experience a wide variety of events and emotions but they are both real and not real. They bear a close relationship to actual places and yet at the same time are landscapes of the mind, invented, endowed with a spirit that does not actually exist, is a fantasy, a chimera, yet as powerful (more so perhaps) as those everyday 'real things' of life.

We see a place through the writer's eyes and it is their place and that of their work and becomes ours for the moment only: another writer will capture the physical aspects of the landscape in a quite different way according to his purpose and outlook, circumstances of the time and necessities of the narrative. London is London is London. London has always been London. But Dickens' London, fog up the river, fog down the river, allies, law courts, railways, debtors' prisons, is not the London of John Betjeman, leafy, middleclass, prosperous Edwardian suburbs, high and handsome. Or the smart neonlit Mayfair of Evelyn Waugh. Beatrix Potter's Mrs Tiggywinkle Lake District of the pretty whitewashed hilltop farmhouse and summer sunshine is not the mighty, holy, brooding and character forming Lake District of Wordsworth's impressionable boyhood.

Writers have often described vividly not merely the scenes of childhood but the impact that those places made upon their early sensitivities, particularly when they spent those years in dramatic, strange and haunting landscapes. Indeed, many impressionable artists have seemed to be more passionately attached to the places of their childhood than to the people, feeling them perhaps to be ultimately more reliable, and unchanging, less fickle and untrustworthy. At least until the years since the Second World War most scenes of childhood could indeed be revisited and recognised, often in every detail: and although the farming landscape of Britain has changed out of all recognition since the war and many towns and cities are quite altered, wilder places, the Scottish Highlands, Exmoor, the Welsh mountains, are still remarkably unchanged.

In *Farewell Happy Fields*, the poet Kathleen Raine's autobiography, she puts into contemporary prose the same emotions and ideas about childhood and landscape so famously expressed by Wordsworth in verse two hundred years previously.

Places have their identity, as flowers or creatures have, their soul or *genius loci*. A place in nature is, after all, only a larger and more complex organism, a symbiosis of many lives. All inviolate places have this wholeness of essence; their perfection lies in their remaining intact, undisturbed by the intrusion of any life which does not itself participate in that harmonious organic unity.

She explains too the sense of inner soul in place to which children and mystics instinctively respond with their whole being.

Perhaps those called nature mystics simply retain longer than others our normal consciousness, our birthright, lost sooner or later, or returning only rarely. Or is it we who return only rarely, and lose Eden by a living away, a refusal to look, our separate identity grows over us like a skin or shroud.

Some places seem particularly to bring out this child-mystic in writers, to call forth a response time and again: that is certainly true of the Welsh border country, the spirit of which so breathed through the work of the diarist Francis Kilvert, the poets Henry Vaughan and Thomas Traherne and the contemporary novelist Bruce Chatwin. In his autobiography, *Landscape with Machines* the chronicler of railways, canals and engineers, L T C Rolt vividly and movingly evokes the spirit of this border country which spoke to him as a small child with a voice he never forgot for the rest of his life.

If ever it is vouchsafed to man to see visions, then it would be in such a place as this valley whose very air seemed to a child to be numinous and charged with magic. No building in Britain has so majestical a setting as Llanthony Abbey. The valley hereabouts is at its widest and most luxuriant. Like some gigantic outflung lion's paw, the high, bracken-furred war of Hatterall Hill encloses its richness in a majestic protective arc terminating in a steep fall. Its slopes were thickly sown with sheep and in that breathless summer stillness the sound of their distant bleating mingled with the singing of birds in the valley below. Everything seemed to conspire to charm my five senses. Nor was this first childish impression in any way delusive. For since this first ever memorable visit I have returned to the Vale of Ewyas countless times at all stages of my life and have seen it in every kind of weather and seasonal mood. Yet is beauty has never failed to equal my expectation; in fact and in recollection it was to prove an unfailing source of spiritual solace to me from that day to this.

But childhood was not always, or perhaps even very often, an idyll, spent in some other Eden; many write evocatively but bitterly in adult life of the oppression of poverty lived out in grim city streets, the coalmining areas of Northumberland where Catherine Cookson

Hazler Hill from Long Mynd, border country between England and Wales: 'Eternity was manifest in the Light of the Day,' wrote Thomas Traherne.

was born, or Dickens' terrible, dark London. Misery and the desperation to escape, the stifling of hope, physical hardship and illness, hunger and claustro-phobia, all scarred many who were imprisoned and who lived out anonymous lives until some genius struggled out and away and then later, spoke for them, remembering and describing, trying to convey the spirit of hell to those outside.

But readers identify with the places an author makes their own, as closely as with their characters often more so, they long not just to visit and see but to live in those landscapes and so they do visit and are sometimes disappointed. For those are so much more than simply outward physical places, viewable, encompassable. Thomas Hardy's Dorset, the Brontës' Yorkshire, Dickens' London have in any case all but vanished now and we are left not with the real setting for George Eliot's *Middlemarch* (also gone and never an especially interesting part of the country in any case) but with another quite different town taken over as a film location for a television dramatisation of the novel and trailed around by those somehow longing to capture the flavour of the fiction at several removes.

But we should not suppose that this is a contemporary phenomenon. It was not very long after the death of the Brontës that complaints were being made about the tourists who were flocking to and spoiling their North Yorkshire village of Haworth. And when Scott chose to set a novel in a particular place and try to capture its spirit on the page, it had the effect of drawing the hoards of admirers to it almost immediately.

He wrote 'The Lady of the Lake' and next year a thousand tourists descended on the Trossachs, watched the sun setting on Loch Katrine and began to take lessons on the bagpipe. Where his muse was one year, a mailcoach and a hotel were the next.

Yet the desire to find those landscapes of a great writer's imagination and once there to be affected by their unique spirit is a universal and understandable one: when we are immersed in a great novel, fired by the evocations of a great poet, we want to get under the skin of the work, somehow walk about within the books, among those people and breathe the air of some magical 'real, unreal' place.

But there are plenty of writers who have no high-flown purpose when choosing settings for their books. They are excited by places because of their atmo-

sphere, something which, as a backdrop, lends a vital dimension to the action of the story in the light of its characters and chimes in well with the book's mood.

I was in a wide semicircle of moorland, with the brown river as radius and the high hills forming the outer circumference. There was not a sign or sound of a human being, only the plashing water and the interminable crying of curlews. Yet, oddly enough, for the first time I felt the terror of the hunted on me.

So writes John Buchan whose novels are steeped in the spirit, atmosphere and intimate local knowledge of the Scottish uplands and the Border country, which he uses as impressive and exciting backgrounds to hunting the hunting, that is, of a man on the run by other men.

The isolated human being, often running in fear of his life, or else in dangerous pursuit of another, is a constant theme of Buchan's, as indeed it is of many a British adventure novelist from Conan Doyle to Graham Greene. Who can ever set foot upon Dartmoor, especially in grim and forbidding weather without thought of the monstrous Hound of the Baskervilles? And Conan Doyle's bleak, wild Devon could as well be Buchan's Scotland.

Over the wide expanse there was no sound and no movement. One great grey bird, a gull or curlew, soared aloft in the blue heaven. He and I seemed to be the only living things between the huge arch of the sky and the desert beneath it. The barren scene, the sense of loneliness and the mystery and urgency of my task all struck a chill into my heart.

Just so does young Mary Yellan feel on crossing Bodmin moor on her way to Jamaica Inn and it is weather which adds its own spirit to Daphne du Maurier's dramatic conjuring up of that godforsaken place.

It was a cold grey day in late November. The weather had changed overnight, when a backing wind brought a granite sky and a mizzling rain with it and although it was now only a little after two o'clock in the afternoon the pallor of a winter evening seemed to have closed upon the hills, cloaking them in mist it would be dark by four.

It is weather which plays such an essential part in the

creation of the atmosphere of the British landscape: weather is as much a character, a presence and a factor of influence upon men as any physical feature, any mountain or moor, lake or river or cliff.

Fine weather makes a scene glorious and the heart high, induces optimism and the sense of physical ease: the play of light on water, the way a warm spring breeze chases small clouds or ripples over ripening corn, and clear air makes distant uplands change colour to soft lavender and so become 'the blue remembered hills', the whole tone and mood of a novel or a poem or a piece of autobiographical prose is lifted and the reader's mood enhanced by descriptions of the countryside in such weathers. And these are by no means necessarily in spring and summertime as Hettie Sorrel, heroine of George Eliot's novel *Adam Bede*, discovered.

Bright February days have a stronger charm of hope about them than any other days in the year. One likes to pause in the mild rays of the sun and look over the gates at the patient plough horses turning at the end of the furrow and think that the beautiful year is all before one. The birds seem to feel just the same: their notes are as clear as the clear air. There are no leaves on the trees and hedgerows, but how green all the grassy fields are! And the dark purplish brown of the ploughed earth and the bare branches is beautiful too. What a glad world this looks like, as one drives or rides along the valleys and over the hills.

It is not difficult for the British writer to be inspired by the combination of place and weather: certain types of scenery allied to the moody, changeable climate of these islands are a gift to the novelist and poet and seductive too, a temptation and a hazard as well as an opportunity for there is always the risk of bathos, always the possibility of over using the Pathetic Fallacy and so taking the easy way out and falling a prey to sentimentality and to the cliché.

The landscape of Britain bears the imprint of the past upon itself: past human lives, past battles won or lost, great tragedies, small defeats, individual moments of glory. The dead are ever present, to Thomas Hardy, to Kilvert, and also the Welsh poet, R S Thomas.

You cannot live in the present.
At least not in Wales.

Barrows and burial grounds, ancient Celtic crosses and stone cairns, derelict chapels, the visible tongues of rock carved by the ice of an age millions of years ago, all are visible still, tangible evidence of the lives of the millions of long dead still seething all around in spirit, clamouring silently to be remembered, recorded.

Casterbridge announced old Rome in every street, alley and precinct. It looked Roman, bespoke the art of Rome, concealed dead men of Rome. It was impossible to dig more than a foot or two deep about the town fields and gardens without coming upon some tall soldier or other of the Empire, who had lain there in his silent unobtrusive rest for a space of fifteen hundred years.

The still air inside churches traps the ghosts of centuries, of past prayers, past petitions, and the echo of the voices of ordinary priests and people reciting the office and the services of the Prayer Book, or singing the old familiar hymns presses in upon the visitor in the silence. And it is hard to imagine what kind of person would fail to sense the eerie presence of dead clansmen in the dreadful atmosphere of Glencoe, or see the ghostly armies marching across the Midlands' battlefields of Edghill or Bosworth Field. For places in Britain, wild and isolated as they may be, are never far from people and the marks they left upon them, for good and ill, changed this or that, in one way or another, forever, and writers have been aware of and recorded this. We are too small for their to be places scarcely touched by men, everywhere may be, has been encompassed, some would say violated.

Each individual region, each country and county and every small local area within that county, has its own particular atmosphere and attributes, differing in many subtle ways from the one next door: the spirit of a place is composed of innumerable elements within the physical contours of the land itself, and its individual characteristics: whether for example there is water and of what kind, and how important it is within the landscape. The land makes small variations in weather, landscape and climate together help to mould the character of the people. It is endlessly fascinating to try and discern all these differences, the British Isles delight and interest, amaze and absorb one in themselves and through literature (and through other arts, notably painting too) and what has been lost in reality can to some extent at least be reinvoked and recaptured through art. To read the work of novelists and poets, diarists and records, whose sense of the spirit of place is very strong, is to be drawn into strange, magical realms, both of the past and of the mind, transmuted by the creative imagination yet still rooted in reality. When we immerse ourselves in them, as well as being aware of character and story we sense that other presence, breathe it in as we read and so come in some measure to understand and to know it, if only vicariously. It is an elusive thing, like a faint scent which, when aggressively and purposefully sought out, evades, vanishes, can never be traced to its source. It has to be come upon, as it were, sideways and be known only indirectly. Where is Wordsworth's Lake District? Where is Hardy's Dorset? Dickens' London? Is the Cornwall of Daphne du Maurier's *Rebecca* and *Jamaica Inn* that same Cornwall of John Betjeman's autobiography? Or Charles Causley's poems? Are these places merely between the pages of their books? And it is not only writers who have sought to capture the spirit of place; composers have frequently attempted to express it in music so that for many the spirit of Britain has been better distilled by Elgar, Vaughan Williams or Britten than by any poetry or descriptive prose.

Yet how can the formation of the land and its vegetation, its past and present, the way the light falls and the water flows, its 'nature' be explained or expressed solely in terms of sound? If we did not know where Elgar was born and lived, walked and worked, but came to his music fresh and ignorant, heard it only as a sequence of notes formed into harmonies and shared out among different instruments, would we picture the Malvern hills and the Vale of Hereford and Worcestershire in the heart of England as we listened? Would there be any pictures at all conjured up in our heads? Which comes first, music or landscape or the spirit of both? Which influences our vision and of what?

There are two essentially contradictory views of place, landscape. That it is merely solid matter, rock and earth, water, trees, its aspect altered by light and weather but otherwise uninfluenced by men, gods or anything other than geological forces controlled by impersonal time. Anything else, any spirit or mood and all sense of the past is merely a projection of human fancy, a poetic fallacy, valid in terms of art and the imagination but having nothing whatsoever to do with the landscape itself.

The other view is Romantic, mystical, religious. That there are within places as within human beings, essences, a spirit, a soul which is perceived and recognised and which casts its influence over the viewer: as Kathleen Raine puts it.

The question is whether the artist paints a prosaic description of what we call the external world or whether the imagination is projected onto it.

Perhaps both are true.

Painters, like poets and composers seem at times to be drawing out the spirit of place from the bare features of the landscape and setting down the received vision, so that Samuel Palmer's Shoreham, Stanley Spencer's Cookham, the great, dark, brooding landscapes of John Martin are based upon the real and visible yet more and other than simply those places.

How much are we projecting an inner landscape, how much are we taking from the outer landscape? In either case it is the imagination which works the transformation.

Is there then such a thing as the spirit of place? Like the human spirit it is experienced and known and artists attempt to capture it yet finally it cannot be held, let alone have its existence proved and then cloned. It is a matter of opinion then, a way of seeing things. A mystery. Nevertheless we greet it and respond to it whether in reality or in art with a universal cry of recognition.

Susan Hill, July 1994

Castle an Dinas in Cornwall, where the legend of Tristan and Isolde flowered again in the novel, **Castle Dor**, *by Daphne du Maurier.*

The West Country

Map 1

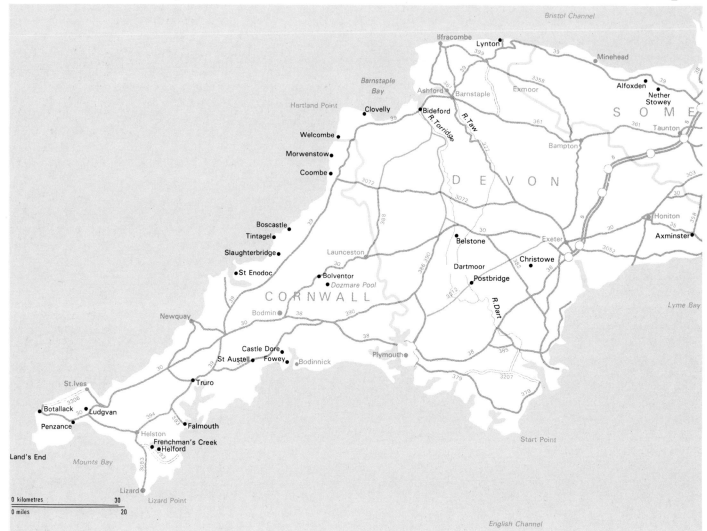

CORNWALL

Bolventor

Site on A30, mid Bodmin Moor, of old coaching inn, subject of Daphne du Maurier novel.

I owe my first sight of Jamaica Inn to a suggestion by Sir Arthur Quiller-Couch that his daughter Foy and I should take a couple of horses and make an expedition to Bodmin Moor, putting up at the Inn.

Bodmin is the greatest and wildest stretch of moorland in Cornwall. The wanderer who is fond of solitude can wander anywhere on either side of the main road and lose himself forthwith, turning, after he has walked barely half a mile in open country, to see no sign of human habitation, nothing but bare brown moor as far as the eye can reach, rising in the distance to frowning tors and craggy rocks that might give shelter if a rain-shower came, but little comfort from the wind which seeks out clefts and crannies even if the day is still.

Like Mary Yellan, who, in the novel, comes to her uncle's Inn from the tranquil hills and valleys of Helford, I came to Bodmin Moor unprepared for its dark, diabolic beauty. In the afternoon we ventured out across the moors, 'desolate, sinister,' I noted in my diary, and foolishly lost our way. To our horror rain and darkness fell upon us, and there we were, exposed to the violence of night with scarcely a hope of returning. Forcing the horses up a steep incline, we plunged onward and struck what we thought was a farm. The cottage was not only empty but part fallen, with rain driving through the empty windows, and what roof there was had been repaired with corrugated tin, so that the cascading rain sounded like hailstones on its surface.

The wind tore at the roof, and the showers of rain, increasing in violence now there was no shelter from the hills, spat against the windows with new venom. On either side the country stretched interminably into space. No trees, no lanes, no cluster of cottages or hamlet, but mile upon mile of bleak moorland, dark and untraversed, rolling like a desert land to some unseen horizon. No human being could live in this wasted country, thought Mary, and remain like other people; the very children would be born twisted, like the blackened shrubs of broom, bent by the force of a wind that never ceased, blow as it would from east and west, from north and south. Their minds would be twisted, too, their thoughts evil, dwelling as they must amidst marshland and granite, harsh heather and crumbling stone.

They would be born of strange stock who slept with this earth as a pillow, beneath this black sky. They would have something of the Devil left in them still . . . Perhaps there was no habitation in all the long one-and-twenty miles that stretched between the two towns of Bodmin and Launceston; perhaps there was not even a poor shepherd's hut on the desolate highway; nothing but the one grim landmark that was Jamaica Inn.

Emerging from the ruins my companion, a better horse-woman than I and owner of both our steeds, looked about her and observed, 'There's nothing for it but to get into the saddle, leave our reins loose on their necks, and let them lead us home.'

I was not impressed by her suggestion, for where was home to the horses? Thirty miles or more to Fowey, or back across the moors to Jamaica Inn? We mounted once again, darkness and silence all about us, save for that dreary patter on the cottage roof.

The horses, sure-footed even amongst dead heather and loose stones, plodded forward without hesitation, and there was some relief at least to be away from the abandoned cottage and in the open, however desolate, for there had been no warmth within its walls, no memories of hearths glowing with turf fire kindled by owners in the past. Surely whoever lived there before he let it fall to ruins had been sullen and morose, plagued by the Withey Brook that ran

somewhere below his door, and in despair went out one night and drowned himself.

I remembered an illustration from a book read long ago in childhood – Sintram, and his Companions – where a dispirited knight had travelled such a journey with the Devil in disguise, who called himself The Little Master. It showed a terrified steed rearing near a precipice. This was to be our fate, and The Little Master would come and claim us.

The horses, bolder now, headed steadily forward, straight across the moor, possibly in the direction of those menacing crags that we had seen in early afternoon, pointing dark fingers to the sky, which, we knew very well, lay contrary to any path for home.

It was seven, it was nine, it was midnight – too dark to see our watches, and fumbling fingers could not strike damp matches. On, forever on, nothing on all sides but waste and moor.

Suddenly my companion cried, 'They've done it . . . they've done it . . . Isn't that the road?'

Peering into the darkness ahead I saw a break in the rising ground, and a new flatness, and there, not a hundred rads distant, the blessed, streaky wetness of the Launceston-Bodmin road, and surprisingly, unbelievably, the gaunt chimneys of Jamaica Inn itself.

Mary stood alone, with the trunk at her feet. She heard a sound of bolts being drawn in the dark house behind her, and the door was flung open. A great figure strode into the yard, swinging a lantern from side to side.

'Who is it?' came the shout. 'What do you want here?'

Mary stepped forward and peered up into the man's face.

The light shone in her eyes, and she could see nothing. He swung the lantern to and fro before her, and suddenly he laughed and took hold of her arm, pulling her roughly inside the porch.

'Oh, it's you, is it?' he said. 'So you've come to us after all? I'm your uncle, Joss Merlyn, and I bid you welcome to Jamaica Inn.' He drew her into the shelter of the house, laughing again, and shut the door, and stood the lantern upon a table in the passage. And they looked upon each other face to face.

Today all is changed at the Inn itself. Coaches, cars, electricity, a bar, dinner of river-trout, baths for the travel-stained instead of the cream-jug of water we were offered. I must take my share of blame because out of that November expedition long ago came a novel which proved so popular that it passed into the folk-lore of the district.

But if you, when you go there, wonder whether the novel was mere fancy, take a walk behind the Inn, and one morning before sunrise, climb Rough Tor and listen to the

Bodmin Moor

Boscastle

wind in the stones. These moors have a fascination unlike any other, they are a survival from another age. They were the first things to be created; afterwards came the forests and the valleys and the sea. Nothing has really changed since Mary Yellan walked the moors, climbed the tors, and rested in low dips beside the springs and streams.

Strange winds blew from nowhere; they crept along the surface of the grass, and the grass shivered; they breathed upon the little pools of rain in the hollowed stones, and the pools rippled. Sometimes the wind shouted and cried, and the cry echoed in the crevices, and moaned, and was lost again. There was a silence on the tors that belonged to another age; an age that is past and vanished as though it had never been, an age when man did not exist, but pagan footsteps trod upon the hills. And there was a stillness in the air and a stranger, older peace, that was not the peace of God.

Enchanted Cornwall by Daphne du Maurier

Boscastle
Coastal village on B3263, 3 miles north of Tintagel.

Most of Thomas Hardy's *A Pair of Blue Eyes* (1873) takes place within a short radius of Boscastle, called Endelstow in the novel. Hardy was architect for the restoration, in 1872, of the church of St Juliot, in the course of which he met Emma Lavinia Gifford, who conducted the music at the church of St Julietta at Lesnewth (West Endelstow), and became the prototype of Elfride in the novel. Two years afterwards she became Hardy's wife.

At dusk, at the tiny harbour (Castle Boterel), it is still possible to imagine this 'region of dream and mystery',

as it appeared to Thomas and Emma when they first met.

'The ghostly birds, the pall-like sea, the frothy wind, the eternal soliloquy of the waters, the bloom of dark purple cast, that seems to exhale from the shoreward precipices, in themselves lend to the scene an atmosphere like the twilight of a night vision.'

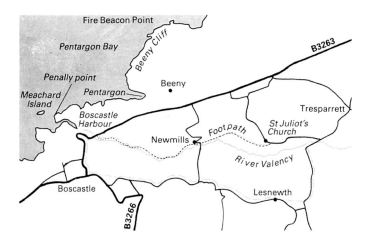

Botallack
Sometime tin mining village on the B3306, 5 miles north of Lands End.

The tinners were at work amongst the rocks and furze of Cornwall as long ago as the Bronze Age and sold their wares as far afield as the Aegean. In the late 19th century foreign competition meant terrible destitution for many and led to charges of wrecking and smuggling, a theme explored in many stories (see Bolventor and

Botallack

Castle Dor

Morwenstow). Botallack inspired stories by Wilkie Collins, a friend and collaborator of Charles Dickens, and *Deep Down* (1868), a novel by R M Ballantyne.

Castle Dor

Ancient Iron Age hill fort, situated off the B3269 out of Fowey, just beyond the turning to Golant.

Also the title of a novel based upon the ancient Cornish legend of Tristan and Iseult, begun by Arthur Quiller Couch. Couch was lecturer in Classics at Oxford and the first editor of *The Oxford Book of English Verse* (1900), but first and foremost a Cornishman, and author of a host of stories about Cornwall and the Cornish.

The legend is one of seduction and betrayal. King Mark, a king of Cornwall in the 5th century, Iseult, the King of Ireland's daughter, and Tristan, King Mark's nephew, formed a triangle of jealous husband, faithless wife and ardent lover respectively, the two young people bent on deceit.

There are many versions of the story, though all deal with the same human condition, which is its emotive appeal – love, betrayal, jealousy, revenge – all imbued with a lusty moral force. Three versions survive from the 12th century, including Beroul's fragment in the Norman dialect. Sir Thomas Malory tells another in Book VIII of *Le Morte D'Arthur*, where Sir Tristram de Liones is a knight of King Arthur's Round Table. Matthew Arnold's 'Tristram and Iseult' (1852) and Swinburne's 'Tristram of Lyonesse' (1882) are among the more modern poetic versions, though Wagner's opera 'Tristan und Isolde' has proved the more en-duringly popular.

Quiller Couch's story, a later flowering of the legend in a romance between Linnet (Iseult), the wife of an innkeeper (Mark), and Amyot (Tristan), a Breton onion seller, is set in motion at Castle Dor itself, believed to have been the site of King Mark's palace. The author's belief took root here, that 'a soil once having brought to birth such a story as Tristan and Iseult would be unable to desist from the effort to throw up secondary shoots.' And in the prologue to the novel, the narrator, clearly Quilller-Couch himself, spends a night on the castle ramparts he has known since a child and unwittingly becomes the medium for the legend's rebirth.

'All England is a palimpsest,' he wrote, 'scored over with writ of hate and love, begettings of children beneath the hazels, betrayals, appeals, curses, concealed travails . . . But this most ancient cirque of Castle Dor, deserted, bramble-grown, was the very nipple of a huge breast in pain, aching for discharge.'

'Q', as Quiller-Couch was known to his many readers, died before he finished *Castle Dor*, and the novel (1962) was completed by Daphne du Maurier.

Dozmare Pool

Large expanse of water, set high up on Bodmin Moor, a mile or so from Bolventor (A30).

Dozmare Pool is claimed (by Tennyson among others) to have been the place where Sir Bedivere threw King Arthur's sword, Excalibur, after he had been mortally wounded by Sir Mordred at Slaughterbridge on the bank of the River Camel.

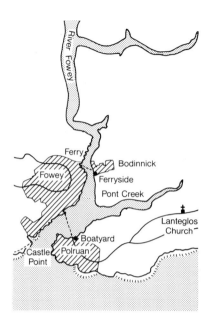

Bodinnick

Hamlet, east side of the River Fowey, opposite Fowey itself, the town and sometime port. Most easily reached by car ferry from Fowey via the A3082.

Daphne du Maurier first lived on her own at Ferryside, Bodinnick, on May 14th, 1927, the day after her twentieth birthday. The house had been bought by her parents as a holiday home – the family lived in Hampstead, London. Daphne, however, immediately took to it as something more significant. She loved the smells and sounds and atmosphere of the river with its big cargo ships, its small boats and yachts at anchor, and warmed at once to the people. Her first novel was based on a local family called Slade; its title, *The Loving Spirit* (1930), came from a poem by Emily Brontë. The novel, which covers four generations of the family, is imbued with a sense that time – past, present, and future – is not a linear progression, that somehow all three are one. It was a theme she would return to many times and grew out of her deep sense of the way landscapes and particular houses held the past. Aspects of the theme had earlier been explored by her Grandfather, George du Maurier, in his novel *Peter Ibbetson*.

Right: *Ferryside at Bodinnick, as Daphne du Maurier first saw it.* Above: *Looking down harbour towards the open sea.*

Frenchman's Creek

The creek lies on the south bank of the Helford Estuary, 1m or so west of Helford village. Can be reached by passenger ferry from Helford Passage on the north bank of the Helford River (5m south west of Falmouth), or on the south side of the Helford, via lanes running east off the B3083.

Frenchman's Creek is the title of a short story by Arthur Quiller-Couch, great friend and sometime near neighbour in Fowey of Daphne du Maurier. She had his permission to use it as the title of her famous novel. The Creek was the place du Maurier and her husband, 'Boy' Browning, chose to honeymoon. 'Here I set the only one of my novels that I am prepared to admit is romantic,' she wrote later, but the romance has its roots in the author's sense of the primitive call of this place.

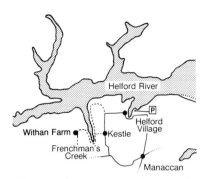

The map shows two ways down to the creek, the shorter from Kestle, the prettiest through Withan Farm. Alternatively you can hire a boat at Helford Village, but beware low tide.

The solitary yachtsman who leaves his yacht in the open roadstead of Helford, and goes exploring up-river in his dinghy on a night in midsummer, when the nightjars call, hesitates when he comes upon the mouth of the creek, for there is something of mystery about it even now, something of enchantment. Being a stranger, the yachtsman looks back over his shoulder to the safe yacht in the roadstead, and to the broad waters of the river, and he pauses, resting on his paddles, aware suddenly of the deep silence of the creek, of its narrow twisting channel, and he feels – for no reason known to him – that he is an interloper, a trespasser in time. He ventures a little way along the left bank of the creek, the sound of the blades upon the water seeming over-loud and echoing oddly among the trees on the farther bank, and as he creeps forward the creek narrows, the trees crowd yet more thickly from enchantment, for what he has seen is not of his world, and what he has heard is beyond his understanding.

Once more he reaches the security of his own ship, and looking back for the last time to the entrance of the creek, he sees the full moon white and shining in all its summer glory rise above the tall trees, bathing the creek in loveliness and light.

A night-jar churrs from the bracken on the hills, a fish breaks the surface of the water with a little plopping sound, and slowly his ship turns to meet the incoming tide, and the creek is hidden from him.

The yachtsman goes below to the snug security of his cabin, and browsing amongst his books he finds at last the thing for which he has been searching. It is a map of Cornwall, ill-drawn and inaccurate, picked up in an idle moment in a Truro bookshop. The parchment is faded and yellow, the marking indistinct. The spelling belongs to another century. Helford river is traced fairly enough, and so are the hamlets of Constantine and Gweek. But the yachtsman looks away from them to the marking of a narrow inlet, branching from the parent river, its short, twisting course running westward into a valley. Someone has scratched the name in thin faded characters – Frenchman's Creek.

The yachtsman puzzles awhile over the name, then shrugs his shoulders and rolls away the map. Presently he sleeps. The anchorage is still. No wind blows upon the water, and the night-jars are silent. The yachtsman dreams – and as the tide surges gently about his ship and the moon shines on the quiet river, soft murmurs come to him, and the past becomes the present.

A forgotten century peers out of dust and cobwebs and he walks in another time. He hears the sound of hoof-beats galloping along the drive to Navron House, he sees the great door swing open and the white, startled face of the manservant stare upward at the cloaked horseman. He sees Dona come to the head of the stairs, dressed in her old gown, with a shawl about her head, while down in the silent hidden creek a man walks the deck of his ship, his hands behind his back, and on his lips a curious secret smile. The farm kitchen of Navron House is a dining-hall once more, and someone crouches on the stairs, a knife in his hand, while from above there rings suddenly the startled cry of a child, and down upon the crouching figure a shield crashes from the walls of the gallery, and two little King

Above: *Frenchman's Creek,
'fascinating, strange, a thing of queer
excitement not fully understood'.*

Below: *Helford Village, remote and
hidden.*

Charles spaniels, perfumed and curled, run yapping and screaming to the body on the floor.

On Midsummer Eve a wood fire burns on a deserted quay, and a man and a woman look at one another and smile and acknowledge their secret, and at dawn a ship sails with the tide, and the sun shines fiercely from a bright blue sky, and the sea-gulls cry.

All the whispers and echoes from a past that is gone teem into the sleeper's brain, and he is with them, and part of them; part of the sea, the ship, the walls of Navron House, part of a carriage that rumbles and lurches in the rough roads of Cornwall, part even of that lost forgotten London, artificial, painted, where link-boys carried flares, and tipsy gallants laughed at the corner of a cobbled mud-splashed street. He sees Harry in his satin coat, his spaniels at his heels, blundering into Dona's bedroom, as she places the rubies in her ears. He sees William with his button mouth, his small inscrutable face. And last he sees La Mouette at anchor in a narrow twisting stream, he sees the trees at the water's edge, he hears the heron and the curlew cry, and lying on his back asleep he breathes and lives the lovely folly of that lost midsummer which first made the creek a refuge, and a symbol of escape.

Frenchman's Creek by Daphne du Maurier

Menabilly

Private estate, west of Fowey on the Gribben Peninsular.

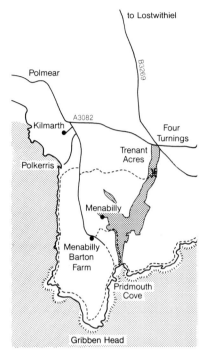

Daphne du Maurier first caught sight of the roofs of Menabilly while on a boat off Gribben Head and discovered that it had been built in the reign of Elizabeth I and had been in the same family's hands since then. She became intrigued, little knowing that not only would she eventually live there, but that it would prove to be a storehouse of ideas to be released in novels such as *The King's General*, *My Cousin Rachel*, and of course *Rebecca* (although the interior of Manderley was inspired by Milton in Cambridge-shire, where Daphne holidayed as a child). She once wrote, 'Who can affirm or deny that the houses which have sheltered us as children, or as adults, and our predecessors too, do not have embedded in their walls, one with the dust and cobwebs, one with the overlay of fresh wallpaper and paint, the imprint of what-has-been?'

Next morning I did a thing I had never done before, nor ever did again, except once in the desert, where to see sunrise is the peak of all experience. In short, I rose at 5.00 am. I pulled across the harbour in my pram, walked through the sleeping town, and climbed out upon the cliffs just as the sun himself climbed out on Pont Hill behind me. The sea was glass. The air was soft and misty warm. And the only other creature out of bed was a fisherman, hauling crab pots at the harbour mouth. It gave me a fine feeling of conceit, to be up before the world. My feet in sand shoes seemed like wings. I came down to Pridmouth Bay, passing the solitary cottage by the lake, and, opening a small gate hard by, I saw a narrow path leading to the woods. Now, at last, I had the day before me, and no owls, no moon, no shadows could turn me back.

I followed the path to the summit of the hill and then, emerging from the woods, turned left, and found myself upon a high grass walk, with all the bay stretched out below me and the Gribben head beyond.

I paused, stung by the beauty of that first pink glow of sunrise on the water, but the path led on, and I would not be deterred. Then I saw them for the first time – the scarlet rhododendrons. Massive and high they reared above my head, shielding the entrance to a long smooth lawn. I was hard upon it now, the place I sought. Some instinct made me crouch upon my belly and crawl softly to the wet grass at the foot of the shrubs. The morning mist was lifting, and the sun was coming up above the trees even as the moon had done last autumn. This time there was no owl, but blackbird, thrush and robin greeting the summer day.

I edged my way on to the lawn, and there she stood. My house of secrets. My elusive Menabilly . . .

The windows were shuttered fast, white and barred. Ivy covered the grey walls and threw tendrils round the windows. The house, like the world, was sleeping too. But later, when the sun was high, there would come no wreath of smoke from the chimneys. The shutters would not be thrown back, or the doors unfastened. No voices would sound within those darkened rooms. Menabilly would sleep on, like the sleeping beauty of the fairy tale, until someone should come to wake her.

I watched her awhile in silence, and then became emboldened, and walked across the lawn and stood beneath the windows. The scarlet rhododendrons encircled her lawns, to south, to east, to west. Behind her, to the north, were the tall trees and

Pridmouth Cove, the 'little narrow cove, the shingle hard and white under our feet', is the cove off which Rebecca drowned. Her boathouse may still be seen. Menabilly featured in The King's General *and* My Cousin Rachel *as well as* Rebecca, *and Kilmarth, the Dower House to the Menabilly Estate, to which Daphne du Muarier moved in 1969, was the inspiration for her time travel novel* The House on the Strand. *It was at Menabilly Barton Farm where she saw the screaming seagulls soaring and diving menacingly about a tractor, and conceived the short story 'The Birds'.*

Menabilly. 'Who can affirm or deny that the houses which have sheltered us . . . do not have embedded in their walls, one with the dust and cobwebs, one with the overlay of fresh wallpaper and paint, the imprint of what-has-been, the suffering, the joy?'

the deep woods. She was a two-storied house, and with the ivy off her would have a classical austerity that her present shaggy covering denied her.

One of her nineteenth-century owners had taken away her small-paned windows and given her plate glass instead, and he had also built at her northern end an ugly wing that conformed ill with the rest of her. But with all her faults, most obvious to the eye, she had a grace and charm that made me hers upon the instant. She was, or so it seemed to me, bathed in a strange mystery. She held a secret – not one, not two, but many – that she withheld from many people but would give to one who loved her well.

As I sat on the edge of the lawn and stared at her I felt as many romantic, foolish people have felt about the Sphinx. Here was a block of stone, even as the desert Sphinx, made by man for his own purpose – yet she had a personality that was hers alone, without the touch of human hand. One family only had lived within her walls. One family who had given her life. They had been born there, they had loved, they had quarrelled, they had suffered, they had died. And out of these emotions she had woven a personality for herself, she had become what their thoughts and their desires had made her.

And now the story was ended. She lay there in her last sleep. Nothing remained for her but to decay and die . . . .

The Rebecca Notebook by Daphne du Maurier

The author of the Civil War novel, The King's General, *looking up at the buttress against the north-west corner of the house. In 1824 it was found to conceal a room, or cell, and the skeleton of a young man dressed as a Cavalier and seated on a stool, a trencher at his feet. In explanation it was discovered that certain members of the Grenville family had hidden at Menabilly before the Cornish rising of 1648. Possibly one of them had taken refuge here from the advancing Parliamentarian troops, and been forgotten. This, and papers made available by the Rashleigh family, who own Menabilly, and the memoirs of Honor Harris, written in 1653, were the basis on which the Daphne du Maurier novel proceeded. A memorial tablet may be seen in Tywardreath church to Honor Harris.*

Last night I dreamt I went to Manderley again. It seemed to me I stood by the iron gate leading to the drive, and for a while I could not enter, for the way was barred to me. There was a padlock and a chain upon the gate. I called in my dream to the lodge-keeper, and had no answer, and peering closer through the rusted spokes of the gate I saw that the lodge was uninhabited.

No smoke came from the chimney, and the little lattice windows gaped forlorn. Then, like all dreamers, I was possessed of a sudden with supernatural powers and passed like a spirit through the barrier before me. The drive wound away in front of me, twisting and turning as it had always done, but as I advanced I was aware that a change had come upon it; it was narrow and unkept, not the drive that we had known. At first I was puzzled and did not understand, and it was only when I bent my head to avoid the low swinging branch of a tree that I realised what had happened. Nature had come into her own again and, little by little, in her stealthy, insidious way had encroached upon the drive with long, tenacious fingers. The woods, always a menace even in the past, had triumphed in the end. They crowded, dark and uncontrolled, to the borders of the drive. The beeches with white, naked limbs leant close to one another, their branches intermingled in a strange embrace, making a vault above my head like the archway of a church. And there were other trees as well, trees that I did not recognise, squat oaks and tortured elms that straggled cheek by jowl with the beeches, and had thrust themselves out of the quiet earth, along with monster shrubs and plants, none of which I remembered.

The drive was a ribbon now, a thread of its former self, with gravel surface gone, and choked with grass and moss. The trees had thrown out low branches, making an impediment to progress; the gnarled roots looked like skeleton claws. Scattered here and again amongst this jungle growth I would recognise shrubs that had been landmarks in our time, things of culture and grace, hydrangeas whose blue heads had been famous. No hand had checked their progress, and they had gone native now, rearing to monster height without a bloom, black and ugly as the nameless parasites that grew beside them.

On and on, now east now west, wound the poor thread that once had been our drive. Sometimes I thought it lost, but it appeared again, beneath a fallen tree perhaps, or struggling on the other side of a muddied ditch created by the winter rains. I had not thought the way so long. Surely the miles had multiplied, even as the trees had done, and this path led but to a labyrinth, some choked wilderness, and not to the house at all. I came upon it suddenly; the approach masked by the unnatural growth of a vast shrub that spread in all directions, and I stood, my heart thumping in my breast, the strange prick of tears behind my eyes.

There was Manderley, our Manderley, secretive and silent as it had always been, the grey stone shining in the moonlight of my dream, the mullioned windows reflecting the green lawns and the terrace. Time could not wreck the perfect symmetry of those walls, nor the site itself, a jewel in the hollow of a hand.

Rebecca by Daphne du Maurier

Morwenstow
One of a group of hamlets west of the A39 between Bideford and Stratton.

This is where North Cornwall and Devon meet and face the roar of the Atlantic across wind-scorched moorland and rocky cliff, a country known to readers of Daphne du Maurier: Stowe Barton, the estate of the King's General, Richard Grenville, stands near Coombe, and monuments to the family can be viewed in Kilkhampton church.

'A new chapter opened,' relates the Guide to the church of St Morwenna and St John the Baptist, Morwenstow, 'with the appointment as resident Vicar in 1834 of a young Oxford man, winner of the Newdigate Prize for poetry ... This was Robert Stephen Hawker, who was to serve at Morwenstow for forty years.' Hawker is the author of 'The Song of the Western Men', more or less regarded as the Cornish anthem, and 'Quest of the Sangraal' (see Tintagel), and numerous poems and stories inspired by the spirit of this out-of-the-way place, and frequently written in his hut made from driftwood on the side of the sheer cliff at the end of the glebe (where he would indulge in a little opium) –

My people were a mixed multitude of smugglers, wreckers, and dissenters of various hue ... But among the legends of local renown a prominent place has always been allotted to a personage whose ... arrival was signalised by a terrific hurricane. The storm came up Channel from the south-

Above: *Hawker's church.* Right: *His inspiration.*

west. The shore and the heights were dotted with watchers for a wreck – those daring gleaners of the harvest of the sea.

As suddenly as if a phantom ship had loomed in the distance, a strange vessel of foreign rig was discovered in fierce struggle with the waves of Harty Race. The sails were blown to rags, and the rudder was apparently lashed for running ashore. But the suck of the current and the set of the wind were too strong for the vessel, and she appeared to have lost her chance of reaching Harty Pool. It was seen that the tall seaman, who was manifestly skipper of the boat, had cast off his garments, and stood prepared upon the deck to encounter a battle with the surges for life and rescue. He plunged over the bulwarks, and arose to sight buffeting the seas. With stalwart arm and powerful chest he made his way through the surf, rose manfully from billow to billow, until with a bound he stood at last upright upon the sand.

A crowd of people had gathered from the land, on horseback and on foot, women as well as men ... Into their midst rushed the dripping stranger: he snatched from a terrified old dame her red Welsh cloak, cast it loosely around him, and bounded suddenly upon the crupper of a young damsel, who had ridden her father's horse down to the beach to see the sight. He grasped her bridle, and, shouting aloud in some foreign language, urged on the double-laden animal into full speed, and the horse naturally took its homeward way. Strange and wild were the outcries that greeted the rider, Miss Dinah Hamlyn, when, thus escorted, she reached her father's door in the very embrace of a wild, rough, tall man, who announced himself by name – never afterwards forgotten in these parts – as Coppinger, a Dane.

He took his immediate place at the family board, and on the settle by the hearth, as though he had been the most welcome and long-invited guest in the land. He soon persuaded the daughter to become his wife, and immediately afterwards his evil nature, so long smouldering, broke out like a wild beast uncaged. All at once the house became the den and refuge of every lawless character on the coast. All kinds of wild uproar and reckless rivalry appalled the neighbourhood day and night. It was discovered that an organised band of desperadoes, smugglers, wreckers, and poachers were embarked in a system of bold adventure, and that Cruel Coppinger was their captain.

> On through the ground-sea, shove!
> Light on the larboard bow!
> There's a nine-knot breeze above
> And a sucking tide below!

'The Smuggler's Song'

Tintagel
Coastal village west of the A39 between Boscastle and Port Isaac.

Go to Morwenstow or Bolventor and Hawker's true stories or Daphne du Maurier's fictional version, *Jamaica Inn*, cast on the same coastline, seem to trap the character of the place in their time — as if that coastline was awaiting the smugglers and wreckers of the 18th and 19th centuries to fulfil itself. But then only a few miles south, almost the same place plays host to a story set centuries earlier, and is yet more apt.

It befell in the days of Uther Pendragon, when he was king of all England, and so reigned, that there was a mighty duke in Cornwall that held war against him long time. And the duke was called the Duke of Tintagel. And so by means King Uther sent for this duke, charging him to bring his wife with him, for she was called a fair lady, and a passing wise, and her name was called Igraine.

The 'drowsy rock of Grim Dundagel, thron'd along the sea,' as R S Hawker described it in his unfinished epic 'Quest of the Sangraal'. According to Thomas Malory (d 1471) and Geoffrey of Monmouth (d 1155) Tintagel Castle was the birthplace of King Arthur.

Then Merlin was bound to come to the king. When King Uther saw him, he said he was welcome.

'Sir,' said Merlin, 'I know all your heart every deal. So ye shall be sworn unto me as ye be a true king anointed, to fulfil my desire, ye shall have your desire.'

Then the king was sworn upon the four Evangelists.

'Sir,' said Merlin, 'this is my desire: the first night that ye shall lie by Igraine ye shall get a child on her, and when that is born, that it shall be delivered to me for to nourish there as I will have it; for it shall be your worship, and the child's avail as mickle as the child is worth.'

'I will well,' said the king, 'as thou wilt have it.'

Then when the lady was delivered, the king commanded two knights and two ladies to take the child, bound in a cloth of gold, 'and that ye deliver him to what poor man ye meet the postern gate of the castle.' So the child was delivered unto Merlin, and so he bare it forth unto Sir Ector, made an holy man to christen him, and named him Arthur; and so Sir Ector's wife nourished him with her own pap.

Le Morte d'Arthur by Thomas Malory

Arthurian myth was made for Tintagel. 'The story grew here,' wrote H V Morton after his first visit. 'On this grey rock above the sea Uther Pendragon took that lovely queen, Igerne; and so began the story that ran through mediaeval Europe challenging the imagination of poet and writer, gathering strength and beauty, to break at last in the splendid climax of the Grail music . . .'

In 1848 Alfred Lord Tennyson travelled to Cornwall, beginning a research itinerary (with a visit to Stephen Hawker, incidentally) for 'The Idylls of the King', his series of 12 connected poems that tell the story of King Arthur from his first meeting with Guinevere to the ruin of his kingdom and his death in the 'last, dim, weird battle of the west.'

'The story grew here,' wrote H V Morton. Looking down from a window of the ruined Tintagel towards crashing waves and Merlin's Cave.

> A deathwhite mist slept over sand and sea:
> Whereof the chill, to him who breathed it, drew
> Down with his blood, till all his heart was cold
> With formless fear; and ev'n on Arthur fell
> Confusion, since he saw not whom he fought.
> For friend and foe were shadows in the mist,
> And friend slew friend not knowing whom he slew;
> And some had visions out of golden youth,
> And some beheld the faces of old ghosts
> Look in upon the battle; and in the mist
> Was many a noble deed, many a base,
> And chance and craft and strength in single fights,
> And ever and anon with host to host
> Shocks, and the splintering spear, the hard mail hewn,
> Shield-breakings, and the clash of brands, the crash
> Of battleaxes on shatter'd helms, and shrieks
> After the Christ, of those who falling down
> Look'd up for heaven, and only saw the mist;
> And shouts of heathen and the traitor knights,
> Oaths, insult, filth, and monstrous blasphemies,
> Sweat, writhings, anguish, labouring of the lungs
> In that close mist, and cryings for the light,
> Moans of the dying, and voices of the dead . . .
>
>   So all day long the noise of battle roll'd
> Among the mountains by the winter sea;
> Until King Arthur's Table, man by man,
> Had fall'n in Lyonesse about their lord,
> King Arthur.

St Austell
Town on the A390, south central Cornwall, south west of Bodmin.

Jack Clemo's life and work is coloured clay. The clay heaps, mountains and lakes of the china clay area, north of St Austell, have become his inner landscape.

Here is the holy ground,
Earth-womb where springs abound,
Some frank for my refreshment, laughing still
If clumsy hand disturb them, others numbed
To poison at an uncouth touch. I thrill,
Sensing these waters yet unplumbed,
Fearful that when I stoop to slake
My thirst I may mistake
Unless you guide and show
Which waters at which hours are mine to know.

From 'Intimate Landscape' by Jack Clemo

St Enodoc
1m north of Rock over Padstow Bay

John Betjeman is buried here. In Volume 1 (1926-1951) of her father's letters, Candida Lycett Green tells us that John Betjeman could be maddening when he insisted on visiting countless old churches on the way to Cornwall for family holidays, and at the start of 'Sunday Afternoon Service in St Enodoc Church, Cornwall' we can imagine it –

Come on! come on! This hillock hides the spire,
Now that one and now none . . .

But then we do arrive, into the churchyard sun –

And so my thoughts this happy Sabbathtide.
   Where deep cliffs loom enormous, where cascade
Mesembryanthemum and stone-crop down,
Where the gull looks no larger than a lark
Hung midway twixt the cliff-top and the sand,
Sun-shadowed valleys roll along the sea.
Forced by the backwash, see the nearest wave
Rise to a wall of huge translucent green
And crumble into spray along the top
Blown seaward by the land-breeze. Now she breaks
And in an arch of thunder plunges down
To burst and tumble, foam on top of foam,
Criss-crossing, baffled, sucked and shot again,
A waterfall of whiteness, down a rock,
Without a source but roller's furthest reach:
And tufts of sea-pink, high and dry for years,
Are flooded out of ledges, boulders seem
No bigger than a pebble washed about
In this tremendous tide. Oh kindly slate!
To give me shelter in this crevice dry.

St Ives
Former fishing town, north coast, A3074.

Favourite holiday haunt of Virginia Woolf's family when she was a child. Her mother died in 1895, when Virginia was 13. Her death caused Virginia bouts of terrible depression. The St Ives holidays ceased. In 1904 she lost her father, and two years later her brother, Thoby, which provoked *Jacob's Room*, a novel with Cornish land- and seascapes.

DEVON

Dartmoor

The moor, 300 square miles of it, is the geographical heart of Devon, nurturing through its rivers two distinctive regions north and south of it. Rising from the heart of the moor and winging its way to the south, is the Dart –

It spills from the Milky Way, pronged with light,
It fuses the flash-gripped earth –

The spicy torrent, that seems to be water
Which is spirit and blood.

From 'West Dart' by Ted Hughes

It has been said that the difference between North and South Devon can be seen in their cows, those of the south, happy and content, cream producers grown fat on the 'milk and honey' sward of the South Hams; while those of the North are angular and tough, self-sufficient, chewing cud a bit on the wild side. There is no question which aspect has inspired its writers more.

Dartmoor itself is breathtakingly sublime, untamed and hilly, host to earliest civilisations, with occasional woods and huge stones stacked in tors, some say by the hand of giants, others by geological movements of pre-civilisation. Order is imposed (as well as at ghastly Princetown prison) by a road, Roman, straight and

The mediaeval Clapperbridge at Postbridge. A short mile north stands Hartland Farm, home of Philip Ouldsbroom, see Postbridge.

true, but frequently thwarted in its diagonal discipline by the activities of the moor's chief natural feature –

Dartmoor, many-fountained Dartmoor, mother of a myriad streams, and wet nurse of a million mists.

R D Blackmore

Christow
West of the B3193, 5m east of Mortonhampstead.

A man's resemblance to a tree has been discovered, and beautifully descanted upon – from nethermost tail of tap-

Dartmoor from Blackingstone Rock.

Dartmoor, mother of a myriad streams.

root, to uttermost twig, and split sky-leaf . . . But thoroughly as [the poets] have worked out the subject, they seem to have missed one most striking analogy. A man (like a tree) can have no avail of comfort, unless there belongs to him the margin of a brook.

'Lark's cot' – as Mr Arthur's home was called by the natives, and even by himself at last – was gifted with a truly desirable brook – the Christow . . . [This] beautiful brook of crystal water, after tumbling by the captain's cot, makes its manner of travelling here. From crags, and big deserts, and gorges full of drizzle, it has scrambled some miles, without leisure for learning self-control or patience. And then it comes suddenly, round a sharp corner, into the quiet of Christowell, whose church is the first work of man it has seen, except that audacious cottage. Then a few little moderate slips lead it with a murmur to a downright road, and a ford where men have spread it gently, and their boys catch minnows. Here it begins to be clad with rushes, and to be chaired by jutting trees, and lintelled by planks, for dear gossip and love; for cottages on either bank come down, and neighbours full of nature inhabit them.

Happy is the village that has no street, and seldom is worried by the groan of wheels. Christowell keeps no ceremonial line of street, or road, or even lane, but goes in and out, as the manner of the land may be, or the pleasure of the landlords. Still there is a place where deep ruts grow, because of having soft rock under them; and this makes it seem to be the centre of the village . . . for the public house is handy. Once upon a time, two carts met here, and here they spent a summer, both being driven by obstinate men. Neither would budge from his own rut, and the horses for several hours rubbed noses, or cropped a little grass, while the men lay down. Being only first cousins, these men would not fight; as they must have done if they had been brothers. Yet neither of them would disgrace his county – fair mother of nobel stubbornness – by any mean compromise, or weak concession; so they waited until it grew dark; and then, with a whistle of good will, began to back away together, and as soon as they found room to turn, went home to supper from a well-spent day.

R D Blackmore, author of *Christowell: A Dartmoor Tale* (1881), wrote that 'in everything, except the accident of birth, I am Devonian; my ancestry were all Devonians; my sympathy and feeling are all Devonian,' and few Devonians would refuse him the honour, for Blackmore's sense of place and people was acute, and his work (see especially *Lorna Doone* – Exmoor) invokes an empathy with the hidden spirit of the county

more complete than any other's.

Postbridge
Hamlet by the East Dart, in the centre of the moor, on the B3212.

Postbridge is more ancient than the road of Roman straightness that strikes through it. Round about are numerous mediaeval monuments. 'Clapper' bridges and miners' smelting houses, ruined dwellings and symbols of the Christian faith all stand within a walk of the hamlet; while, more ancient yet, though of yesterday contrasted with the stone man's relics, shall be seen a fragment of the Great Central Trackway or Fosseway, which extended from Caithness to Mounts Bay before the Roman landed. Fragments of this ancient cobbled road still lie northerly of Postbridge, and traverse Dart at a shallow beneath Hartland Farm. Next, plunging into the prehistoric past, your antiquary enters behind the veil of time to trace Neolithic man through Dartmoor. Menhirs and parallelitha, hypaethral circles and hidden graves, the ruins of lodges and the shattered walls of many an aboriginal hamlet still stand upon these naked hills.

Hartland Farm is the home of Philip Ouldsbroom, the hero of *The Thief of Virtue* (1910), a novel by Eden Phillpotts, in which Postbridge is the focus of the action. Phillpotts wrote eighteen novels set on Dartmoor, and in his day he was hailed as being 'for Devonshire something of what Hardy had been for the neighbouring county of Dorset'. His knowledge of Dartmoor was extraordinary, but he never courted the spirit of the place like Hardy with Dorset.

Eden Phillpotts' novels cover the whole moor. One of the most popular, The Secret Woman, highlights a particular beauty in the north, Belstone village (bottom left) 'beneath the mean dwelling house' of Watchett Hill (above).

At mid-day in summer, shadows, very purple under the ambient splendour of the hour, roamed over Dartmoor, sometimes in thronging companies, and sometimes alone. They leapt the rivers, raced the level heaths, and climbed the hills. Upon the sky there worked two separate winds, and each drove its own flock. At lower level advanced the cumuli and threw their shades upon the earth; and, above them, great lines of transparent but visible vapour filmy against the blue, sailed in upper zones, and by their direction marked another stream of air. The cirri, like fingers that rose out of a palm beneath the horizon, spread fanwise from a point unseen. Then to the zenith, in majestic and unfolding perspective they ascended. Beneath the sun these cloud-lances of the height, flying arrowy, burnt like flame, and by contrast dimmed the round, golden heads of the greater clouds beneath them. Most delicate and dazzling bright were they – mere flakes of fire upon the solar face that no way dimmed the downbeat of his glory; but that they, too, flung shadows and spread invisible gauze of shade among the darker umbrage might not be doubted, though the unseen passing of them cooled no cheek. Upon their aerial way they went, and closed their ranks again and narrowed as they sank to the farther horizon.

The Thief of Virtue by Eden Phillpotts

The Grimpen Mire

We had come to a point where a narrow grassy path struck off from the road and wound away across the moor. A steep, boulder-sprinkled hill lay upon the right which had in bygone days been cut into a granite quarry. The face which was turned towards us formed a dark cliff, with ferns and brambles growing in its niches. From over a distant rise there floated a gray plume of smoke.

'A moderate walk along this moor-path brings us to Merripit House,' said he. 'Perhaps you will spare an hour that I may have the pleasure of introducing you to my sister.'

My first thought was that I should be by Sir Henry's side. But then I remembered the pile of papers and bills with which his study table was littered. It was certain that I could not help with those. And Holmes had expressly said that I should study the neighbours upon the moor. I accepted Stapleton's invitation, and we turned together down the path.

'It is a wonderful place, the moor,' said he, looking round over the undulating downs, long green rollers, with crests of jagged granite foaming up into fantastic surges. 'You never tire of the moor. You cannot think the wonderful secrets which it contains. It is so vast, and so barren, and so mysterious.'

'You know it well, then?'

'I have only been here two years. The residents would call me a newcomer. We came shortly after Sir Charles settled. But my tastes led me to explore every part of the country round, and I should think that there are few men who know it better than I do.'

'Is it hard to know?'

'Very hard. You see, for example, this great plain to the north here with the queer hills breaking out of it. Do you observe anything remarkable about that?'

'It would be a rare place for a gallop.'

'You would naturally think so and the thought has cost several their lives before now. You notice those bright green spots scattered thickly over it?'

'Yes, they seem more fertile than the rest.'

Stapleton laughed.

'That is the great Grimpen Mire,' said he. 'A false step yonder means death to man or beast. Only yesterday I saw one of the moor ponies wander into it. He never came out. I saw his head for quite a long time craning out of the bog-hole, but it sucked him down at last. Even in dry seasons it is a danger to cross it, but after these autumn rains it is an awful place. And yet I can find my way to the very heart of it and return alive. By George, there is another of those miserable ponies!'

Something brown was rolling and tossing among the green sedges. Then a long agonized, writhing neck shot

'This most God-forsaken corner of the world. The longer one stays here the more does the spirit of the moor sink into one's soul.'

upward and a dreadful cry echoed over the moor. It turned me cold with horror, but my companion's nerves seemed to be stronger than mine.

'It's gone!' said he. 'The mire has him. Two in two days, and many more, perhaps, for they get in the way of going there in the dry weather and never know the difference until the mire has them in its clutches. It's a bad place, the great Grimpen Mire.'

'And you say you can penetrate it?'

'Yes, there are one or two paths which a very active man can take. I have found them out.'

'But why should you wish to go into so horrible a place?'

'Well, you see the hills beyond? They are really islands cut off on all sides by the impassable mire, which has crawled round them in the course of years. That is where the rare plants and the butterflies are, if you have the wit to reach them.'

'I shall try my luck some day.'

He looked at me with a surprised face.

'For God's sake put such an idea out of your mind,' said he. 'Your blood would be upon my head. I assure you that there would not be the least chance of your coming back alive. It is only by remembering certain complex landmarks that I am able to do it!'

'Halloa!' I cried. 'What is that?'

A long, low moan, indescribably sad, swept over the moor. It filled the whole air, and yet it was impossible to say whence it came. From a dull murmur it swelled into a deep roar, and then sank back into a melancholy, throbbing murmur once again. Stapleton looked at me with a curious expression in his face.

Wild beasts are more than a legend on the moor; sightings of pumas and wild cats have been made even in modern times. Conan Doyle's hound of the Baskervilles – 'never in the delirious dream of a disordered brain could anything more savage, more appalling, more hellish be conceived than that dark form and savage face which broke upon us out of the wall of fog' – materialises out of the dread Grimpen Mire, indulging our wildest fantasies of the place. But so adept is he in his preparations that when the beast is delivered, there is no need for us to suspend belief, any more than there is for poor Watson:

Baskerville Hall, October 13th

My Dear Holmes:

My previous letters and telegrams have kept you pretty well up to date as to all that has occurred in this most God-forsaken corner of the world. The longer one stays here the more does the spirit of the moor sink into one's soul, its vastness, and also its grim charm. When you are once out upon its bosom you have left all traces of modern England behind you, but, on the other hand, you are conscious everywhere of the homes and the work of the prehistoric people. On all sides of you as you walk are the houses of these forgotten folk, with their graves and the huge monoliths which are supposed to have marked their temples. As you look at their gray stone huts against the scarred hillsides you leave your own age behind you, and if you were to see a skin-clad, hairy man crawl out from the low door, fitting a flint-tipped arrow on to the string of his bow, you would feel that his presence there was more natural than your own.

The Torridge
River rising on Dartmoor and flowing north into Barnstaple (or Bideford) Bay.

The river walks in the valley singing
Letting her veils blow –

A novelty from the red side of Adam

From 'Torridge' by Ted Hughes

The primitive spirit of the moor flowed out through the Torridge and the Taw into the veins of the county's most popular writer this century. Henry Williamson rode to Georgeham on a motorbike after a furious row with his father, and began a quest for that 'ancient, forgotten beauty that our fathers knew and loved with

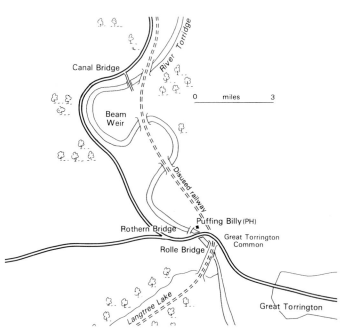

Right: *Route from the Puffing Billy pub to Canal Bridge (above) where Tarka was born and died. The hunt was filmed here on the day Henry Williamson himself died.* Below right: *Torridge weir.*

Full Guide available from The Tarka Project, Torrington, EX38 8EZ.

a passionate love'. He found it in the story of Tarka, whose real-life progenitor he helped rescue from a drain. At Skirr Cottage Tarka became part a menagerie of dogs, cats, gulls, buzzards and magpies. Then one night the otter strayed and Henry, with the help of his dog, found it caught in a gin-trap. He threw his jacket over the chattering animal and managed to release the trap, but the otter ran off, apparently having lost three of its toes in the jaws of the trap. For hours Henry searched, but failed to find him.

At the end of Tarka, the novel, comes the terrible hunt itself. After six hours of wearying chase up the river, there is a pause, a stillness, a peace. Tarka is hiding by a fallen willow bough. Most of the hounds, now silent, are sat still on the banks. A girl is watching a scarlet dragonfly whirring and darting 'over the willow snag'. Then she, who through childhood has walked this river 'seeing a Spirit everywhere, gentle in thought to all her eyes beheld', watches as the dragonfly settles on what she thinks is part of the willow . . . until she hears the otter's sneeze.

Williamson delivered Tarka's fate into the hands of an innocent because he accepted the hunter mentality of man and animal, and loved all animals (and some humans) for their whole spirit. In *Tarka*, Williamson is not decrying the hunting of wild animals. He is saying this *is* nature, the darkness and the light, we should not be deceived. This is what is on offer. Wonder at it in all its glory.

During the sixth hour the otter disappeared. The river grew quiet. People not in uniform sat down on the grass. The huntsman was wading slowly upstream feeling foothold with pole and keeping an eye on Deadlock. Stickle stood slack, but ready to bar the way with pole-strokes. Look-outs gazed at the water before them. It was known that the otter might leave the river at any moment. The boy with the warped pole, on whose cheeks were two patches of dried otter-blood, was already opening his knife, ready to cut another notch on the handle in the form of a cross.

But for more than an hour the sun-thongs flickered across the placid water; and in softening light the owl returned, flying high over the bridge, to the mouse runs in the quiet meadow beyond.

A fallen bough of willow lay in the pool near one bank, and Tarka lay beside it. His rudder held a sunken branch. Only his wide upper nostrils were above the water. He never moved. Every yard of the banks between the stickles was searched again. Poles were thrust into branches, roots, and clumps of flag-lilies. The wading huntsman prodded Peal Rock and the rock above it. Hounds sat on the banks, shivering, and watching Deadlock, Render, and Harper working the banks. The crack of a whip, a harsh voice rating – Rufus had turned a rabbit out of a bramble and was chasing it across the meadow. He returned to the river in a wide circle, eyeing the whip.

At the beginning of the eighth hour a scarlet dragonfly whirred and darted over the willow snag, watched by a girl sitting on a bank. Her father, an old man lank and humped as a heron, was looking out near her. She watched the dragonfly settle on what looked like a piece of bark beside the snag; she heard a sneeze, and saw the otter's whiskers scratch the water. Glancing round she realised that she alone had seen the otter. She flushed, and hid her grey eyes with her lashes. Since childhood she had walked the Devon rivers with her father, looking for flowers and the nests of birds, passing some rocks and trees as old friends, seeing a Spirit everywhere, gentle in thought to all her eyes beheld.

For two minutes the maid sat silent, hardly daring to look at the river. The dragonfly few over the pool, seizing flies and tearing them apart in its horny jaws. Her father watched it as it settled on the snag, rose up, circled, and lit on the water, it seemed. Tarka sneezed again, and the dragonfly flew away. A grunt of satisfaction from the old man, a brown hand and wrist holding aloft a hat, a slow intake of breath, and, 'TALLY-HO!'

Tarka the Otter by Henry Williamson

Tarka was a triumph for Williamson in that it is a story completely faithful to nature, as he painstakingly observed her process.

He was not decrying hunting as such. He put nature under a microscope and reproduced his findings without sentiment, with an eye to truth.

Exmoor

Far to the north, a high moorland area, largely forested until the 19th Century, part in Devon, part in Somerset.

Francis Kilvert's Diaries

A visit to the Castle Hotel, Lynton

I got up at 6 o'clock as the sun was rising behind the Tors. The house was silent and no one seemed to be about. I unlocked the door and let myself out into the garden. It was one of the loveliest mornings that ever dawned upon this world. A heavy dew had fallen in the night and as I wandered down the beautiful winding terraced walks every touch sent a shower from the great blue globes of the hydrangeas, and on every crimson fuchsia pendant flashed a diamond dew drop.

The clear pure crisp air of the early morning blew fresh and exhilarating as the breeze came sweet from the sea. No one was astir, everything was silent, and I seemed to have the beautiful world to myself. The only sound that broke the stillness was the roaring of the Lynn far below. The scene which was clothed in darkness as we came in last night now lay suddenly revealed in the full splendour of the brilliant morning light, glowing with all its superb colouring, the red cliffs of the mighty Tors, the purple heather slopes and the rich brown wilderness of rusting fern, the snowy foam fringe chafing the feet of the cliffs, and the soft blue playing into green in the shoaling water of the bay where the morning was spread upon the sea.

In the quiet early sunny morning it seemed to me as if that place must be one of the loveliest nooks in the Paradise of this world.

In 1835, when Richard Doddridge Blackmore was 10, he came with his family from Culmstock in East Devon to live at Ashford, just north of Barnstaple, a few miles only from Exmoor.

It was perfect timing. Blackmore's imagination was at its most impressionable, and he thrilled to the legends of the place. 'Any son of Exmoor, chancing on this volume,' he wrote in the preface to the first edition of *Lorna Doone* (1869), 'cannot fail to bring to mind the nurse-tails of his childhood – the savage deeds of the Doones.' Sixteen years earlier T H Cooper, in *A Guide to Lynton*, had recorded the tradition of a ruined village where the Doones lived, terrorising the country and escaping with their booty across the wild hills of Exmoor.

Besides the stories, he felt a genetic affinity with the area. There had been Blackmores here since the late 16th century, and his grandfather had been Rector at Combe Martin and over the border at Oare, the moorland village from which John Ridd would emerge in *Lorna Doone.*

Blackmore's memory of his own self as a child, trailing around the country with his grandfather, seems to fit the 17th-century world that John Ridd inhabits – 'I behold an old man, with a keen profile, under a parson's shovel hat, riding a tall chestnut horse up the western slope of Exmoor, followed by his little grandson upon a shaggy and stuggy pony.'

Lorna Doone was a flowering from the roots, and in the end, as Blackmore saw, the proof of the endeavour was that it won the 'attention and kind regard, not of the general public only, but also of those who are at home with the scenery, people, life, and language, wherein a native cannot always satisfy a native.'

'The valley into which I gazed was fair with early promise . . . The willow bushes over the stream hung as if they were angling with tassel'd floats of gold and silver, bursting like a bean-pod . . . I feel with every blade of grass, as if it had a history; and make a child of every bud, as though it knew and loved me. And being so, they seem to tell me of my own delusions, how I am no more than they, except in self-importance. While I was letting of my thoughts go wild to sounds and sights of nature, a sweeter note than thrush or ouzel ever wooed a mate in, floated on the valley breeze at the quiet turn of sundown. The words were of an ancient song, fit to cry or laugh at.'
John Ridd in Lorna Doone

Here the 14-year-old John Ridd first discovers Doone Valley by chance and begins his 'boyish slavery' to Lorna:

Doone Valley – 'a deep green valley, carved from out the mountains in a perfect oval.'

Lorna Doone Farm, Malmsmead. 'Everybody knows . . . how soft the fall of land is round about.'

Now the day was falling fast behind the brown of the hill-tops; and the trees, being void of leaf and hard, seemed giants ready to beat me. And every moment, as the sky was clearing up for a white frost, the cold of the water got worse and worse, until I was fit to cry with it. And so, in a sorry plight, I came to an opening in the bushes, where a great black pool lay in front of me, whitened with snow (as I thought) at the sides, till I saw it was only foam-froth. . . . And the look of this black pit was enough to stop one from diving into it, even on a hot summer's day with sunshine on the water; I mean, if the sun ever shone there. As it was, I shuddered and drew back; not alone at the pool itself, and the black air there was about it, but also at the whirling manner, and wisping of white threads upon it, in stripy circles round and round; and the centre still as jet.

But soon I saw the reason of the stir and depth of that great pit, as well as of the roaring sound which long had made me wonder. For skirting round one side, with very little comfort, because the rocks were high and steep, and the ledge at the foot so narrow, I came to a sudden sight and marvel, such as I never dreamed of. For, lo! I stood at the foot of a long pale slide of water, coming smoothly to me, without any break or hindrance, for a hundred yards or more, and fenced on either side with cliff, sheer. and straight, and shining. The water neither ran nor fell, nor leaped with any spouting, but made one even slope of it, as if it had been combed or planed, and looking like a plank of deal laid down a deep black staircase. However there was no side-rail, nor any place to walk upon, only the channel a fathom wide, and the perpendicular walls of crag shutting out the evening. . . .

I girt up my breeches anew, with each buckle one hole tighter, for the sodden straps were stretching and giving, and mayhap my legs were grown smaller from the coldness of it. Then I bestowed my fish around my neck more tightly, and not stopping to look much, for fear of fear, crawled along over the fork of rocks, where the water had scooped the stone out; and shunning thus the ledge from whence it rose, like the mane of a white horse, into the broad black pool, softly I let my feet into the dip and rush of the torrent.

And here I had reckoned without my host . . . for the green wave came down, like great bottles upon me, and my legs were gone off in a moment, and I had not time to cry out with wonder, only to think of my mother and Annie, and knock my head very sadly, which made it go round so that brains were no good, even if I had any. But all in a moment, before I knew aught, except that I must die out of the way, with a roar of water upon me, my fork, praise God, stuck fast in the rock, and I was borne up upon it. . . . I gathered my legs back slowly, as if they were fish to be landed, stopping whenever the water flew too strongly off my shin-bones, and in this manner I won a footing, leaning well forward like a draught-horse. To me it seemed half-a-mile at least of sliding water above me, but in truth it was little more than a furlong, as I came to know afterwards. It would have been

'About two miles below our farm, the Bagworthy water runs into the Lynn, and makes a real river of it. Thence it hurries away, with strength and force of wilful waters, under the foot of a bare-faced hill, and so to rocks and woods again, where the stream is covered over, and dark, heavy pools delay it.' John Ridd in Lorna Doone

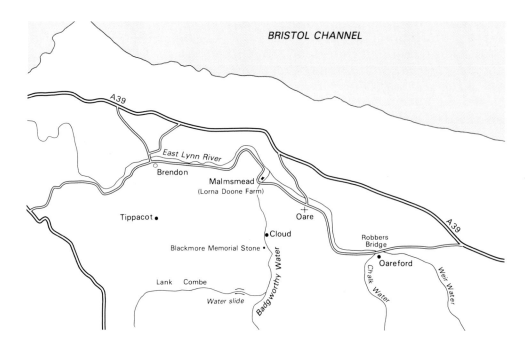

Lorna Doone Country. A Guidebook,
The Lorna Doone Trail *by S H*
Burton, is available by post from
Minehead Tourist Information, 0643
702624.

a hard ascent, even without the slippery slime, and the force of the river over it, and I had scanty hope indeed of ever winning the summit. Nevertheless my terror left me, now I was face to face with it, and had to meet the worst; and I set myself to do my best, with a vigour and sort of hardness, which did not then surprise me, but have done so ever since. . . . The greatest danger of all was just where I saw no jeopardy, but ran up a patch of black ooze-weed in a very boastful manner, being now not far from the summit. Here I fell very piteously, and was like to have broken my knee-cap, and the torrent got hold of my other leg, while I was indulging the bruised one. . . . At last the rush of forced water, where first it came over the lips of the fall, drove me into the middle, and I stuck awhile with my toe-balls on the slippery links of the pop-weed, and the world was green and gliddery, and I durst not look behind me. Then I made up my mind to die at last; for so my legs would ache no more, and my breath not pain my heart so; only it did seem such a pity, after fighting so long, to give in, and the light was coming upon me, and again I fought towards it; then suddenly I felt fresh air, and fell into it headlong.

When I came to myself again, my hands were full of young grass and mould; and a little girl kneeling at my side was rubbing my forehead tenderly, with a dock-leaf and a handkerchief.

'Oh, I am so glad,' she whispered softly, as I opened my eyes and looked at her; 'now you will try to be better, won't you?'

I had never heard so sweet a sound as came from between her bright red lips, while there she knelt and gazed at me; neither had I ever seen anything so beautiful as the large dark eyes intent upon me, full of pity and wonder. And then, my nature being slow, and perhaps, for that matter, heavy, I wandered with my hazy eyes down the black shower of her hair, as to my jaded gaze it seemed; and where it fell on the turf, among it (like an early star) was the first primrose of the season.

SOMERSET

Alfoxden

An estate just south of Holford, off the A39 between Bridg-water and Watchet. Now a hotel called Alfoxton Park.

Some times when I earnestly look at a beautiful object or landscape, it seems as if I were on the brink of a fruition still denied – as if a vision were an appetite . . .

Samuel Taylor Coleridge

In December 1796, Coleridge moved with his wife Sara and their first child, Hartley, to Nether Stowey, a village in the shadow of the Quantocks, now on the A39. While there, he persuaded William Wordsworth, whom he had met 18 months earlier in Bristol, and Dorothy, Wordsworth's sister, to rent Alfoxden – 'a gentleman's seat, with a park and woods, elegantly and completely furnished, with nine lodging rooms, three parlours, and a hall, in the most beautiful and roman-tic situation by the seaside, four miles from Stowey – this we have got for Wordsworth at the rent of twenty-three pounds a year, taxes included! The park and woods are his for all purposes he wants them, and the large gardens are altogether and entirely his.'

Once installed, the northern accents of the Words-worths and their penchant for carrying stools on night-time walks are said to have aroused the suspicions of the locals, who mistook them for French spies. It was a time when England was in the grip of an invasion scare. Owing to Coleridge's association with radical politicians such as Thelwall, the suspicions were taken seriously by the Home Office and an Investigator was sent to take up a watching brief from the Globe Inn.

It must have lent a strange frisson to what was a time of inestimable importance in the growth of Coleridge's spiritual awareness and poetic imagination, his first real exposure to nature in the company of 'the only man to whom at all times and in all modes of excellence I feel myself inferior.' In 'Frost at Midnight', he promises his newborn son that he will have, from the start, what he, Coleridge, had been denied:

. . . For I was reared
In the great city, pent 'mid cloisters dim,
And saw nought lovely but the sky and stars.

But thou, my babe! shalt wander like a breeze
By lakes and sandy shores, beneath the crags
Of ancient mountains, and beneath the clouds,
Which image in their bulk both lakes and shores
And mountain crags: so shalt thou see and hear
The lovely shapes and sounds intelligible
Of that eternal language, which thy God
Utters, who from eternity doth teach
Himself in all, and all things in himself.
Great universal Teacher! he shall mould
Thy spirit, and by giving make it ask.

For the Wordsworths too it is a period of equally intense creativity, the three of them walking and talk-ing 'as three persons with one soul,' as Coleridge described it. The daily round of walks and creativity Dorothy described in her *Alfoxden Journal*.

ALFOXDEN, *January 20th*, 1798. The green paths down the hill-sides are channels for streams. The young wheat is streaked by silver lines of water running between the ridges, the sheep are gathered together on the slopes. After the wet dark days, the country seems more populous. It peoples itself in the sunbeams. The garden, mimic of spring, is gay with flowers. The purple-starred hepatica spreads itself in the sun, and the clustering snow-drops put forth their white heads, at first upright, ribbed with green, and like a rosebud when completely opened, hanging their heads downwards, but slowly lengthening their slender stems. The slanting woods of an unvarying brown, showing the light through the thin net-work of their upper boughs. Upon the highest ridge of that round hill covered with planted oaks, the shafts of the trees show in the light like the columns of a ruin.

January 26th. Walked upon the hill-tops; followed the sheep tracks till we overlooked the larger coombe. Sat in the sunshine. The distant sheep-bells, the sound of the stream; the woodman winding along the half-marked road with his laden pony; locks of wool still spangled with the dewdrops; the blue-grey sea, shaded with immense masses of cloud, not streaked; the sheep glittering in the sunshine. Returned through the wood. The trees skirting the wood, being exposed more directly to the action of the sea breeze, stripped of the net-work of their upper boughs, which are stiff and erect, like black skeletons; the ground strewed with the red berries of the holly. Set forward before two o'clock. Returned a little after four.

'Lines Written in Early Spring', William himself re-

Alfoxden, Holford, where William and Dorothy Wordsworth stayed.

called, were 'composed while I was sitting by the side of a brook that runs down from the Coomb, in which stands the village of Alford, through the grounds of Alfoxden.'

I heard a thousand blended notes,
While in a grove I sat reclined,
In that sweet mood when pleasant thoughts
Bring sad thoughts to the mind.

To her fair works did nature link
The human soul that through me ran;
And much it grieved my heart to think
What man has made of man.

Through primrose-tufts, in that sweet bower,
The periwinkle trailed its wreaths;
And 'tis my faith that every flower
Enjoys the air it breathes.

The birds around me hopped and played:
Their thoughts I cannot measure,
But the least motion which they made,
It seemed a thrill of pleasure.

The budding twigs spread out their fan,
To catch the breezy air;
And I must think, do all I can,
That there was pleasure there.

January 31st. Set forward to Stowey at half-past five. A violent storm in the wood; sheltered under the hollies. When we left home the moon immensely large, the sky scattered over with clouds. These soon closed in, contracting the dimensions of the moon without concealing her.

The thin gray cloud is spread on high,
It covers but not hides the sky.
The moon is behind, and at the full;
And yet she looks both small and dull.
The night is chill, the cloud is gray.
Christabel

The sound of the pattering shower, and the gusts of wind, very grand. Left the wood when nothing remained of the storm but the driving wind, and a few scattering drops of rain. Presently all clear, Venus first showing herself between the struggling clouds; afterwards Jupiter appeared. The hawthorn hedges, black and pointed, glittering with millions of diamond drops; the hollies shining with broader patches of light. The road to the village of Holford glittered like another stream. On our return, the wind high – a violent storm of hail and rain at the Castle of Comfort. All the

The brook where Wordsworth heard 'a thousand blended notes'.

Heavens seemed in one perpetual motion when the rain ceased; the moon appearing, now half veiled, and now retired behind heavy clouds, the stars still moving, the roads very dirty.

March 7th. William and I drank tea at Coleridge's. A cloudy sky. Observed nothing particularly interesting – the distant prospect obscured. One only leaf upon the top of a tree – the sole remaining leaf – danced round and round like a rag blown by the wind.

The one red leaf, the last of its clan,
That dances as often as dance it can,
Hanging so light, and hanging so high,
On the topmost twig that looks up at the sky.

Christabel

March 19th. Wm. and Basil and I walked to the hill-tops, a very cold bleak day. We were met on our return by a severe hailstorm. William wrote some lines describing a stunted thorn.

March 23rd. Coleridge dined with us. He brought his ballad finished. We walked with him to the Miner's house. A beautiful evening, very starry, the horned moon.

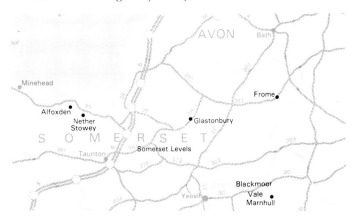

Glastonbury
Town on the A39, east of the M5 at J23.

The extraordinariness of Glastonbury Tor begins with its physical characteristics, its visibility for miles about, the smooth greenness and shape of the mound, which makes it look suspiciously man-made, the narrow terraces that circle the summit which appear to form a convoluted maze with the ruin of the chapel of St Michael at its core, and the qualities of the spring that flows from its flank – the Chalice Well, crystal clear water that trails red wherever it spreads.

'Glastonbury Tor'

the dance moves in us
we turn to the measure of stars
    of the hidden waters
we follow the bird's flight
    and the song
            always beyond us
the shifting of leaves is our music
our pattern the shadow of cloud
we dance to the sun
on the white hill we dance
we dance to the stillness
    at the heart of the dance

by Frances Horovitz

In fact the hill is composed of clays and limestones in horizontal strata that have gradually eroded, except at the top which is a layer of very hard Midford sand. And the phenomenon of the red water is the oxidising of the naturally high iron content upon contact with the air. None of which challenges the spirit of the place that has been irrepressible, it seems, for thousands of years and in very different cultures.

Originally, the Tor, the Abbey, and the Chalice Well constituted an island, the low flat Somerset plain, stretching westwards to Bridgwater Bay, being liable to flooding in winter from the Axe, Brue and Parrett rivers. Its pre-Saxon name was Ynyswitrin (Glass Island). In summer, the water receded to reveal a 'summer pasture', hence the Saxon name, 'somer saete', for the whole county.

Today, the western boundary of the lowland area of the Somerset plain is known as the Somerset Levels, and its eastern flood plains as the Moors. Behind the clay banks of the Levels, tides rise many feet higher than the Moors, and even as late as 1607, after considerable engineering works first by the Romans and in the 12th, 13th and 15th centuries, sea water could still come in as far as Glastonbury.

Long before the 18th Century, when ditches, or rhynes, were dug, enclosing fields and organising the drainage better, the area had developed its own culture, the willows along the flowery edges of the rhynes supporting a thriving basket-making industry. In 1987 it became the setting for a novel by Peter Benson, called *The Levels*.

Towards the end of the 19th Century two Iron Age lake villages, built as huts on platforms raised above the marshland, were unearthed at Godney and at Mere. Presumably the area would have been rich in fish and bird life, but it is possible that settlers were drawn here for other reasons and even earlier than Celtic times. There is no evidence for this but there is speculation concerning its name, Glass Island. Glass had early pagan associations with death and burial, quartz stone (nature's glass) being used in Bronze Age tombs in Ireland and as ceremonially significant pillars in stone circles, places of ritual sacrifice, as at the Boscawen-Un stone circle in Penwith in Cornwall.

Speculation that Glastonbury was a seat of the Old Religion or a sacred burial site was fuelled by legend. St Collen was an early Christian settler who built his cell at Glastonbury and upset the locals by denying that the tor was the entrance to the Underworld, the domain of Gwyn ap Nudd. When, so the story goes, he was introduced to it – a fine castle within the hill, he sprinkled his holy water so that it all disappeared.

In the etheric atmosphere about those two, as they stood there, quivered the immemorial Mystery of Glastonbury. Christians had one name for this Power, the ancient heathen inhabitants of this place had another, and a quite different one. Everyone who came to this spot seemed to draw something from it, attracted by a magnetism too powerful for anyone to resist, but as different people approached it they changed its chemistry, though not its essense, by their own identity, so that upon none of them it had the same psychic effect. This influence was personal and yet impersonal, it was a material centre of force and yet an immaterial fountain of life. It had its own *sui generis* origin in the nature of the Good-Evil First Cause, but it had grown to be more and more an independent entity as the centuries rolled over it. This had doubtless come about by reason of the creative energies pouring into it from the various cults, which, consciously or unconsciously, sucked their life-blood from its wind-blown, gossamer-light vortex. Older than Christianity, older than the Druids, older than the gods of Norsemen or Romans, older than the gods of the neolithic men, this many-named Mystery had been handed down to subsequent generations . . .

A Glastonbury Romance by John Cowper Powys

It is possible that Glastonbury received the first Christians in Britain. William of Malmesbury, a 12th-century monk from Malmesbury Abbey in Wiltshire and author of various authoritative historical works, wrote from his research in the library of Glastonbury Abbey, *De Antoquitate Glastoniensis Ecclesiae*, which is the primary Christian source about Glastonbury.

He records a 2nd-century Foundation of Christianity in Britain under the auspices of Pope Eleutherias, but cautiously entertains the possibility that when the Pope's Christian messengers arrived at Glastonbury they discovered a church already there, a wattle and daub structure dedicated to St Mary, and set amongst a dozen huts or cells, later a great draw for pilgrims and known as the Old Church.

At about the same time other historians began to build on Glastonbury's earlier reputation as a sacred burial ground or kingdom of the Underworld. Geoffrey of Monmouth first mentioned Avalon as King Arthur's burial site in his *Historia Regum Britanniae*:

Arthur himself, our renowned King, was mortally wounded and was carried off to the Isle of Avalon, so that his wounds might be attended to.

Malory's more romantic account in *Le Morte D'Arthur* came a few hundred years later –

Then Sir Bedevere took the king upon his back, and so went with him to that water side. And when they were at the water side, even fast by the bank hoved a little barge with many fair ladies in it, and among them all was a queen, and all they had black hoods, and all they wept and shrieked when they saw King Arthur.

'Now put me into the barge,' said the king.

And so he did softly; and there received him three queens with great mourning; and so they set them down, and in one of their laps King Arthur laid his head.

And then that queen said, 'Ah, dear brother, why have ye tarried so long from me? Alas, this wound on your head hath caught over-much cold.'

And so then they rowed from the land, and Sir Bedevere beheld all those ladies go from him.

Then Sir Bedevere cried, 'Ah my lord Arthur, what shall become of me, now ye go from me and leave me here alone among mine enemies?'

'Comfort thyself,' said the king, 'and do as well as thou mayest, for in me is no trust for to trust in; for I will into the vale of Avilion to heal me of my grievous wound: and if thou hear never more of me, pray for my soul . . . '

By this time, Giraldus Cambrensis had already identified 'insula Avallonia' with Glastonbury. Malory formalises it, leaving Sir Bedevere with the hermit 'in a chapel beside Glastonbury' with Arthur's tomb 'new graven . . . and so they lived in their prayers, and fastings, and great abstinence.'

With their wholly compatible codes, Christian and Arthurian myth were inseparable at the start. But when the Arthurian stories began to be more popular and important than the ethics they had been devised to engender, problems arose.

Robert de Boron's early 13th-century romance, *Joseph d'Arimathie* (which he followed with *Merlin*, and *Perceval*) cast Joseph, the rich disciple who obtained permission from Pilate to remove Christ's body to his own tomb, into the role of earliest founder of Christianity in Britain. In the context of William of Malmesbury's work, this was an acceptable idea to the monks of Glastonbury. But de Boron also had Joseph bring with him the Cup of the Last Supper in which he had caught the blood of the crucified Christ, identifying it with the Holy Grail (see Dinas Bran, Clwyd, Wales), and raising the standing of that great totem of Arthurian myth to the most exalted heights. When the word spread that the Holy Grail had been kept at Glastonbury in a stony nook beneath the waters of the Chalice Well, the stream of pilgrims became a flood. Then in 1190 or 1191, rather than tempering the

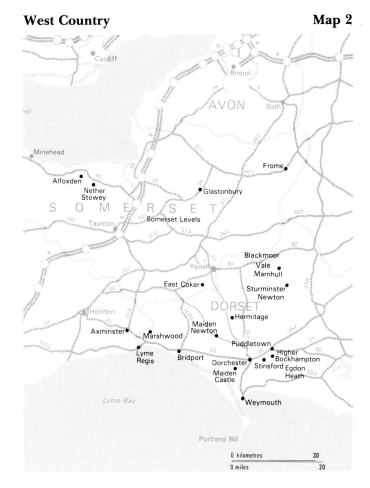

West Country   **Map 2**

rumours, the monks declared they had turned up Arthur's body in an oak coffin from 16 feet underground, and the flood became tidal.

In the 16th Century, a poem 'The Lyfe of Ioseph of Aramathia', probably written by a monk of Glastonbury, began to tone the stories down. The poet confirms that Joseph had brought Christianity to Britain –

Then hyther into brytayne Ioseph dyd come,
And this was by kyng Aueragas dayes;
So dyd Ioseph and also Iosephas his sonne,
With many one mo, as the old boke says.
This kynge was hethen & lyued on fals layes,
And yet he gaue to Ioseph au[i]lonye,
Nowe called Glastenbury . . .
There Ioseph lyued with other hermyttes twelfe,
That were the chyfe of all the company,
But Ioseph was the chefe hym-selfe;
There led they an holy lyfe and gostely.

The withy beds and part of the flat dividing grid of the rhines of the Somerset Levels. As late as 1607 sea water came in as far as Glastonbury (Avalon), turning it into an island.

And Joseph had come with blood that had fallen upon his shirt from the wound in Christ's side, and 'thys blode in two cruettes Ioseph dyd take.' But significantly there was no mention of the Holy Grail.

If the stories had run away with themselves, it did nothing to diminish the power of the place to inspire, whatever the 'denomination' of its pilgrims:

'Well, of course to our old-fashioned Protestant ancestors Glastonbury must have reeked with what you call "superstition". Three famous Saxon kings are buried here, something like six well-known saints are buried here. All the Holy Grail legends gather to a head here. The Druids played a great part here; and long before the Druids there was a Lake Village' – he gave a grave, characteristically West-country jerk with his head to indicate the northwestern point of the compass – 'whose mounds you can still see in the fields. Ancient British that probably was; older anyway than History! But I expect the deepest-rooted superstition here, if you could compel Glastonbury Tor to speak, would turn out to be the religion of the people who lived before the Ancient Britons; perhaps even before the Neolithic Men. At any rate we have some excuse for being "superstitious" in these parts. Don't you think so, Miss Drew?'

'I think you are very kind, dear Vicar, to answer Mr Crow's question at all,' said the old lady severely. 'For myself I would answer it rather differently. I would assure him that what he calls superstition WE call the Only True Faith.'

A Glastonbury Romance by John Cowper Powys

AVON

Bath
Town south west of Bristol on the A4 and south of the M4 on the A46, famous for its remedial hot springs.

Hudbras' son Bladud finally succeeded him and ruled the kingdom for twenty years. It was he who built the town of Kaerbadum, which is now called Bath, and who constructed the hot baths there which are so suited to the needs of mortal men. He chose the goddess Minerva as the tutelary deity of the baths. In her temple he lit fires which never went out and which never fell away into ash, for the moment that they began to die down they were turned into balls of stone . . . Bladud was a most ingenious man who encouraged necromancy throughout the kingdom of Britain.

From *Historia Regum Britanniae* by Geoffrey of Monmouth

A temple of Minerva was uncovered at Bath in the 12th century, after Geoffrey was writing, and it has been argued that the connection between Bladud, Bath, and Minerva, the Moon Goddess, and Bladud's experiments with necromancy (which led to his death after attempting flight over the town of Trinovantum) are evidence that the Baths were, in the Iron Age and possibly earlier, a place of pagan spiritual significance.

In 'The Myth of King Bladud' (1980), R J Stewart shows that the original spelling of Bladud's name would have been (in its two parts) Bel or Bal, and Duddydd or Derydd, the first referring to the orgiastic Celtic sun god Bel, and the second referring to divinity or priesthood.

'Springs were focal points for worship,' Stewart explains, 'they were thought of as the gateways to the Underworld . . . places of regeneration, where secret powers made life re-occur . . . Springs were proof that fertile powers resided within the earth, and hot-springs attracted particular attention.'

Clearly, as is so often the case with the sacred sites of previous cultures, the Romans' Aquae Sulis took up where Bladud left off, but when the Saxons arrived, they left the place a ruin, as this contemporary poem shows:

Wondrous is this stone-wall, wrecked by fate;
the city-buildings crumble, the works of the giants decay.

Roofs have caved in, towers collapsed,
barred gates are broken, hoar frost clings to mortar,
houses are gaping, tottering and fallen,
undermined by age. The earth's embrace,
its fierce grip, holds the mighty craftsmen;
they are perished and gone. A hundred generations
have passed away since then. This wall, grey with lichen
and red of hue, outlives kingdom after kingdom,
withstands tempests; its tall gate succumbed.
The city still moulders, gashed by storms . . .

From 'The Ruin'

By 1687, when Celia Fiennes visited the baths, they are once again in use but all orgiastic pretensions are long gone.

There is 5 baths the hot bath the most hot springs – its but small and built all round, which makes it ye hotter – out if it runns the water into a bath called the Le pours.

The third bath is called the Cross bath which is some thing bigger then the former and not so hot.

. . . The Kings bath is very large, . . . in it is the hot pumpe that persons are pumpt at for Lameness or on their heads for palsyes. I saw one pumpt, they put on a broad brim'd hatt with the Crown cut out so as ye brims Cast off ye water from ye face. So . . . The Ladyes goes into the bath with Garments made of a fine yellow canvas, which is stiff and made large with great sleeves like a parsons gown . . . The Gentlemen have drawers and waistcoates of the same sort of canvas.

. . . Ye queens bath is a degree hotter than ye Cross bath and ye Kings bath much hotter, these have all galleryes round and the pump is in one of these gallery's at ye Kings bath which ye Company drinks of, it is very hot and tastes like the water that boyles Eggs, has such a smell, but ye nearer the pumpe you drink it, ye hotter and less offencive and more spiriteous.

And by the time of Jane Austen's *Northanger Abbey* (1818), the primitive spirit is not even straining at the leash:

'How uncomfortable is it,' whispered Catherine, 'not to have a single acquaintance here!'

'Yes, my dear,' replied Mrs Allen, with perfect serenity, 'it is very uncomfortable, indeed.'

'What shall we do? The gentlemen and ladies at this table look as if they wondered why we came here; we seem forcing ourselves into their party.'

'*Springs were focal points for worship . . . gateways to the Underworld . . . proof that fertile powers resided within the earth, and hot-pools attracted particular attention.*' R J Stewart

'Aye, so we do. That is very disagreeable. I wish we had a large acquaintance here.'

'I wish we had *any*; it would be somebody to go to.'

'Very true, my dear; and if we knew anybody, we would join them directly. The Skinners were here last year; I wish they were here now.'

'Had not we better go away as it is? Here are no tea-things for us, you see.'

'No more there are, indeed. How very provoking! But I think we had better sit still, for one gets so tumbled in such a crowd. How is my head, my dear? Somebody gave me a push that has hurt it, I am afraid.

'No, indeed, it looks very nice. But, dear Mrs Allen, are you sure there is nobody you know in all this multitude of people? I think you *must* know somebody.'

'I don't, upon my word; I wish I did. I wish I had a large acquaintance here with all my heart, and then I should get you a partner. I should be so glad to have you dance. There goes a strange-looking woman! What an odd gown she has got on! How old-fashioned it is! Look at the back.'

After some time they received an offer of tea from one of their neighbours; it was thankfully accepted, and this introduced a light conversation with the gentleman who offered it, which was the only time that anybody spoke to them during the evening, till they were discovered and joined by Mr Allen when the dance was over.

'Well, Miss Morland,' said he, directly, 'I hope you have had an agreeable ball.'

'Very agreeable, indeed,' she replied, vainly endeavouring to hide a great yawn.

DORSET

No county is so dominated by a single writer's perception of it, at a crucial point in its cultural history, as Dorset is by Thomas Hardy. He lived from 1840 to 1928, an extraordinary period of change, but in fact the way of life he wrote about was well past when, in 1871, his first novel (*Desperate Remedies*) was published.

Egdon Heath

When Hardy was a boy in the 1840s, Egdon Heath began outside the backdoor of his cottage in Higher Bockhampton. Seventy years later his friend and topographical commentator, Hermann Lea, could describe it as 'that vast expanse of moorland which stretches, practically without a break, from Dorchester to Bournemouth.' But today there is virtually none of it left. Photographer Tim Hawkins found a little piece 'overlooked by Corfe Castle to the south . . .

'It was a spot which returned upon the memory of those who loved it with an aspect of peculiar and kindly congruity. Smiling champaigns of flowers and fruit hardly do this . . . Indeed, it is a question if the exclusive reign of this orthodox beauty is not aspproaching its last quarter. The new Vale of Tempe may be a gaunt waste in Thule: human souls may find themselves in closer and closer harmony with external things wearing a sombreness distasteful to our race when it was young,' wrote Hardy. In fact civilisation has encroached on a primitive piece of England that not only lived through Hardy's novels – through The Return of the Native, *and scenes from* The Dynasts *and* Tess of the D'Urbervilles *– but actually took its name from them.*

A Saturday afternoon in November was approaching the time of twilight, and the vast tract of unenclosed wild known as Egdon Heath embrowned itself moment by moment. Overhead the hollow stretch of whitish cloud shutting out the sky was as a tent which had the whole heath for its floor.

The heaven being spread with this pallid screen and the earth with the darkest vegetation, their meeting-line at the horizon was clearly marked. In such contrast the heath wore the appearance of an instalment of night which had taken up its place before its astronomical hour was come: darkness had to a great extent arrived hereon, while day stood distinct in the sky. Looking upwards, a furze-cutter would have been inclined to continue work; looking down, he would have decided to finish his faggot and go home. The distant rims of the world and of the firmament seemed to be a division in time no less than a division in matter. The face of the heath by its mere complexion added half an hour to evening; it could in like manner retard the dawn, sadden noon, anticipate the frowning of storms scarcely generated, and intensify the opacity of a moonless midnight to a cause of shaking and dread.

In fact, precisely at this transitional point of its nightly roll into darkness the great and particular glory of the Egdon waste began, and nobody could be said to understand the heath who had not been there at such a time. It could best be felt when it could not clearly be seen, its complete effect and explanation lying in this and the succeeding hours before the next dawn: then, and only then, did it tell its true tale. The spot was, indeed, a near relation of night, and when night showed itself an apparent tendency to gravitate together could be perceived in its shades and the scene. The sombre stretch of rounds and hollows seemed to rise and meet the evening gloom in pure sympathy, the heath exhaling darkness as rapidly as the heavens precipitated it. And so the obscurity in the air and the obscurity in the land closed together in a black fraternization towards which each advanced half-way.

The place became full of a watchful intentness now; for when other things sank brooding to sleep the heath appeared slowly to awake and listen. Every night its Titanic form seemed to await something; but it had waited thus, unmoved, during so many centuries, through the crises of so many things, that it could only be imagined to await one last crisis – the final overthrow.

The Return of the Native by Thomas Hardy

Hermitage
Hamlet to the west of the village of Middlemarsh, which lies on the A352 between Charminster and Sherborne.

As in *Under the Greenwood Tree* (see Higher Bockhampton), we have a close, wholly integrated community cut off from the outside world. Little Hinton is 'one of those sequestered spots,' Hardy wrote, 'where, from time to time, dramas of a grandeur and unity truly Sophoclean are enacted in the real, by virtue of the concentrated passions and closely-knit interdependence of the lives therein.' But the story of *The Woodlanders* is sad and its tragedy goes beyond the community into Hardy's view of life in the world at large. The clue to what it is all about lies of course in the wood itself –

Although the time of bare boughs had now set in there were sheltered hollows amid the Hintock plantations and copses in which a more tardy leave-taking than on windy summits was the rule with the foliage. This caused here and there an apparent mixture of the seasons; so that in some of the dells they passed by holly-berries in full red growing beside oak and hazel whose leaves were as yet not far removed from green, and brambles whose verdure was rich and deep as in the month of August. To Grace these well-known peculiarities were as an old painting restored.

Now could be beheld that change from the handsome to the curious which the

The neighbourhood of The Woodlanders. *Hermann Lea, with whom Hardy would cycle round the countryside verifying the real sites in his works, states in his* Hardy's Wessex *that Little Hintock, the focus of the action, is Hermitage.*

Hardy was not well disposed to tourists chasing round after him. He once complained about some Japanese 'Kodaking' him from behind a hedge.

features of a wood undergo at the ingress of the winter months. Angles were taking the place of curves, and reticulations of surfaces – a change constituting a sudden lapse from the ornate to the primitive on Nature's canvas, and comparable to a retrogressive step from the art of an advanced school of painting to that of the Pacific Islander . . .

The tragedy of The Woodlanders *is the tragedy of life's Unfulfilled Intention, a 'thwarted purposing', as he reiterated in his poem 'Yell'ham-Wood's Story' – 'That we come to live, and are called to die . . . Life offers to deny.'*

They went noiselessly over mats of starry moss, rustled through interspersed tracts of leaves, skirted trunks with spreading roots whose mossed rinds made them like hands wearing green gloves; elbowed old elms and ashes with great forks, in which stood pools of water that overflowed on rainy days, and ran down their stems in green cascades. On older trees still than these huge lobes of fungi grew like lungs. Here, as everywhere, the Unfulfilled Intention, which makes life what it is, was as obvious as it could be among the depraved crowds of a city slum. The leaf was deformed, the curve was crippled, the taper was interrupted; the lichen ate the vigour of the stalk, and the ivy slowly strangled to death the promising sapling.

The Woodlanders by Thomas Hardy

Higher Bockhampton
Hamlet south of the A35, 3m east of Dorchester.

The cottage where Hardy was born and lived for much of his first 30 years lies just outside the hamlet, a little to the north, then north east up a lane.

His memories of it were precious to his work, as so much of times-gone-

Hardy's cottage: a focal place, scene of Tranter Dewy's party in that work most evocative of rural England – Under The Greenwood Tree.

by had been imbibed here in the company of his mother and grandmother.

It faces west, and round the back and sides
High beeches, bending, hang a veil of boughs,
And sweep against the roof. Wild honeysucks
Climb on the walls, and seem to sprout a wish
(If we may fancy wish of trees and plants)
To overtop the apple-trees hard by.

Red roses, lilacs, variegated box
Are there in plenty, and such hardy flowers
As flourish best untrained. Adjoining these
Are herbs and esculents; and farther still
A field; then cottages and trees, and last
The distant hills and sky.

Behind, the scene is wilder. Heath and furze
Are everything that seems to grow and thrive
Upon the uneven ground. A stunted thorn
Stands here and there, indeed; and from a pit
An oak uprises, springing from a seed
Dropped by some bird a hundred years ago.

From 'Domicilium' by Thomas Hardy

Hardy chose the cottage as Tranter Dewy's house in *Under the Greenwood Tree*, perhaps the novel that fulfils best our expectations of Hardy as the literary harvester of rural England at its zenith.

In Under the Greenwood Tree *Hardy looks in upon a phase of rustic life already extinct in his time. 'A quarter of a century ago a string-choir might still be heard in some of the village churches in Wessex,' wrote his friend Hermann Lea in 1913, 'but the only instances today are where certain vicars have endeavoured to revive the string-music for some special service — a proceeding which has not always proved to be the success anticipated.' In the novel the Mellstock Choir is displaced by the new-fangled organ.*

The guests had all assembled, and the tranter's party had reached that degree of development which accords with ten o'clock P.M. in rural assemblies. At that hour the sound of a fiddle in process of tuning was heard from the inner pantry.

'That's Dick,' said the tranter. 'That lad's crazy for a jig.'

The fictitious name of Mellstock [around which the story is laid] included the several villages, hamlets, and isolated houses comprised in the parish of Stinsford,' wrote Hermann Lea. This is in the area of Hardy's birthplace, Higher Bockhampton.

And now a further phase of rural revelry had disclosed itself. It was the time of night when a guest may write his name in the dust upon the tables and chairs, and a bluish mist pervades the atmosphere, becoming a distinct halo round the candles; when people's nostrils, wrinkles, and crevices in general, seem to be getting gradually plastered up; when the very fiddlers as well as the dancers get red in the face, the dancers having advanced farther still towards incandescence, and entered the cadaverous phase; the fiddlers no longer sit down, but kick back their chairs and saw madly at the strings, with legs firmly spread and eyes closed, regardless of the visible world. Again and again did Dick share his Love's hand with another man, and wheel round; then, more delightfully, promenade in a circle with her all to himself, his arm holding her waist more firmly each time, and his elbow getting farther and farther behind her back, till the distance reached was rather noticeable; and, most blissful, swinging to places shoulder to shoulder, her breath curling round his neck like a summer zephyr that had strayed from its proper date. Threading the couples one by one they reached the bottom, when there arose in Dick's mind a minor misery lest the tune should end before they could work their way to the top again, and have anew the same exciting run down through. Dick's feelings on actually reaching the top in spite of his doubts were supplemented by a mortal fear that the fiddling might even stop at this supreme moment; which prompted him to convey a stealthy whisper to the far-gone musicians, to the effect that they were not to leave off till he and his partner had reached the bottom of the dance once more, which remark was replied to by the nearest of those convulsed and quivering men by a private nod to the anxious young man between two semiquavers of the tune, and a simultaneous 'All right, ay, ay,' without opening his eyes. Fancy was now held so closely, that Dick and she were practically one person. The room became to Dick like a picture in a dream; all that he could remember of it afterwards being the look of the fiddlers going to sleep, as humming-tops sleep – by increasing their motion and hum, together with the figures of grandfather James and old Simon Crumpler sitting by the chimney-corner, talking and nodding in dumb-show, and beating the air to their emphatic sentences like people in a railway train.

The dance ended, 'Piph-h-h-h!' said tranter Dewy, blowing out his breath in the very finest stream of vapour that a man's lips could form. 'A regular tightener, that one, sonnies!' He wiped his forehead, and went to the cider-mug on the table.

Under the Greenwood Tree by Thomas Hardy

Lyme Regis
Coastal town south of the A35, mid-way between Axminster and Bridport, a part of the coastline noted for its fossils.

The Cobb has invited what familiarity breeds for at least seven hundred years, and the real Lymers will never see much more to it than a long claw of old grey wall that flexes itself against the sea. In fact, since it lies well apart from the main town, a tiny Piraeus to a microscopic Athens, they seem almost to turn their backs on it.

Certainly it has cost them enough in repairs through the centuries to justify a certain resentment. But to a less tax-paying, or more discriminating, eye it is quite simply the most beautiful sea-rampart on the south coast of England. And not only because it is, as the guide-books say, redolent of seven hundred years of English history, because ships sailed to meet the Armada from it, because Monmouth landed beside it . . . but finally because it is a superb fragment of folk-art.

Primitive yet complex, elephantine but delicate; as full of subtle curves and volumes as a Henry Moore or a Michelangelo; and pure, clean, salt, a paragon of mass. . .

It stood right at the seawardmost end, apparently leaning against an old cannon-barrel up-ended as a bollard. Its clothes were black. The wind moved them, but the figure stood motionless, staring, staring out to sea, more like a living memorial to the drowned, a figure from myth, than any proper fragment of the petty provincial day.

The French Lieutenant's Woman by John Fowles

'These are the very steps that Jane Austen made Louisa Musgrove fall down in Persuasion,' says a character in John Fowles novel, *The French Lieutenant's Woman* (1969), from which the description of the Cobb also comes. Few people now think of Louisa Musgrove falling down steps when they walk the Cobb, for the image of John Fowles's woman, standing, staring out to sea, so concentrated the promise of his story that it now transcends the particularity of any such single occurrence, and, like a mythic landscape, holds us in thrall as it were the whole tale.

The image, Fowles suggests at the beginning of Chapter 1, came from the first stanza of Thomas Hardy's poem, 'The Riddle':

'A very strange stranger it must be, who does not see charms in the immediate environs of Lyme, to make him wish to know it better,' wrote Jane Austen in Persuasion. But it is never more than the setting for the human drama that unfolds. In John Fowles' French Lieutenant's Woman, the figure by the cannon-bollard becomes part of the 'folk-art' of the Cobb . . .

> Stretching eyes west
> Over the sea,
> Wind foul or fair,
> Always stood she
> Prospect-impressed;
> Solely out there
> Did her gaze rest,
> Never elsewhere
> Seemed charm to be.

Ernestina peered – her grey, her very pretty eyes, were short-sighted, and all she could see was a dark shape.

'Is she young?'

'It's too far to tell.'

'But I can guess who it is. It must be poor Tragedy.'

'Tragedy?'

'A nickname. One of her nicknames.'

'And what are the others?'

'The fishermen have a gross name for her.'

'My dear Tina, you can surely -'

The Cobb at Lyme – 'as full of subtle curves and volumes as a Henry Moore or a Michelangelo.' John Fowles

'They call her the French Lieutenant's . . . Woman.' . . .

She turned to look at him – or as it seemed to Charles, through him. It was not so much what was positively in that face which remained with him after that first meeting, but all that was not as he had expected; for theirs was an age when the favoured feminine look was the demure, the obedient, the shy. Charles felt immediately as if he had trespassed; as if the Cobb belonged to that face, and not to the Ancient Borough of Lyme. It was not a pretty face, like Ernestina's. It was certainly not a beautiful face, by any period's standard or taste. But it was an unforgettable face, and a tragic face. Its sorrow welled out of it as purely, naturally and unstoppably as water out of a woodland spring. There was no artifice there, no hypocrisy, no hysteria, no mask; and above all, no sign of madness. The madness was in the empty sea, the empty horizon, the lack of reason for such sorrow; as if the spring was natural in itself, but unnatural in welling from a desert.

Again and again, afterwards, Charles thought of that look as a lance; and to think so is of course not merely to describe an object but the effect it has. He felt himself in that brief instant an unjust enemy; both pierced and deservedly diminished.

The woman said nothing. Her look back lasted two or three seconds at most; then she resumed her stare to the south.

Maiden Castle
Ancient earthwork, a mile or so south west of Dorchester, off the A354.

Maiden Castle, like 'the mysterious nest of some gigantic jurassic-age bird-dragon.' John Cowper Powys

This has been the subject of a novel by John Cowper Powys – *Maiden Castle* (1936), where there is an attempt to get in touch with the old gods of Mai-Dun; and more recently, Christopher Priest speculates in *A Dream of Wessex* (1977) about a 22nd-century Wessex reachable through this ancient site.

They both walked with such rapid strides that it was not long before they reached the couple of isolated cottages, with a vegetable garden in front of them, that marks the halfway point to the ancient earthwork. Their road was both treeless and hedgeless and around it in all directions extended wide stretches of arable land where not a hedge or a tree was visible.

In fact nothing seemed visible from that long, straight, pilgrim's road except the object of the pilgrimage. Towards this object, towards this low-lying and yet grandly rising mass of *fossae* and *valla*, this man-made promontory of earth in an expanse of natural earth, this man-made city of turf in an expanse of natural turf, this Titanic erection of the demented mould-warp man, heaved up between the roots of the grass and the highways of the winds, the narrow road led as directly and undeviatingly as if this vast Polis, for so the classical geographer designated it, this mystical City of Dunium, had been an antediluvian monster – a monster compared with whom Leviathan himself were but a field-mouse – whose long straight dragon's tongue lay supine as a strip of seaweed so that the Beings it intended to swallow might advance at ease along it, undeterred by any distraction from advancing to their doom.

Dud stared in fascinated awe at the great earth-monument.

From this halfway distance it took all sorts of strange forms to his shameless mind. It took the shape of a huge "dropping" of supermammoth dung.

It took the shape of an enormous seaweed-crusted shell, the shell of the fish called Kraken, whom some dim motion of monstrous mate-lust had drawn up from the primeval slime of its sea-bed.

It took the shape of that vast planetary Tortoise, upon whose curved back, sealed with the convoluted inscriptions of the Nameless Tao, rested the pillar of creation.

But above all as he surveyed that dark-green bulk rising at the end of the long, narrow road he was compelled to think of the mysterious nest of some gigantic jurassic-age bird-dragon, such as, in this May sunshine, he could imagine even now hatching its portentous egg.

Maiden Castle by John Cowper Powys

Marnhull
The Marlott of Hardy's Tess of the D'Urbervilles. *Village south of the A30, off the B3092.*

Tess of the D'Urbervilles caused considerable controversy when first published. In those days a woman was responsible for the illegitimacy of her children. Tess, who is cruelly used and abused in the book, was thought immoral by some, and although after a brief period of joy she pays the civilised price for her 'liberation' (she is tried and hanged for the murder of her persecutor Alec D'Urberville), what Hardy thought about Tess was in the sub-title for all to see – 'A Pure Woman'.

It was a hazy sunrise in August. The denser nocturnal vapours, attacked by the warm beams, were dividing and shrinking into isolated fleeces within hollows and coverts, where they waited till they should be dried away to nothing.

The sun, on account of the mist, had a curious sentient, personal look, demanding the masculine pronoun for its adequate expression. His present aspect, coupled with the lack of all human forms in the scene, explained the old-time heliolatries in a moment. One could feel that a saner religion had never prevailed under the sky. The luminary was a golden-haired, beaming, mild-eyed, God-like creature, gazing down in the vigour and intentness of youth upon an earth that was brimming with interest for him.

The completion of a sheaf drew the women together 'like dancers at a quadrille . . . every one placing her sheaf on end against those of the rest, till a shock . . . was formed.'

His light, a little later, broke through chinks of cottage shutters, throwing stripes like red-hot pokers upon cupboards, chests of drawers, and other furniture within; and awakening harvesters who were not already astir.

But of all ruddy things that morning the brightest were two broad arms of painted wood, which rose from the margin of a yellow cornfield hard by Marlott village. They, with two others below, formed the revolving Maltese cross of the reaping-machine, which had been brought to the field on the previous evening to be ready for operations this day. The paint with which they were smeared, intensified in hue by the sunlight, imparted to them a look of having been dipped in liquid fire.

The movements of the other women were more or less similar to Tess's, the whole bevy of them drawing together like dancers in a quadrille at the completion of a sheaf by each, every one placing her sheaf on end against those of the rest, till a shock, or 'stitch' as it was here called, of ten or a dozen was formed.

They went to breakfast, and came again, and the work proceeded as before. As the hour of eleven drew near a person watching her might have noticed that every now and then Tess's glance flitted wistfully to the brow of the hill, though she did not pause in her sheafing. On the verge of the hour the heads of a group of children, of ages ranging from six to fourteen, rose above the stubbly convexity of the hill.

The face of Tess flushed slightly, but still she did not pause.

The eldest of the commers, a girl who wore a triangular shawl, its corner draggling on the stubble, carried in her arms what at first sight seemed to be a doll, but proved to be an infant in long clothes. Another brought some lunch. The harvesters ceased working, took their provisions, and sat down against one of the shocks. Here they fell to, the men plying a stone jar freely, and passing round a cup.

Tess Durbeyfield had been one of the last to suspend her labours. She sat down at the end of the shock, her face turned somewhat away from her companions. When she had deposited herself a man in a rabbit-skin cap and with a red handkerchief tucked into his belt, held the cup of ale over the top of the shock for her to drink. But she did not accept his offer. As soon as her lunch was spread she called up the big girl her sister, and took the baby of her, who, glad to be relieved of the burden, went away to the next shock and joined the other children playing there. Tess, with a curiously stealthy yet courageous movement, and with a still rising colour, unfastened her frock and began suckling the child.

Tess of the D'Urbervilles by Thomas Hardy

Puddletown
The Weatherbury of Far From The Madding Crowd, *a village on the A35, 5m east of Dorchester.*

The power of the central images of Hardy's work, which ensures their survival, derives not least from his ability to show the way rural people, wholly independent of the wider world, enter into a special communion with the spirit of place.

It was the first day of June, and the sheep-shearing season culminated, the

Puddletown (Weatherbury): 'In comparison with cities, Weatherbury was immutable . . . Ten generations failed to alter the turn of a single phrase . . .'

Right: The Great Barn – 'vast porches . . . dusky, filmed'. Searching for the one Hardy described is fruitless as there is none near Puddletown. As Hermann Lea suggests, Hardy probably imported its features into the story 'from a neighbouring place, there being two or three barns in South Dorset of which this would be a faithful description.' The picture shows the Great Barn at Abbotsbury, nearly 100 yards long and at least 500 years old.

'In these Wessex nooks the busy outsider's ancient times are only old; his old times are still new; his present is futurity. So the barn was natural to the shearers, and the shearers were in harmony with the barn.' Thomas Hardy

landscape, even to the leanest pasture, being all health and colour. Every green was young, every pore was open, and every stalk was swollen with racing currents of juice. God was palpably present in the country, and the devil had gone with the world to town.

They sheared in the great barn, called for the nonce the Shearing-barn, which on ground-plan resembled a church with transepts. It not only emulated the form of the neighbouring church of the parish, but vied with it in antiquity. Whether the barn had ever formed one of a group of conventual buildings nobody seemed to be aware; no trace of such surroundings remained. The vast porches at the sides, lofty enough to admit a waggon laden to its highest with corn in the sheaf, were spanned by heavy-pointed arches of stone, broadly and boldly cut, whose very simplicity was the origin of a grandeur not apparent in erections where more ornament has been attempted. The dusky, filmed, chestnut roof, braced and tied in by huge collars, curves, and diagonals, was far nobler in design, because more wealthy in material, than nine-tenths of those in our modern churches. Along each side wall was a range of striding buttresses, throwing deep shadows on the spaces between them, which were perforated by lancet openings, combining in their proportions the precise requirements both of beauty and ventilation.

One could say about this barn, what could hardly be said of either the church or the castle, akin to it in age and style, that the purpose which had dictated its original erection was the same with that to which it was still applied. Unlike and superior to either of those two typical remnants of mediaevalism, the old barn embodied practices which had suffered no mutilation at the hands of time. Here at least the spirit of the ancient builders was at one with the spirit of the modern beholder. . . .

Far From the Madding Crowd by Thomas Hardy

Portland Bill
Southernmost point of the Isle of Portland, south of Weymouth.

I cannot conceive of any portion of English coast more calculated to arouse a boy's imagination than the Chiswell end of the Chesil Beach. It is possible even when the weather is rough to stand in comparative safety and look down into the dragon throat of the terrible bay. A prodigious Atlantic roller, visible for a long time to a rain-drenched onlooker above the turbulence of all lesser waves far out at sea, dashes itself at last against this huge natural breakwater, and a second later, its pride broken, withdraws with an irresistible suction down, down, down, foam and tumbling pebbles together, until with a snarl, the very ocean floor is, for the duration of a moment, exposed under the curved suspended arch of a tottering wall of water, high towering as a church steeple, broad and awe-inspiring as the Niagara in flood . . .

It is best to come to the Bill when the summer visitors have dispersed to their distant homes. On a dim afternoon in November one can listen to sermons of excellent import at the foot of the pulpit rock. Thomas Hardy was aware of this or he could never have written *The Souls of the Slain*.

Dorset Essays by Llewelyn Powys

'There pass by the Bill, clinging to the necks of their runaway stallions lashed to desperation by the whips of the wind, the Thuellai, women-spirits of the storm. They go shrieking over the Race.' Llewellyn Powys

The thick lids of Night closed upon me
  Alone at the Bill
  Of the Isle by the Race –
Many-caverned, bald, wrinkled of face –
And with darkness and silence the spirit was on me
  To brood and be still.

No wind fanned the flats of the ocean,
  Or promontory sides,
  Or the ooze by the stand,
Or the bent-bearded slope of the land,
Whose base took its rest amid everlong motion
  Of criss-crossing tides.

Soon from out of the Southward seemed nearing
  A whirr, as of wings
  Waved by mighty-vanned flies,
Or by night-moths of measureless size,
And in softness and smoothness well-nigh beyond hearing
  Of corporal things.

And they bore to the bluff, and alighted –
  A dim-discerned train
  Of sprites without mould,
Frameless souls none might touch or might hold –
On the ledge by the turreted lantern, far-sighted
  By men of the main.

And I heard them say 'Home!' and I knew them
  For souls of the felled
  On the earth's nether bord
Under Capricorn, whither they'd warred,
And I neared in my awe, and gave heedfulness to them
  With breathings inheld . . .

From 'The Souls of the Slain' by Thomas Hardy

HAMPSHIRE

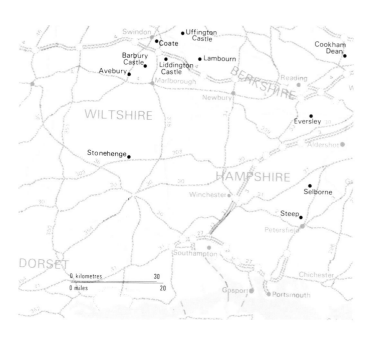

Eversley
A327 on the Hampshire Berkshire border.

Charles Kingsley, author of *The Water Babies*, was first curate then rector of Eversley, and when he first came here in 1842, at the age of 23, he wrote of its beauty to his future wife, Frances.

Kingsley at Eversley, 'drinking in all the forms of beauty . . . all the lowly intricacies of nature which no-one stoops to see.'

The view is beautiful. The ground slopes upward from the windows to a sunk fence and road, without banks or hedges, and then rises in the furze hill in the drawing, which hill is perfectly beautiful in light and shade, and colour . . . Behind the acacia on the lawn you get the first glimpse of the fir-forests and moors, of which the five-sixths of my parish consist. Those delicious self-sown firs! Every step I wander they whisper to me of you, the delicious past melting into the more delicious future.

It is hotter than yesterday, if possible, so I wandered out into the fields, and have been passing the morning in a lonely woodland bath – a little stream that trickles off the moor – with the hum of bees, and the sleepy song of birds around me, drinking in all the forms of beauty which lie in the pebbles, and mossy nooks of damp tree roots, and all the lowly intricacies of nature which no one stoops to see.

Here Kingsley developed grounds for his Faith in God from the forms and patterns of Nature. He writes of –

. . . the belief which is becoming every day stronger with me that all symmetrical natural objects, aye, and perhaps all forms, colours, and scents which show organisation or arrangement, are types of some spiritual truth or existence . . . When I walk the fields I am oppressed every now and then with an innate feeling, that everything I see has a meaning, if I could understand it . . . Everything seems to be full of God's reflex, if we could but see it.

Selborne
Village west of the A325 between Farnham and Petersfield.

Selborne, so poorly served by its hollow lanes that it would invariably be cut off from the rest of the world in winter.

See, Selborne spreads her boldest beauties round
The varied valley, and the mountain ground,
Wildly majestic! what is all the pride,
Of flats, with loads of ornaments supply'd?
Unpleasing, tasteless, impotent expense,
Compar'd with nature's rude magnificence.

   Arise, my stranger, to these wild scenes haste;
The unfinish'd farm awaits your forming taste:
Plan the pavilion, airy, light and true;
Thro' the high arch call in the length'ning view;
Expand the forest sloping up the hill;
Swell to a lake the scant, penurious rill;
Extend the vista, raise the castle mound
In antique taste, with turrets ivy-crown'd;
O'er the gay lawn the flow'ry shrub dispread,
Or with the blending garden mix the mead;
Bid China's pale, fantastic fence, delight,
Or with the mimic statue trap the sight.

The parish of Selborne lies in the extreme eastern corner of the county of Hampshire, bordering on the county of Sussex, and not far from the county of Surrey . . . The high part of the south-west consists of a vast hill of chalk, rising 300 feet above the village, and is divided into a sheep-down, the high wood and a long hanging wood, called the Hanger. The covert of the eminence is altogether beech . . . The prospect is bounded to the south-east and east by a vast range of mountains called the Sussex Downs . . . The village consists of one single, straggling street, three-quarters of a mile in length, in a sheltered vale.

The Natural History and Antiquities of Selborne (1789) by
Gilbert White

So deeply lined with one gauge of cartwheels (the local wheelwright's gauge) was the one street, that in winter it was impassable unless your wheels matched it, and so poorly served was that one street by its 'hollow lanes' (one of which survives still) that the village was cut off for months at a time.

The book, delivered in the form of letters, is remarkable for the painstaking observations of nature of its author, many of which took place in the 7-acre garden behind his house, The Wakes, where he constructed two alcoves and connected them to the house by a brick path, so that he could reach them even in bad weather. The one farthest from the house was set in among 20-foot field hedges of beech and thorn, an ideal environment for birds.

White also kept a herb, fruit and rose garden and had a special liking for the Cantaloupe melon, priding himself to an almost obsessive degree on the size he could grow them. 'On his return from Oxford or from visits to friends,' wrote his friend the rose gardener, Dean Hole, 'he hastens to inspect his beds of Cantaloupes, as a young mother rushes to the nursery after absence, or a schoolboy home for the holidays to his pony in the stable.'

So White's scientific approach to nature, which was rigorous and which did much to win the hearts of his many readers (the book went through 150 editions in as many years), did involve him occasionally in a certain amount of irrepressible feeling, although his 7-pound pet tortoise Timothy might have demured. Used to watching the ancient creature retreat from the sun under his plants of *Mirabilis jalapa* (Marvel of Peru), White was driven to marvel that God had

All that remains of White's fruit wall, his initials inscribed in stone, G W 1761. Beneath it grew the Marvel of Peru into which Timothy would retreat from the sun.

bestowed 'such a profusion of days' on Timothy, 'such a seeming waste of longevity, on a reptile that appears to squander more than two-thirds of its existence in joyless stupor.'

Steep
Off the A325 north of Petersfield.

A century or so after White, Edward Thomas, the poet and topographical prose writer living 5 miles south of Selborne, considered (in *The South Country*, 1909) a similarly scientific approach to unravelling the spirit of a place.

Some day there will be a history of England written from the point of view of one parish, or town, or great house. Not until there is such a history will all our accumulations of information be justified. It will begin with a geological picture, something large, clear, architectural, not a mass of insignificant names. It must be imaginative: it might, perhaps, lean sometimes upon Mr Doughty's *Dawn in Britain*. The peculiar combination of soil and woodland and water determines the direction and position and importance of the ancient trackways; it will determine also the position and size of the human settlements. The early marks of these – the old flint and metal implements, the tombs, the signs of agriculture, the encampments, the dwellings – will have to be clearly described and interpreted. Folk-lore, legend, place-names must be learnedly, but bravely and humanly used, so that the historian who has not the extensive sympathy and

The enormous yew at the Wakes, White, who lived there for 63 years from about 1730, almost certainly knew. The ha-ha was built by him, but his labourers overdid the digging out and made a 6-foot fall at one end which had to be chained off.

imagination of a great novelist will have no chance of success. What endless opportunities will he have for really giving life to past times in such matters as the line made by the edge of an old wood with the cultivated land, the shapes of the fields, with their borders of streams or hedge or copse or pond or wall or road, the purpose and interweaving of the roads and footpaths that suggest the great permanent thoughts and the lesser thoughts and dreams of the brain.

In the end Thomas either decided against the endeavour, or he was thwarted in it by a tragically early death (he was killed at Arras in 1917). On the whole it seems unlikely that the piece was more than a conceptualising of the broad purpose of Thomas's topographical work, for in his poetry he accepts that there will always be 'short-lived happy-seeming things' in nature 'that we no naught of'. Place is a vibrant living thing that you could never 'bite to the core':

The glory of the beauty of the morning,
The cuckoo crying over the untouched dew;
The blackbird that has found it, and the dove
That tempts me on to something sweeter than love;
White clouds ranged even and fair as new-mown hay;
The heat, the stir, the sublime vacancy
Of sky and meadow and forest and my own heart:–
The glory invites me, yet it leaves me scorning
All I can ever do, all I can be,
Beside the lovely of motion, shape, and hue,
The happiness I fancy fit to dwell
In beauty's presence. Shall I now this day
Begin to seek as far as heaven, as hell,
Wisdom or strength to match this beauty, start
And tread the pale dust pitted with small dark drops,
In hope to find whatever it is I seek,
Hearkening to short-lived happy-seeming things
That we know naught of, in the hazel copse?
Or must I be content with discontent
As larks and swallows are perhaps with wings?
And shall I ask at the day's end once more
What beauty is, and what I can have meant
By happiness? And shall I let all go,
Glad, weary, or both? Or shall I perhaps know
That I was happy oft and oft before,
A while forgetting how I am fast pent,
How dreary-swift, with naught to travel to,
Is Time? I cannot bite the day to the core.

'The Glory' by Edward Thomas

WILTSHIRE

Let us get out of these indoor narrow modern days, whose twelve hours somehow have become shortened, into the sunlight and the pure wind. A something that the ancients thought divine can be found and felt there still.

There was a hill to which I used to resort . . . The labour of walking three miles to it, all the while gradually ascending, seemed to clear my blood of the heaviness accumulated at home. On a warm summer day the slow continued rise required continual effort, which carried away the sense of oppression . . .

Moving up the sweet short turf, at every step my heart seemed to obtain a wider horizon of feeling; with every inhalation of rich pure air, a deeper desire. The very light of the sun was whiter and more brilliant here. By the time I had reached the summit I had entirely forgotten the petty circumstances and the annoyances of existence. I felt myself, myself. There was an intrenchment on the summit, and going down into the fosse I walked round it slowly to recover breath. On the south-western side there was a spot where the outer bank had partially slipped, leaving a gap. There the view was over a broad plain, beautiful with wheat, and inclosed by a perfect amphitheatre of green hills. Through these hills there was one narrow groove, or pass, southwards, where the white clouds seemed to close in the horizon. Woods hid the scattered hamlets and farmhouses, so that I was quite alone.

I was utterly alone with the sun and the earth. Lying down on the grass, I spoke in my soul to the earth, the sun, the air, and the distant sea far beyond sight. I thought of the earth's firmness – I felt it bear me up; through the grassy couch there came an influence as if I could feel the great earth speaking to me, I thought of the wandering air – its pureness, which is its beauty; the air touched me and gave me something of itself. I spoke to the sea; though so far, in my mind I saw it, green at the rim of the earth and blue in deeper ocean; I desired to have its strength, its mystery, and glory. Then I addressed the sun, desiring the soul equivalent of his light and brilliance, his endurance and unwearied race. I turned to the blue heaven over, gazing into its depth, inhaling its exquisite colour and sweetness. The rich blue of the unattainable flower of the sky drew my soul towards it, and there it rested, for pure colour is rest of heart. By all these I prayed; I felt an emotion of the soul beyond all definition; prayer is a puny thing to it, and the word is a rude sign to the feeling, but I know no other.

The Story of My Heart by Richard Jefferies

Coate Farm, 3 miles from the ridgeway of Barbury, Liddington, and Uffington castles to which he would resort. Right: *Coate Water.*

Coate
A mile or so south east of Swindon on the A4259.

Coate Water, just a few steps south from the farm where Richard Jefferies was born in 1848, covers well over 50 acres. In *Bevis: The Story of a Boy*, Jefferies showed, in an autobiographical boy's adventure story, how the lake, its islands, the woods, and the reeded swampland became a battleground for him and his friends. But Jefferies gives us more —

A broad, cool shadow from the trees had fallen over the

hatch, for the afternoon had gone on, and the sun was declining behind them over the western hills. A broad, cool shadow, whose edges were far away, so that they were in the midst of it. The thrushes sang in the ashes, for they knew that the quiet evening, with the dew they love, was near. A bullfinch came to the hawthorn hedge just above the hatch, looked in and out once or twice, and then stepped inside the spray near his nest. A yellow-hammer called from the top of a tree, and another answered him across the field. Afar in the mowing-grass the crake lifted his voice, for he talks more as the sun sinks.

The swirling water went round and round under the fall, with lines of white bubbles rising, and quivering masses of yellowish foam ledged on the red rootlets under the bank and against the flags. The swirling water, ceaselessly beaten by the descending stream coming on it with a long-continued blow, returned to be driven away again. A steady roar of the fall, and a rippling sound above it of bursting bubbles and

crossing wavelets of the hastening stream, notched and furrowed over stones, frowning in eager haste. The rushing and the coolness, and the song of the brook and the birds, and the sense of the sun sinking, stilled even Bevis and Mark a little while. They sat and listened, and said nothing; the delicious brook filled their ears with music.

They dashed open the gate, and ran down to the beach. It was a rough descent over large stones, but they reached the edge in a minute, and as they came there was a splashing in several places along the shore. Something was striving to escape, alarmed at their approach. Mark fell on his knees, and put his hand where two or three stones, half in and half out of water, formed a recess, and feeling about drew out two roach, one of which slipped from his fingers.

Stonehenge

Stone circle, north of the A303, 6m north of Salisbury, probably erected between 1700 and 1500BC.

Today I paid my first visit to Stonehenge. . . .

The sun was hot, but a sweet soft air moved over the Plain 'wafting' the scent of the purple heather tufts and the beds of thyme and making the delicate blue harebells tremble on their fragile stems. A beautiful little wheatear flitted before us from one stone heap to another along the side of the wheel track as we struck across the firm elastic turf. Around us the Plain heaved mournfully with great and solemn barrows, the 'grassy barrows of the happier dead'. It seemed to be holy ground and the very Acre of God. Beyond Ambresbury the Plain swelled into bolder hills, and dark clumps of trees here and there marked the crests and high places of the downs, while the white and dusty road glared away northwards in full sweep for Devizes across the great undulations of the rolling Plain.

. . . The grey cluster of gigantic Stones stood in the mist of a green plain, and the first impression they left on my mind was that of a group of people standing about and talking together. It seemed to me as if they were ancient giants who suddenly became silent and stiffened into stone directly anyone approached, but who might at any moment become alive again, and at certain seasons, as at midnight and on Old Christmas and Midsummers Eve, might form a true 'Chorea Gigantum' and circle on the Plain in a solemn and stately dance.

It is a solemn awful place. As I entered the charmed circle of the sombre Stones I instinctively uncovered my head. It was like entering a great Cathedral Church. A great silent service was going on and the Stones inaudibly whispered to each other the grand secret. The Sun was present at the service in his Temple and the place was filled with his glory. During the service we sat under the shadow of the great leaning stone upon the vast monolith which has fallen upon and crushed and which now nearly covers the Hearth or Altar Stone. Many Stones still stood upright, one leaned forward towards the East, as if bowing to the rising sun, while some had fallen flat on their faces as if prostrate with adoration before the Lamp of Heaven, or as if like Dragon they had fallen across the theshold of the Temple before the advent of a purer faith, and in reluctant acknowledgment and worship of One Greater then They.

It must be a solemn thing to pass a night among the silent shadows of the awful Stones, to see the Sun leave his Temple in the evening with a farewell smile, and to watch for him again until at morning he enters once more by the great Eastern gate and takes his seat upon the altar stone.

As we went down the southern slope of the green plain we left the Stones standing on the hill against the sky, seeming by turns to be the Enchanted Giants, the Silent Preachers, the Sleepless Watchers, the great Cathedral on the Plain.

Striking across the country we came at twilight to the edge of the downs and saw Old Sarum looming before us. Up and down we climbed, the hardest steepest way through moat and over mound, till we came at dusk into the strange sad mysterious deserted city, silent but for the voices of some children at play amongst the bushes within the desolate mounds and broken walls.

Francis Kilvert's *Diaries*

'The heathen temple . . . older than the centuries; older than the D'Urbervilles.' Thomas Hardy

'It is a solemn awful place. As I entered the charmed circle of the sombre Stones I instinctively uncovered my head.' Francis Kilvert

When we came to the edge of this sacred Place, we tethered our Horses to the Posts provided and then, with the Sunne direct above us, walked over the short grass which (continually cropt by the flocks of Sheep) seemed to spring us forward to the great Stones. I stood back a little as Sir Chris. walked on, and I considered the Edifice with steadinesse: there was nothing here to break the Angles of Sight and as I gaz'd I opened my Mouth to cry out but my Cry was silent; I was struck by an exstatic Reverie in which all the surface of this Place seemed to me Stone, and the Sky itelf Stone, and I became Stone as I joined the Earth which flew on like a Stone through the Firmament. And thus I stood until the Kaw of a Crow rous'd me: and yet even the call of the black Bird was an Occasion for Terrour, since it was not of this Time. I know not how long a Period I had transversed in my Mind, but Sir Chris. was still within my Sight when my Eyes were clear'd of Mist. He was walking steadily towards the massie Structure and I rushed violently to catch him, for I greatly wished to enter the Circle before him. I stopped him with a Cry and then ran on: when Crows kaw more than ordinary, *said I* when I came up to him all out of Breath, we may expect Rain. Pish, *he replied*. He stopped to tye his Shooe, so then I flew ahead of him and first reached the Circle which was the Place of Sacrifice. And I bowed down.

Master Jones says it is erected on the Cubit measure, *says Sir Chris.* coming after me and taking out his Pocket-Book, and do you see, Nick, its beautiful Proportions?

It is a huge and monstrous Work, *I answered* standing straight, and it has been called the Architecture of the Devil.

But he paid no heed to me: They must have used tall trees for Levers, *he continu'd* squinting up at the Stones, or they discover'd the art of ordering Engines for the raising of Weights.

Some said Merlyn was the Father, *I replied*, and raised these Stones by the hidden Mysteries of Magick.

Sir Chris. laughed at this and sat upon the Stone in the inner Circle. There is an old rhyme, Nick, *says he*, which goes thus:

> This Fame saies, Merlyn to perfection brought
> But Fame said more than ever Merlyn wrought.

And he learn'd forward with a Smile.

You are sitting on the Altar Stone, *I said*; and he jumped up quickly like one bitten. Do you see, *I continu'd*, how it is of a harder Stone and designed to resist Fire?

I see no Scorch marks, *he replied*: but then he wandred among the other Stones as I recall'd another merry Verse:

These are all places of Sacrifice, I cried out, and these stones are the Image of God raised in Terrour!
Hawksmoor by Peter Ackroyd

Will you wake him?
No, not I,
For if I do
He's sure to Cry.

When we were not close about each other I could talk freely again: For these are all places of Sacrifice, *I call'd out*, and these Stones are the Image of God raised in Terrour! . . .

The skie was getting wonderful Dark with a strong Winde which swirled around the Edifice: Do you see, *I said*, how the Architraves are so stangely set upon the

'It is a huge and monstrous Work, I answered standing straight, and it has been called the Architecture of the Devil.'

heads of the Upright stones that they seem to hang in the Air? But the winde took my words away from him as he crouched with his Rule and Crayon. Geometry, *he called out*, is the Key to this Majesty: if the Proportions are right, I calculate that the inner part is an Exagonall Figure raised upon the Bases of four Equilaterall Triangles! I went up to him saying, Some believe they are Men metamorphosised into Stone, but he payed no Heed to me and stood with his Head flung back as *he continue'd*: And you see, Nick, there is an Exactness of Placing them in regard to the Heavens, for they are so arranged as to estimate the positions of the Planets and the fixed Starres. From which I believe they had magneticall compass Boxes.

Then the Rain fell in great Drops, and we sheltered beneath the Lintel of one great Stone as it turned from gray to blew and green with the Moisture. And when I lean'd my Back against that Stone I felt in the Fabrick the Labour and Agonie of those who erected it, the power of Him who enthrall'd them, and the marks of Eternity which had been placed there. I could hear the Cryes and Voices of those long since gone but I shut my Ears to them and, to keep away Phrensy, stared at the Moss which grew over the Stone. Consider this, *I told Sir Chris.*, the Memphitic pyramid has stood about three thousand and two hundred years, which is not as long as this Edifice: but it was twenty years in building, with three hundred and sixty thousand men continually working upon it. How many laboured here, and for how long? And then I went on after a Pause: the Base of the pyramidde is the exact size and shape of Lincolns-Inn-Fields, and I have some times in my Mind's Eye a Pyrammide rising above the stinking Streets of London. The sky had cleared as I spoke, the clowds rowled away, and as the Sun struck the Ground I looked towards Sir Chris. But he seemed altered in Feature: he had heard nothing of my Matter but sat leaning his Head back upon the Stone, pale as a Cloth and disconsolate to a strange Degree. I lay no Stress upon the Thing called a Dream, *he said*, but I just now had a Vision of my Son dead.

Hawksmoor by Peter Ackroyd

Wales

To live in Wales is to be conscious
At dusk of the spilled blood
That went to the making of the wild sky,
Dyeing the immaculate rivers
In all their courses.
It is to be aware,
Above the noisy tractor
And hum of the machine
Of strife in the strung woods,
Vibrant with sped arrows.
You cannot live in the present,
At least not in Wales.
There is the language for instance,
The soft consonants
Strange to the ear.
There are cries in the dark at night
As owls answer the moon,
And thick ambush of shadows,
Hushed at the fields' corners
There is no present in Wales,
And no future;
There is only the past,
Brittle with relics,
Wind-bitten towers and castles
With sham ghosts;
Mouldering quarries and mines;
And an impotent people,
Sick with inbreeding,
Worrying the carcase of an old song.

'Welsh Landscape' by RS Thomas

Left: *view from the Black Mountains, north up the Honddu Valley.*

GWYNEDD

Caernafon
Approached by the A487, Caernafon lies at the south-west end of the Menai Straits opposite the Isle of Anglesey, on the site of the Roman outpost of Segontium.

Caernafon is the fount of the oldest story about the Roman occupation of Britain. *The Dream of Maxen* is part of the *Mabignogian*, a collection of eleven stories sustained orally since earliest times and written down in the 14th Century. They turn on historical fact, very often depicting pivotal events

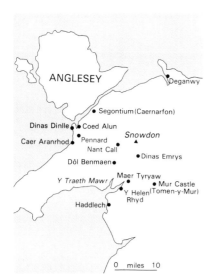

The Gwynedd map of the Mabignogian, itself the mythic spirit map of Wales.

in our culture, and are couched inspirationally in the romantic magical mythical landscape of Wales.

Dinas Dinlle

Impressive coastal Iron Age hill fort, west of the A499 at Llandwrog, 5m from Caernafon.

Dinas Dinlle takes us way back before the Roman occupation and *Math Son of Mathonwy*, the story associated with the fort, seems to tell of a time even before the Iron Age Celts, who came to Britain around 400BC.

It is said locally that at lowest tide the rocky remnants of an ancient castle, Caer Arianrhod, are visible below Dinas Dinlle. The figure of Arianrhod appears both in the in the story of *Math son of Mathonwy* and in the Welsh Triads, a collection of ancient aphorisms arranged epigrammatically in threes.

Robert Graves identifies Arianrhod with 'Caridwen, or Cerridwen, the White Goddess of Life-in-Death and Death-in-Life', an aspect of the original feminine principle whence all creative inspiration flows (see also Narberth, Dyfed). Historically he argues for matriarchy as the oldest human culture, placing it in Sumeria, 8 to 10,000 years BC, giving his poetic muse the status of the all-powerful Sumerian goddess, ultimately fruitful and creative, but utterly ruthless – her story, 'the story [Math] is at least as old as the Babylonian Gilgamish epic.'

In the magical and unsettling tale of *Math Son of Mathonwy*, Arianrhod is portrayed first as Virgin Mother – (in matriarchal Goddess mythology the role of men in the reproduction process is negligible) – and then as Blodeuwedd, Love Goddess made of 'the blossoms of the oak, and the blossoms of the broom, and the blossoms of the meadow-sweet . . . a maiden, the fairest and most graceful that man ever saw', who betrays her lover – (in myth the Goddess's lovers are emasculated and disposed of like drones to preserve the mystique of her virginity) – and finally as sow, devourer of her son's dead flesh.

Math's Court retains remnants of the old matriarchal system, both symbolically – 'at that time he could not live unless his feet were in the folds of a virgin's lap' (the virgin is called Goewin), and in terms of the royal succession, which appears to be matrilinear – it is Math's sister's son, Gwydion, who inherits his magical powers. Finally, Gwydion is known in the tale as son of Don, establishing his descent from the Pelasgian tribe of Danaans, who came to Britain during the Bronze Age in the second millennium BC, and worshipped the Goddess Danu,

Gwydion has used his magic to steal Pryderi's sacred swine, symbolically usurping the power of this southern king, whose kingdom (see Narberth, Dyfed) had been the ancient seat of another goddess figure, Rhiannon. The battles that follow, between the forces of Math, and Pryderi are fought in the plain between Snowdonia and Dinas Dinlle (see map): between Coed Alun and Pennardd, and, as Pryderi retreats, at Nant Call. At Dol Benmaen, Pryderi seeks a truce; thereafter both forces travel under a white flag to Y Traeth Mawr (the Big Strand) and Y Velen Rhyd (the Yellow Ford) in the esturial silt plain of the River Glaslyn as it makes its way to

The tide falls at Dinas Dinlle to reveal the Kingdom of Arianrhod.

Tremadoc Bay. The business is finally settled in single combat between Gwydion and Pryderi when the truce breaks down and the foot soldiers of both sides cannot resist getting at each other.

'The two men were set apart. They armed themselves and fought, and by reason of strength and skill and magic and enchantment Gwydion was the victor and Pryderi was killed; he was buried at Maen Tryryawg, above Y Velen Rhyd, and there his grave is.' This is modern Moentwrog.

The suggestion that what we are witnessing here is a usurpation of the power of the goddess culture from the south is given credence with the introduction of Arianrhod to the story and the exposure of the mystique of her virginity, followed by a strange reappraisal of the role of men in the business of procreation (the ultimately creative act). It was this swing which, according to Graves in his story, produced the major cultural shift from matriarchy to patriarchy in ancient times. After it, the idea of a male progenitor of the universe was no longer considered absurd.

First, the royal virgin foot bearer is raped by Gwydion's brother – 'the other girls were forced out of the chamber, and Goewin taken against her will' – and after a succession of weird situations when Gwydion and his brother are turned by Math into animals, male and female alternately,

Looking out from the ramparts of the Bronze Age ramparts of Dinas Dinlle towards Snowdon, across the battle plain of Math and Pryderi.

which mate with one another and procreate, Arianrhod is wheeled in as replacement virgin foot bearer and found wanting –

Math took his wand and bent it, saying, 'Step over that, and if you are a virgin I will know.' Arianrhod stepped over the wand, and with that step she dropped a sturdy boy with thick yellow hair; the boy gave a loud cry, and with that cry she made for the door, dropping a second small something on the way, but before anyone could get a look at it Gwydion snatched it up and wrapped it in a silk sheet and hid it in a little chest at the foot of his bed.

The fair-haired boy is baptised Dylan, son of the Wave, and runs off into the sea, where he swims 'as well as the best fish that was therein'. The 'something' in Gwydion's chest turns out to be Dylan's brother. Gwydion rears him at Dinas Dinlle and tries again and again to get Arianrhod at her nearby castle to accept him. She refuses, seeing the boy as the cause of her dishonour. There follows a sequence of curses laid on the boy by Arianrhod – first that he will remain nameless unless named by her, second that he should never have arms or armour until she gives him them, third that he will 'never have a wife of the race that now inhabits the earth'.

Gwydion overcomes all three. Arianrhod is tricked into naming the boy Llew Llaw Gyffes (Lion with the Steady Hand), hence Dinas Din-lle, Din-Llew, Llew's fort. But when, to beat the third curse, Blodeuwedd is created as Llew Llaw's wife, and Llew Llaw is given Mur Castle as his stronghold,

Blodeuwedd plots with her lover, a passing chieftain called Gronw Pebyr, to kill him. This is not an easy matter as Llew Llaw cannot be 'slain within a house, nor without . . . [nor] on horseback [nor] on foot'. Blodeuwedd discovers Llew's secret however –

'By making a bath for me by the side of a river, and by putting a roof over the cauldron, and thatching it well and tightly, and bringing a buck, and putting it beside the cauldron. Then if I place one foot on the buck's back, and the other on the edge of the cauldron, whosoever strikes me thus will cause my death.'

Gronw delivers the fatal dart 'on the hill which is now called Bryn Kyvergyr, on the band of the River Cynvael'. Mur Castle is Tomen-y-Mur today and the valley of the Cynfal, from which this legend arises, is perfectly in accord. There is about it something of what the poet Hugh MacDiarmid calls the 'universal' history of place . . . ' the possible in the present, the infinite in the intrinsic of the present . . . a value, a principle-value, a motive-value', a spirit of place which the priest and poet R S Thomas prefers to call God, though it is not the God of Sunday School story.

God is in the sound of the white water
Falling at Cynfal. God is in the flowers
Sprung at the foot of Olwen, and Melangell
Felt his heart beating in the wild hare.
Wales is in fact His peculiar home,
Our fathers knew Him. But where is that voice now?
Is it in the chapel vestry, where Davies is using
The logic of the Smithfield?

From 'The Minister' by R S Thomas

Bottom left: *Hell's Mouth, the Llyn peninsular, pointing towards Bardsey Island, graveyard of 10,000 saints.* Below: *the simple cottage of R S Thomas, poet and priest, overlooks the bay.*

Harlech

The castle built by Edward I c1283 dominates the town, 7m or so south west of Moentwrog, overlooking Tremadog Bay.

Robert Graves spent many holidays as a child here, as he describes in his autobiography, *Goodbye to All That* (1929), and it is here too that one of the key figures in ancient British mythology, which became his great interest, once held sway.

This country (and I known no other like it) seemed to be independent of formal nature. One hardly noticed the passage of the seasons there; the wind always blew across the stunted grass, the black streams always ran cold and clear, over black stones. The mountain sheep were wild and free, capable of scrambling over a six-foot stone wall (unlike the slow, heavy, smutty-fleeced South-down flocks that fattened in the fields beyond Wimbledon) and, when in repose, easily mistaken for the lichen-covered granite boulders strewn everywhere. Few trees grew except hazels, rowans, stunted oaks and thorn bushes in the valleys. Winters were always mild, so that last year's bracken and last year's heather survived in a faded way through to the next spring. We saw hardly any birds, bar an occasional buzzard, and curlews wheeling in the distance; and wherever we went the rocky skeleton of the hill seemed only an inch or two beneath the turf. . . .

Had this been Ireland, we would have self-consciously learned Irish and the local legends; but we did not go to Ireland, except once when I was an infant in arms. Instead we came to know Wales more purely, as a place with a history too old for local legends; while walking there we made up our own. We decided who lay buried under the Standing Stone, and who had lived in the ruined round-hut encampment, and in the caves of the valley where the big rowans grew. On our visits to Germany I had felt a sense of home in a natural human way, but above Harlech I found a personal peace independent of history or geography. The first poem I wrote as myself concerned those hills.

Goodbye to all That by Robert Graves

Harlech Castle, site of the fortress of Bran, King of Britain, looks out over Tremadog Bay.

This is a wild land, country of my choice,
With harsh craggy mountain, moor ample and bare.
Seldom in these acres is heard any voice
But voice of cold water that runs here and there
Through rocks and lank heather growing without care.
No mice in the heath run, no song-birds fly
For fear of the buzzard that floats in the sky . . .

Time has never journeyed to this lost land,
Crakeberry and heather bloom out of date,
The rocks jut, the streams flow singing on either hand,
Careless if the season be early or late,
The skies wander overhead, now blue, now slate;
Winter would be known by his cutting snow
If June did not borrow his armour also.

From 'Rocky Acres' by Robert Graves

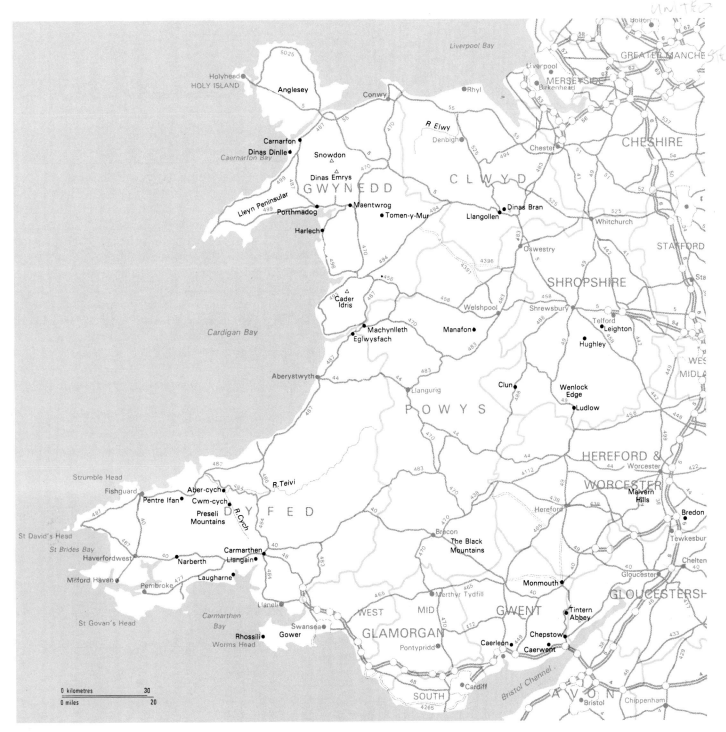

Bran the Blessed son of Llyr was the crowned king of this island, having been raised to the throne of London. One afternoon he was sitting on the rock of Harddlech overlooking the sea . . . [and] saw thirteen ships coming from the south of Ireland and making for the coast, moving easily and swiftly, running before the

Wales and the border counties, Shropshire and Hereford & Worcester, see pages 67 to 90.

wind and approaching rapidly. 'I see ships out there making boldly for our land,' said Bran. 'Tell the men of the court to equip themselves and go learn what our visitors want.'

Branwen Daughter of Llyr from the *Mabignogian*, see Dinas Dinlle, establishes the site of the court of Bran, the most eminent pre-Celtic King of Britain (in early literature he is as much a god as a king) at Harlech, and tells the story of his defeat and decapitation at the hands of King Mallolwch's forces from Ireland.

In *The White Goddess* (1961) Robert Graves describes Bran's defeat as 'the most important religious event in pre-Christian Britain . . . the expulsion of a long-established Bronze Age priesthood from the national necropolis by an alliance of . . . worshippers of the Danaan god Bel, Beli, Belus or Belinus, with an invading Brythonic [Celtic] tribe.'

After the battle Bran's head is returned to Harlech before being transported eventually to 'the White Mount in London', where it is buried according to Bran's dying wish, 'with the face turned towards France' to protect Britain from invasion.

If the White Mount is Tower Hill, the hill of the white tower, as has been suggested, then the story may explain the legend that while there are ravens at Tower Hill Britain is safe from invasion, for 'Bran' means raven.

Snowdon
At 3,560ft, the highest peak in Wales, Snowdon is contained within the A4085, 4086, and 498.

In the summer of 1791 it was climbed by William Wordsworth, who recorded his experience at the summit in Book XIII of his autobiographical poem, 'The Prelude':

'To the Welsh, besides being the hill of the Awen or Muse, it has always been the hill of hills, the loftiest of all mountains, the one whose snow is the coldest, to climb to whose peak is the most difficult of all feats; and the one whose fall will be the most astounding catastrophe of the last day.' George Borrow (1862)

> I looked about, and lo!
> The Moon stood naked in the heavens, at height
> Immense above my head, and on the shore
> I found myself of a huge sea of mist,
> Which, meek and silent, rested at my feet.
> A hundred hills their dusky backs upheaved
> All over this still ocean; and beyond,
> Far, far beyond, the vapours shot themselves,
> In headlands, tongues, and promontory shapes,
> Into the sea, the real sea, that seemed
> To dwindle and give up its majesty,
> Usurped upon as far as sight could reach.
> Meanwhile the Moon looked down upon this show
> In single glory, and we stood, the mist
> Touching our very feet; and from the shore
> At distance not the third part of a mile
> Was a blue chasm; a fracture in the vapour,
> A deep and gloomy breathing-place through which
> Mounted the roar of waters, torrents, streams

Innumerable, roaring with one voice!
The universal spectacle throughout
Was shaped for admiration and delight,
Grand in itself alone, but in that breach
Through which the homeless voice of waters rose,
That dark deep thoroughfare, had Nature lodged
The soul, the imagination of the whole.

Here 'Nature lodged The soul, the imagination of the whole.' William Wordsworth

On the third morning after our arrival at Bangor we set out for Snowdon.

Snowdon or Eryri is no single hill, but a mountainous region, the loftiest part of which, called Y Wyddfa, nearly four thousand feet above the level of the sea, is generally considered to be the highest point of Southern Britain. The name Snowdon was bestowed upon this region by the early English on account of its snowy appearance in winter; Eryri by the Britons, because in the old time it abounded with eagles, Eryri in the ancient British language signifying an eyrie or breeding-place of eagles. . . .

Perhaps in the whole world there is no region more picturesquely beautiful than Snowdon, a region of mountains, lakes, cataracts and groves, in which Nature shows herself in her most grand and beautiful forms . . .

It was to Snowdon that Vortigern retired from the fury of his own subjects, caused by the favour which he showed to the detested Saxons. It was there that he called to his counsels Merlin, said to be begotten on a hag by an incubus, but who was in reality the son of a Roman consul by a British woman.

Wild Wales by George Borrow

George Borrow draws his reference to Vortigren and Merlin from Geoffrey of Monmouth's *Historia Regum Britanniae* (1136). Vortigern, the 5th Century King of Britain, having foolishly encouraged a Saxon called Hengist into Britain, set up an assembly at the Cloister of Ambrius, near Salisbury, and invited some 500 English counts and earls to sign a peace treaty, but each of Hengist's soldiers turned up with a dagger concealed in his boot, and on the call of 'Nimet oure saxes!' the throats of 460 Englishmen were cut. Vortigern, a cowardly, deceitful king, and hopelessly shortsighted as a strategist, fled in horror to Snowdon (Eryri), and summoned magicians to tell him what he should do.

They advised him to build a tower into which he could retreat should he lose all his other fortresses to the Saxons. This appealed to Vortigern's desperate insecurity, but every time his stonemasons laid the foundations, the following day the earth swallowed them up. The magicians tell him to look for a lad without a father, and kill him, 'So that the mortar and the stones could be sprinkled with the lad's blood.'

It is then that the boy Merlin enters myth.

Vortigern's messengers choose him because he fulfils the peculiar conditions of the King's magicians, but before his blood can be let, Merlin says, '"My Lord King, summon your workmen. Order them to dig in the earth, and, underneath, you will find a pool. That is what is preventing the tower from standing." This is done and a pool is found, clearly it is this which made the ground unsteady.

'Ambrosius Merlin went up to the magicians a second time and said: 'Tell me, now, you lying flatterers. What lies beneath the pool?" They remained silent, unable to utter a single sound. "Order the pool to be drained," said Merlin, "and at the bottom you will observe two hollow stones. Inside the stones you will see two Dragons which are sleeping."

' . . . While Vortigern, King of the Britons, was still sitting on the bank of the pool which had been drained of its water, there emerged two Dragons, one white, one red. As soon as they were near enough to each other, they fought bitterly, breathing out fire as they panted. The White Dragon began to have the upper hand and to force the Red One back to the edge of the pool. The Red Dragon bewailed the fact that it was driven out and then turned upon the White One and forced it backwards in its turn. As they struggled on in this way, the King ordered Ambrosius Merlin to explain just what this battle of the Dragons meant. Merlin immediately burst into tears . . .'

A very similar story occurs in *Historia Britonum* by Nennius (c830), who gives the name of the lad as Ambros, not Melin, hence Geoffrey's 'Ambrosius Merlin', probably after Ambrosius Aurelianus, a highly successful soldier around that time. Yet earlier Welsh sources, however, call him Emrys, and the site is very likely Dinas Emrys, a hill in the southern foothills of Snowdon, near Llyn Dinas.

Lludd and Lleflys, a story in the *Mabignogian* about the Roman invasion of Britain, confirms the burial site of the dragons as 'Dinas Emries . . . the most secure place in Eryri', their interment the means whereby peace can be assured. Lludd and Lleflys being sons of Beli, are the last of the Celtic rulers of Britain. Geoffrey allowed Merlin knowledge of this earlier event, probably through Lludd and Llleflys. History, Merlin says rightly, is about to repeat itself:

Alas for the Red Dragon, for its end is near. Its cavernous dens shall be occupied by the White Dragon, which stands for the Saxons whom you have invited over. The Red Dragon represents the people of Britain, who will be overrun by the White One: for Britain's mountains and valleys shall be levelled, and the streams in its villeys shall run with blood.

He adds a rider, however – 'The Red One will grieve for what has happened, but after an immense effort it will regain its strength. Calamity will next pursue the White One and the buildings in its little garden will be torn down.' Some believe that this refers to the crowning of Owen Glendower in 1402 as King of Wales.

Remarkably, Michael Senior in his authoritative *Myths of Britain*, tells of the discovery, during an excavation of Dinas Emrys, of 'a man-made pool, a cistern, probably cut during the early-Roman period of the hill's occupation . . . [and] on the banks of this pool and over an area of the pool where it had silted, a paved stone platform was discovered, thought, this time, to belong to the Dark Age period. Under the circumstances one can hardly resist the speculation that paving would have covered the whole pool and the rest of it had been removed by Vortigern's magicians in their earlier excavations carried out under the direction of Emrys-Merlin.'

Dinas Emrys, birthplace of the Merlin myth.

CLWYD

Dinas Bran
Bronze Age hill fort, off the A539 north of Llangollen.

At last there appeared a free open space at the end of their path; and at the sight of this both man and horse strained eagerly forward, the young human body and the old equine body fusing themselves together, in that excited rush, as if they were one creature.

There it was! There before him, towering up beneath a great bank of white clouds and against a jagged ridge of bare and desolate rock, rose the castle of his imagination.

For some minutes he remained spell-bound, absolutely caught out of himself, lost to everything but that majestic sight. It was not less, *it was more*, than the picture he had in his mind.

All ramparts ever built, all towers, all fortresses, all castles, seemed to him mere clumsy reproductions of the ideal perfection of *Dinas Brān*. It wasn't that it was so large – and he could see clearly, even from this distance, that it was in a battered, broken condition – but it took into itself that whole hill it was built upon! Yes, that was the thing. Dinas Brān was not the stones of its human walls, not the majestic outlines of its towering battlements, not its soaring arches and turrets and bastions; it was an impregnable mountain called up out of that deep valley by some supernatural mandate. Its foundations were sunk in the earth, but they were sunk in more than the earth; they were sunk in that mysterious underworld of beyond-reality whence rise the eternal archetypes of all the refuges and all the sanctuaries

Castle Bran, Castle of Wonders, Keeper of the Holy Grail.

of the spirit, untouched by time, inviolable ramparts not built by hands! . . .

It was as if Dinas Brān were really in some extraordinary manner not as solidly *material* as other places. And why shouldn't there be spots like this on the surface of the earth where the electric currents of good and evil have clashed and contended for so long that they had drawn the opacity out of 'matter,' showing it to be, what Aristotle said it was, entirely malleable by mind?

From *Owen Glendower* by John Cowper Powys

Dinas Bran exerts a shadowy pagan influence on all stories about the Holy Grail. The castle was the pre-Celtic King Bran's stronghold in East Wales and a 13th-century French romance set in the Welsh Marches names it as Grail Castle, the Castle of Wonders where the Grail was kept (see also Glastonbury, Somerset), perhaps suggesting, as indeed many stories in the Mabignogian do, that the Christian concepts of resurrection and eternal life, which the Grail embody, also belonged to an earlier, pagan period.

WEST GLAMORGAN

Rhossili
The Gower Peninsular.

Gower, as a matter of fact, is one of the loveliest sea-coast stretches in the whole of Britain, and some of its tiny villages are as obscure, as little inhabited, and as lovely as they were a hundred years ago.

Dylan Thomas wrote that in a letter and in the margin, 'this sounds like a passage from a Tourists' Guide.' It was a favourite haunt, especially the Worm, 'a seaworm of rock pointing into the channel . . . the very promontory of depression.'

Laughing on the cliff above the very long golden beach, we pointed out to each other, as though the other were blind, the great rock of the Worm's Head. The sea was out. We crossed over on slipping stones and stood, at last, triumphantly on the windy top. There was monstrous, thick grass there that made us spring-heeled, and we laughed and bounced on it, scaring the sheep who ran up and down the

The Worm, the 'very promontory of depression'.

battered sides like goats. Even on this calmest day a wind blew along the Worm. At the end of the humped and serpentine body, more gulls than I had ever seen before cried over their new dead and the droppings of ages. On the point, the sound of my quiet voice was scooped and magnified into a hollow shout, as though the wind around me had made a shell or cave, with blue, intangible roof and sides, as tall and wide as all the arched sky, and the flapping gulls were made thunderous. Standing there, legs apart, one hand on my hip, shading my eyes like Raleigh in some picture, I thought myself alone in the epileptic moment near bad sleep, when the legs grow long and sprout into the night and the heart hammers to wake the neighbours and breath is a hurricane through the elastic room. Instead of becoming small on the great rock poised between sky and sea, I felt myself the size of a breathing building, and only Ray in the world could match my lovely bellow as I said: 'Why don't we live here always? Always and always. Build a bloody house and live like bloody kings!' The word bellowed among the squawking birds, they carried it off to the headland in the drums of their wings; like a tower, Ray pranced on the unsteady edge of a separate rock and beat about with his stick, which could turn into snakes or flames; and we sank to the ground, the rubbery, gull-limed grass, the sheep-

pilled stones, the pieces of bones and feathers, and crouched at the extreme point of the Peninsula. We were still for so long that the dirty-grey gulls calmed down, and some settled near us.

Then we finished our food.

From 'Who Do You Wish Was With Us?'
by Dylan Thomas

GWENT

Carleon
Just north of the M4 at J25.

Caer Llion features in *The Story of Maxen* (see Caernafon, Gwynedd) about the Roman occupation of Britain. But from the 5th or 6th Century the fortress is inseparable from Arthurian myth as the place where King Arthur held court.

Arthur may have been, as Nennius describes him in his 9th-century *Historia Britonum*, a real chieftain or general in history, or he may have been assigned the reputation of a real-life 'dux bellorum' for the purpose of mythology. Certainly there is mention of Arthur in apparently very ancient tales, for example in *Kilhwch and Olwen* (frequently found in modern editions of *The Mabignogian*), suggesting that the concept of Arthur was taken up from the past, probably for the purpose of boosting morale in the present. The legend grew after the Saxon invasion (see Snowdon, Dinas Emrys, Gwynedd) with a widespread nostalgia for life as it had once been led in Britain, and swelled once more after the Norman invasion for similar reasons. In his *History*, Geoffrey of Monmouth claims that Arthur's legendary code revolutionised the morality of the nation –

Britain had reached such a standard of sophistication that it excelled all other kingdoms in its general affluence, the richness of its decorations, and the courteous behaviour of its inhabitants. Every knight in the country who was in any way famed for his bravery wore livery and arms showing his own distinctive colour; and women of fashion often displayed the same colours. They scorned to give their love to any man who had not proved himself three times in battle. In this way the womenfolk became chaste and more virtuous and for their love the knights were ever more daring.

Carleon, City of Legions and Court of King Arthur.

Situated as it is in Glamorganshire [now Gwent], on the River Usk, not far from the Severn Sea, in a most pleasant position, and being richer in material wealth than other twonships, this city was eminently suitable for such a ceremony. The river which I have named flowed by it on one side, and up this the kings and princes who were to come from across the sea could be carried in a fleet of ships. On the other side, which was flanked by meadows and wooded groves, they had adorned the city with royal palaces, and by the gold-painted gables of its roofs it was a match for Rome. What is more it was famous for its two churches. One of these, built in honour of the martyr Julius, was graced by a choir of most lovely virgins dedicated to God. The second, founded in the name of the blessed aaron, the companion of Julius, was served by a monastery of canons, and counted as the third metropolitan see of Britain. The city also contained a college of two hundred learned men, who were skilled in astronomy and the other arts, and who watched with great attention the courses of the stars and so by their careful computations prophesied for King Arthur any prodigies due at that time.

Lady Charlotte Guest, 19th-century translator of the Mabignogian other ancient Welsh texts, wrote that so long as the Arthurian world remained an ideal for us, Arthur would not die, and the tradition of Arthur simply sleeping, awaiting his time to return, is an integral part of the myth as perpetuated in the 14th century by Malory in *Le Morte D'Arthur* – 'Some men say in many parts of England that king Arthur is not dead, but had by the will of our Lord Jesu into another place; and men say that he shall come again, and he shall win the holy cross . . . [and] that there is written upon his tomb this verse: "Hic Iacet Arthurius, Rex Quondam Rexque Futurus" ("Here Lies Arthur, Sometime And Future King").'

In 'A Welshman to an Tourist' the poet R S Thomas writes that 'He and his knights are the bright ore that seams our history', and this idea of the spirit of Arthur being held in the Welsh landscape is taken up by the poet and artist, David Jones:

. . . you never know *what* may be
     – not hereabouts.
No wiseman's son *born* do know
     not in these whoreson March-lands
of this Welshry.

Yet he sleeps on
     very deep is his slumber:
how long has he been the sleeping lord?
are the clammy ferns
     his rustling vallance
does the buried rowan
     ward him from evil, or
does he ward the tanglewood
     and the denizens of the wood
are the stunted oaks his gnarled guard
     or are their knarred limbs
strong with his sap?

Do the small black horses
     grass on the hunch of his shoulders?
are the hills his couch
     or is he the couchant hills?
Are the slumbering valleys
     him in slumber
     are the still undulations
the still limbs of him sleeping?
Is the configuration of the land
     the furrowed body of the lord
and the scarred ridges
     his dented greaves
do the trickling gullies
     yet drain his hog-wounds?

Does the land wait the sleeping lord
     or is the wasted land
that very lord who sleeps?

From 'The Sleeping Lord' by David Jones

Tintern Abbey

14th-century Cistercian Abbey beside the River Wye, a few miles north of Chepstow. A466, J22 on the M4.

Tintern Abbey at first sight seemed to me to be bare and almost too perfect to be entirely picturesque. One wants a little more ruin and ivy and the long line of the building should be broken by trees, but within the precincts of the Abbey the narrow aisled vistas, the graceful lightness of the soaring arches and the exquisite and perfect tracery of the east and west windows are singularly beautiful.

It was a solemn grey day, very quiet, a perfect day for seeing a ruined Abbey which is less imposing in glaring sunshine and under a cloudless blue sky. Rain had begun to fall lightly and the soft grey mist which came creeping up the valley with the rising tide, veiling the crests of the wooded cliffs with light woolly clouds, seemed in harmony with the spirit of the place. For a long time I was alone in the ruins. There was no sound amongst the lofty walls and

Tintern – 'how oft, In darkness, have I turned to thee.' William Wordsworth.

vast grey arches but the chattering of the jackdaws, the gentle singing of birds from the orchard and gardens without the walls, and the soft falling of the quiet rain as it dropped tenderly like the tears of Heaven weeping upon the greensward floor of the ruined Church and the richly crossed but nameless tombs of the Abbots of Tintern.

Francis Kilvert's *Diaries*

POWYS

Manafon

A village on the River Rhiw, 5m south west of Welshpool

In the hill country at the moor's edge
There is a chapel, religion's outpost
In the untamed land west of the valleys,
The marginal land where flesh meets spirit
Only on Sundays and the days between
Are mortgaged to the grasping soil.

This is the land of green hay
And greener corn, because of the long
Tarrying of winter and the late spring.
This is the land where they burn peat
If there is time for cutting it,

And the weather improves for drying it,
And the cart is not too old for carrying it
And doesn't get stuck in the wet bog.

This is the land where men labour
In silence, and the rusted harrow
Breaks its teeth on the grey stones.
Below, the valleys are an open book,
Bound in sunlight; but the green tale
Told in its pages is not true.

From 'The Minister' by R S Thomas

'The Minister' is about the time, from 1942, that R S Thomas was Rector of Manafon. He wanted to fight for the farmers he was among – 'I was conscious of the modern industrial technological world, and I felt I wanted to say, "Look, these people also have their part in the general pattern."' But the area is a 'marginal land' and there wasn't much room for the spirit among these 'anglicised people of the border'. His first poem, 'A Peasant', came when on a raw November day he saw a labourer docking swedes – 'docking mangles, chipping the green skin from the yellow bones with a half-witted grin of satisfaction'. At night we see the same labourer 'fixed in his chair motionless except when he leans to gob in the fire. There is something frightening in the vacancy of his mind.'

When Wales is his subject Thomas is uncompromising –

Where can I go, then, from the smell
Of decay, from the putrefying of a dead Nation?'

He has been quoted as supporting Meibion Glyndwr (the Sons of Glendower), radicals who burn down the homes of English settlers –

. . . I have walked the shore
For an hour and seen the English
Scavenging among the remains
Of our culture, covering the sand
Like the tide and, with the roughness
Of the tide, elbowing our language
Into the grave that we have dug for it.

From 'Reservoirs'

He notices – 'a general view' – that the most beautiful parts of Wales are those inhabited by Welsh speakers

and that these people do make an effort to read and imbibe the spirit of the place. In 'The Face' he imagines a figure ploughing on a hill and how linked he is with the valleys, the changing landscape, the mines and villages.

'Wales is a living entity, with its streams and its mountains,' he says, but its spirit has been driven out of its people. His nationalism, political and linguistic, arose out of this, particularly 'what technology and the industrial life has done to Wales.'

POWYS/DYFED

Machynlleth
Where the A487 and 489 meet in Dovey Valley, 15m north east of Aberystwyth.

I have been all men known to history,
Wondering at the world and at time passing;
I have seen evil, and the light blessing
Innocent love under a spring sky.

I have been Merlin wandering in the woods
Of a far country, where the winds waken
Unnatural voices, my mind broken
By sudden acquaintance with man's rage.

I have been Glyn Dŵr set in the vast night,
Scanning the stars for the propitious omen,
A leader of men, yet cursed by the crazed women
Mourning their dead under the same stars.

I have been Goronwy, forced from my own land
To taste the bitterness of the salt ocean;
I have known exile and a wild passion
Of longing changing to a cold ache.

King, beggar and fool, I have been all by turns,
Knowing the body's sweetness, the mind's treason;
Taliesin still, I show you a new world, risen,
Stubborn with beauty, out of the heart's need.

'Taliesin 1952' by R S Thomas

The Taliesin of R S Thomas's poem is the inspired child-poet Gwion. The name is given him spontaneously by Elphin, the wayward son of Gwyddno, whose kingdom lies 'on the strand between Dyvi [the Dovey Estuary] and Aberystwyth', when Elphin discovers Gwion in a 'leathern bag' hanging on a pole in the weir of Gwyddno. The name means 'radiant brow', the first aspect Elphin perceives of this extraordinary child.

The Story of Taliesin, sometimes part of the *Mabignogian* and sometimes not, is a kind of metaphysical reference point for the other tales in that it concerns the spirit not just of Wales, but for all times and all cultures. There is a real enough landscape for the story, which is authoritatively set in the high country of West Powys and at Gwyddno's court just a few miles south west of Machynlleth in Cardigan Bay, Dyfed. It is an appropriate landscape, rich in the spirit of the imagination. R S Thomas came to live and work five miles away from Machynlleth, at Eglwysfach, and wrote 'The Moor' about the high country in West Powys:

It was like a church to me.
I entered it on soft foot,
Breath held like a cap in the hand.
It was quiet.
What God was there made himself felt,
Not listened to, in clean colours
That brought a moistening of the eye,
In movement of the wind over grass.

There were no prayers said. But stillness
Of the heart's passions – that was praise
Enough; and the mind's cession
Of its kingdom. I walked on,
Simple and poor, while the air crumbled
And broke on me generously as bread.

'The Moor' by R S Thomas

How Taliesin came to be trussed up in the leathern bag is the first part of the story. Caridwen gives birth to a child so ugly that she decides to 'boil a cauldron of Inspiration and Science for her son, that his reception might be honourable because of his knowledge of the mysteries of the future state of the world.' She consults 'the books of the Fferyllt' (literally the magician or chemist) and puts Gwion from Llanfair in Caereinion (between Machynlleth and Welshpool) in charge of stirring it for a year and a day.

And one day, towards the end of the year, as Caridwen was culling plants and making incantations, it chanced that three

drops of the charmed liquor flew out of the cauldron and fell upon the finger of Gwion Bach. And by reason of their great heat he put his finger to his mouth, and the instant he put those marvel-working drops into his mouth, he foresaw everything that was to come, and perceived that his chief care must be to guard against the wiles of Caridwen, for vast was her skill.

We hear how Gwion flees and Caridwen chases after, how Gwion changes himself into a hare and she into a greyhound, how then he runs to a river and becomes a fish and she an otter bitch, 'until he was fain to turn himself into a bird of the air. Then she, as a hawk, followed him and gave him no rest in the sky.' Finally he becomes a grain of wheat and she, as a high-crested black hen, swallows him. 'And, as the story goes, she bore him nine months, and when she was delivered of him, she could not find it in her heart to kill him, by reason of his beauty, and cast him into the sea to the mercy of God, on the twenty-ninth day of April.'

The rest of the story, beyond Elphin's finding Gwion and naming him Taliesin, need not concern us, except that Taliesin exhibits an extraordinary talent, silencing the sycophantic court bards so that they can only 'play "blerwm"' with their fingers on their lips, and offering them riddles like this –

Discover what it is –
The strong creature from before the flood,
Without flesh, without bone,
Without vein, without blood,
Without head, without feet;
It will neither be older nor younger
Than at the beginning . . .
In field, in forest . . .
Without hand, without foot
Without signs of old age . . .
It is also so wide
As the surface of the earth;
And it was not born,
Nor was it seen . . .

And so on. Before the court can come up with an answer, the spirit of Taliesin answers for them and 'there arose a mighty storm of wind, so that the king and all his nobles thought that the castle would fall upon their heads.'

The wind is itself a physical clue to the nature of the spirit that Taliesin embodies. 'Idno and Heinin called me Merddin [Merlin]', he says. Taliesin is a spirit omnipresent in the world, he does not scorn cultural boundaries, he delights in the diversity, he is the poetic spirit that resides in the landscape of Wales but also he is the spirit that infuses the imagination of all cultures throughout all ages –

I was with my Lord in the highest sphere,
On the fall of Lucifer into the depth of hell:
I have borne a banner before Alexander . . .
I was in Canaan when Absalom was slain;
I conveyed the divine Spirit to the level of the valley of
  Hebron;
I was in the court of Don before the birth of Gwydion . . .
I was at the place of the crucifixion of the merciful Son of
  God;
I have been three periods in the prison of Arianrhod . . .
I am a wonder whose origin is not known . . .

Narberth
Situated a mile or so south of the A40 between St Clears and Haverfordwest on the A478.

This area of Wales, surrounded on three sides by the sea and including the Preseli Mountains and the most impressive chamber tomb in Wales at Pentre Ifan, is as redolent of ancient myth as Gwynedd in the north. We have already met King Pryderi of Dyfed (see Dinas Dinlle, Gwynedd) from whom Gwydion stole the sacred swine. Now, we go back a generation to Pwyll Lord of Dyfed, and Rhiannon, Pryderi's mother. This,

The immense late Stone Age chamber tomb, Pentre Ifan.

one of the oldest stories of the Mabignogian, probably belonging to the second millennium BC, brings us among some of the very earliest invader inhabitants of Wales.

Pwyll Lord of Dyved ruled over the seven cantrevs of that land. One day, when he was in his chief court at Arberth [Narberth], his thoughts and desires turned to hunting. Glynn Cuch [Glen Cych, between Aber Cych and Cwm Cych] was the part of his realm he wanted to hunt, so he set out that evening from Arberth and went as far as Penn Llwyn on Bwya, where he spent the night. At dawn the next day he rose and made for Glynn Cuch, in order to turn his hounds loose in the forest; he blew his horn and began to muster the hunt, but in riding after the hounds he became separated from his companions. As he listened to the baying of his pack he perceived the cry of another pack, a different cry which was advancing towards him. He spied a clearing in the forest, a level field, and as his pack reached the edge of the field he saw the other pack with a stag running before it, and near the centre of the clearing this other pack overtook the stag and brought it down. Pwyll at once remarked the pack's colour, without bothering to look at the stag, for no hound he had ever seen was the colour of these: a dazzling shining white with red ears, and as the whiteness of the dogs shone so did the redness of their ears.

What is happening here is that Pwyll has met Arawn King of Annwvyn, the Underworld or Otherworld, whose pack of hounds are the Hounds of Hell. Perhaps the stag is Pwyll's soul; for sure, things look pretty bad for Pwyll. He asks how he can earn Arawn's friendship, and Arawn sends him into the Underworld in his place to rid him of an enemy, Havgan King of Annwvyn, while Arawn stays in Dyfed.

The burial mounds and cromlechs of the landscape of this early Bronze Age era bear witness to it as a time obsessed with death and monuments to the dead and the passage of the soul after death to the Underworld. In Glen Cych it is not difficult to imagine an 'otherworld' breaking through.

On another day Pwyll walks from the court at Arberth to Gorsedd Arberth, 'the hill which rose above the court. One of the men said, "Lord, it is the property of this hill that whenever a man of royal blood sits on it, one of two things happens: he receives blows or wounds, or else he sees a wonder." "I do not expect to receive blows or wounds in the company of such a host," said Pwyll, "and I would be glad to see a wonder. I will go and sit on the hill."'

There is a mound just south of Narberth with a 13th century castle on it and the suggestion of its phenomenal property is not unique – on Cader Idris in Gwynedd there is a spot where if you spend the night you will end up dead, mad or a poet.

The Preseli Mountains, source of the bluestone pillars – the inner most sacred ring – of Stonehenge. The story of Pwyll suggests a reason why they would have been transported.

Seated on the mound Pwyll sees a woman 'dressed in shining gold brocade and riding a great pale horse approaching'. She appears to be travelling at a steady pace but the horseman Pwyll sends to find out who she is, cannot catch up with her. This happens time and again. Finally on the third day Pwyll himself climbs into the saddle and pushes his horse 'to its utmost speed', but pursuit is hopeless and he calls out to her. Then she stops, and she introduces herself as Rhiannon daughter of Heveydd the Old and admits, 'My most important errand was to try to see you.' And the romance begins.

Rhiannon is no ordinary woman. When eventually she bears him a son, Pryderi, he disappears and there is a suggestion that she has eaten him. But then a foal is taken from its mother in similar circumstances and when the foal is found so is Pryderi. Rhiannon is made to do penance and stand at a horse box outside Pwyll's house and carry people up to the house on her back.

The identification of Rhiannon with the horse, symbol of otherworldy power (man's domination of the horse being the domination of reason over intuition, the animal sixth sense) and of fertility (as, for example,

at the Hobby Horse, the May Eve fertility rite at Padstow in Cornwall) identifies Rhiannon as a Goddess, pre-dating the Roman horse goddess Epona, perhaps a throwback to Robert Graves's White Goddess, the ruthless Virgin 'Queen Bee' figure of earliest times (see Dinas Dinlle, Gwynedd, and Machynlleth, Powys). The suspicion that she has devoured her child is certainly a feature common to Rhiannon, Arianrhod and Caridwen, and probably a reference to child sacrifice.

If so, and Dyfed was her seat of power, it might explain why bluestone of the Preseli mountains near here was mined and carried all the way to Stonehenge to consruct its inner circle of pillars. Transportation to what has been described as Britain's national necropolis – a monstrous undertaking – can reasonably be explained in terms of the religious symbolic value of the stone – either as a means to defeat or harness Rhiannon's power.

Laugharne
3m south of the A40 at St Clears.

Dylan Thomas lived here. The first poem he wrote about it, the first place poem he ever wrote, was 'Poem in October':

> It was my thirtieth year to heaven
> Woke to my hearing from harbour and neighbour wood
> And the mussel pooled and the heron
>   Priested shore
>   The morning beckon
> With water praying and call of seagull and rook
> And the knock of sailing boats on the net webbed wall …

SHROPSHIRE

Into my heart an air that kills
  From yon far country blows:
What are those blue remembered hills,
What spires, what farms are those?

That is the land of lost content,
  I see it shining plain,
The happy highways where I went
  And cannot come again.

Alfred Edward Housman was born in the Valley House, Fockbury, near Bromsgrove, Worcestershire (where the family shortly moved) in 1859. 'I had,' he once wrote, 'a sentimental feeling for Shropshire because its hills were our western horizon. I know Ludlow and Wenlock, but my topographical details, Hughley, Abdon under Clee – are sometimes quite wrong. Remember that Tyrtaeus was not a Spartan.'

The Welsh Marches

High the vanes of Shrewsbury gleam
Islanded in Severn stream;
The bridges from the steepled crest
Cross the water east and west.

The flat of morn in conqueror's state
Enters at the English gate:
The vanquished eve, as night prevails,
Bleeds upon the road to Wales.

Ages since the vanquished bled
Round my mother's marriage-bed;
There the ravens feasted far
About the open house of war:

When Severn down to Buildwas ran
Coloured with the death of man,
Couched upon her brother's grave
The Saxon got me on the slave.

The sound of fight is silent long
That began the ancient wrong;
Long the voice of tears is still
That wept of old the endless ill.

In my heart it has not died,
The war that sleeps on Severn side;
They cease not fighting, east and west,
On the marches of my breast.

Here the truceless armies yet
Trample, rolled in blood and sweat;
They kill and kill and never die;
And I think that each is I.

None will part us, none undo
The knot that makes one flesh of two,
Sick with hatred, sick with pain,
Strangling – When shall we be slain?

When shall I be dead and rid
Of the wrong my father did?
How long, how long, till spade and hearse
Put to sleep my mother's curse?

A Shropshire Lad (1896) is a set of 63 poems that carry an 'underlying streak or shadow' of melancholic and a singularly truthful tone, as myth rings true. They sing a song by or about a farming lad or soldier, to rhythms that pick out the military beat of a borderland endlessly fraught with feuding, the Welsh Marches.

The Recruit

Leave your home behind, lad,
  And reach your friends your hand,
And go, and luck with you
  While Ludlow tower shall stand.

Oh, come you home of Sunday
  When Ludlow streets are still
And Ludlow bells are calling
  To farm and lane and mill,

Or come you home of Monday
  When Ludlow market hums
And Ludlow chimes are playing
  'The conquering hero comes,'

Come you home a hero,
  Or come not home at all,
The lads you leave will mind you
  Till Ludlow tower shall fall.

Clun Castle, looking across – 'Tracks of ancient occupation. Frail ironworks rusting in the thorn thicket. Hearthstones; charred lullabies. A solitary axe-blow that is the echo of a lost sound.'
Mercian Hymns *by Geoffrey Hill*

And you will list the bugle
    That blows in lands of morn,
And make the foes of England
    Be sorry you were born.

And you till trump of doomsday
    On lands of morn may lie,
And make the hearts of comrades
    Be heavy where you die.

Leave your home behind you,
    Your friends by field and town:
Oh, town and field will mind you
    Till Ludlow tower is down.

This mixture of melancholy and the military may have something to do with why it was only during the First World War – many years after publication – that sales of *A Shropshire Lad* burgeoned. Housman's 'land of lost content', while possibly referring to the poet's own childhood up to his mother's tragically early death when he was 12, would have found parallels in people's minds in Wartime England. First-hand experience of the horror of war consigned blissful childhood visions to doubtful memory, and post-war technological and economic changes seemed set finally to dismantle England's already crumbling rural culture, leaving much that was good behind:

When smoke stood up from Ludlow,
And mist blew off from Teme,
And blithe afield to ploughing
Against the morning beam
I strode beside my team,

The blackbird in the coppice
Looked out to see me stride,
And hearkened as I whistled
The trampling team beside,
And fluted and replied:

'Lie down, lie down, young yeoman;
What use to rise and rise?
Rise man a thousand mornings
Yet down at last he lies,
And then the man is wise.'

'The lads you leave will mind you Till Ludlow tower shall fall.'
A E Housman

Dawn over A E Housman's 'land of lost content'.

HEREFORD & WORCESTERSHIRE

The Malvern Hills
Range of hills, west of the M5 between J7 and 9.

One summer season, when the sun was warm, I rigged myself out in shaggy woollen clothes, as if I were a shepherd; and in the garb of an easy-living hermit I set out to roam far and wide through the world, hoping to hear of marvels. But on a morning in May, among the Malvern Hills, a strange thing happened to me, as though by magic. For I was tired out by my wanderings, and as I lay down to rest under a broad bank by the side of a stream, and leaned over gazing into the water, it sounded so pleasant that I fell asleep.

And I dreamt a marvellous dream: I was in a wilderness, I could not tell where, and looking Eastwards I saw a tower high up against the sun, and splendidly built on top of a hill; and far beneath it was a great gulf, with a dungeon in it, surrounded by deep, dark pits, dreadful to see. But between the tower and the gulf I saw a smooth plain, thronged with all kinds of people, high and low together, moving busily about their worldly affairs . . .

Now I will show you the meaning of the mountain, the dark valley, and the plain full of people.

A fair lady, clothed in linen, came down from a castle and called me gently, saying, 'My son, are you asleep? Do you see these people, moving about in such a turmoil of activity? Most people who pass through this world wish for nothing better than worldly success: the only heaven they think about is on earth.'

Lovely as she was, something in her face made me uneasy, and I said, 'Forgive me, Lady, but what does it all mean?'

'The tower on the hill,' she replied, 'is the home of Truth.'

Piers Ploughman by William Langland (c1330–86)

The Malvern Hills: 'There is no more English spot in all England, and few more beautiful.' Bernard Levin

Hereford
Town on the A49, 10m south of Leominster.

How like an Angel came I down!
I nothing in the World did know.
But 'twas Divine.

The corn was orient and immortal wheat which never should be reaped nor was ever sown. I thought it had stood from everlasting to everlasting. The dust and stones of the street were as precious as gold: the gates were at first the end of the world. The green trees when I saw them first through

*'On a morning in May, among the Malvern Hills, a strange thing happened
to me, as though by magic. For I was tired out by my wanderings, and as I lay
down to rest I dreamt a marvellous dream . . .'*

one of the gates transported and ravished me; their sweetness and unusual beauty made my heart to leap, and almost mad with ecstacy, they were such strange and wonderful things . . . Eternity was manifest in the Light of the Day, and something infinite beyond everything appeared, which talked with my expectation and moved my desire.

Thomas Traherne was born here in 1636. His *Centuries* were discovered on a London bookstall and bought for a few pence in 1896. They are a mystical expression of the glory of the world, of the spirit in nature, of the spirit in man.

Traherne's belief in the divinity of the imagination, as opposed to a fallen world, puts him 200 years ahead of his time. He believed that children have an intuitive grasp loosened by the world, and that they should teach the teachers, so that they might unlearn.

These pure and virgin apprehensions I had in my infancy, and that divine light wherewith I was born, are the best unto this day wherein I can see the universe.

Heart of England and South East

GLOUCESTERSHIRE

Adlestrop
Village on the Gloucestershire/Oxfordshire border, 2m north east of Stow-on-the-Wold.

Yes. I remember Adlestrop –
The name, because one afternoon
Of heat the express-train drew up there
Unwontedly. It was late June.

The steam hissed. Someone cleared his throat.
No one left and no one came
On the bare platform. What I saw
Was Adlestrop – only the name.

And willows, willow-herb, and grass,
And meadowsweet, and haycocks dry,
No whit less still and lonely fair
Than the high cloudlets in the sky.

Adlestrop Station, one afternoon, late June.

And for that minute a blackbird sang
Close by, and round him, mistier,
Farther and farther, all the birds
Of Oxfordshire and Gloucestershire.

'Adlestrop' by Edward Thomas

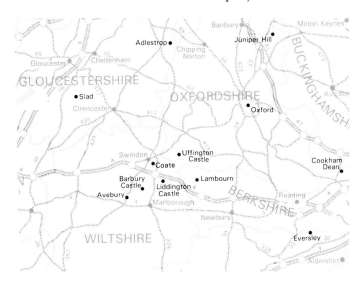

Slad

Cotswold village, 2m north east of Stroud.

In the second decade of the 20th Century, Slad Valley was a warm, sleepy, loving cocoon, lost to the changes of the world outside. 'Living down there,' Laurie Lee wrote, 'was like living in a bean-pod; one could see nothing but the bed one lay in.'

The day Rosie Burdock decided to take me in hand was a motionless day of summer, creamy, hazy, and amber-coloured, with the beech trees standing in heavy sunlight as though clogged with wild wet honey. It was the time of hay-making, so when we came out of school Jack and I went to the farm to help.

The whirr of the mower met us across the stubble, rabbits jumped like firecrackers about the fields, and the hay smelt crisp and sweet. The farmer's men were all hard at work, raking, turning, and loading. Tall, whiskered fellows forked the grass, their chests like bramble patches. The air swung with their forks and the swathes took wing and rose like eagles to the tops of the wagons. The farmer gave us a short fork each and we both pitched in with the rest . . .

I stumbled on Rosie behind a haycock, and she grinned up at me with the sly, glittering eyes of her mother. She wore her tartan frock and cheap brass necklace, and her bare legs were brown with hay-dust.

'Get out a there,' I said. 'Go on.'

Rosie had grown and was hefty now, and I was terrified of her. In her cat-like eyes and curling mouth I saw unnatural wisdoms more threatening than anything I could imagine. The last time we'd met I'd hit her with a cabbage stump. She bore me no grudge, just grinned.

'I got sommat to show ya.'

'You push off,' I said.

I felt dry and dripping, icy hot. Her eyes glinted, and I stood rooted. Her face was wrapped in a pulsating haze and her body seemed to flicker with lightning.

Rosie Burdock.

'You thirsty?' she said.

'I ain't, so there.'

'You be,' she said. 'C'mon.'

So I stuck the fork into the ringing ground and followed her, like doom.

We went a long way, to the bottom of the field, where a wagon stood half-loaded. Festoons of untrimmed grass hung down like curtains all around it. We crawled underneath, between the wheels, into a herb-scented cave of darkness. Rosie scratched about, turned over a sack, and revealed a stone jar of cider.

'It's cider,' she said. 'You ain't to drink it though. Not much of it, any rate.'

Huge and squat, the jar lay on the grass like an unexploded bomb. We lifted it up, unscrewed the stopper, and smelt the whiff of fermented apples. I held the jar to my mouth and rolled my eyes sideways, like a beast at a waterhole. 'Go on,' said Rosie. I took a deep breath. . . .

Never to be forgotten, that first long secret drink of golden fire, juice of those valleys and of that time, wine of wild orchards, of russet summer, of plump red apples, and Rosie's burning cheeks. Never to be forgotten, or ever tasted again. . . .

I put down the jar with a gulp and a gasp. Then I turned to look at Rosie. She was yellow and dusty with buttercups and seemed to be purring in the gloom; her hair was rich as a wild bee's nest and her eyes were full of stings. I did not know what to do about her, nor did I know what not to do. She looked smooth and precious, a thing of unplumbable mysteries, and perilous as quicksand.

'Rosie . . . ' I said, on my knees, and shaking.

'The valley was . . . a funnel for winds, a channel for floods, a jungly, bird-crammed, insect-hopping sun-trap whenever there happened to be any sun.'

'Living down there was like living in a bean-pod; one could see nothing but the bed one lay in.'

She crawled with a rustle of grass towards me, quick and superbly assured. Her hand in mine was like a small wet flame which I could neither hold nor throw away. Then Rosie, with a remorseless, reedy strength, pulled me down from my tottering perch, pulled me down, down into her wide green smile and into the deep subaqueous grass.

Then I remember little, and that little, vaguely. Skin drums beat in my head. Rosie was close-up, salty, an invisible touch, too near to be seen or measured. And it seemed that the wagon under which we lay went floating away like a barge, out over the valley where we rocked unseen, swinging on motionless tides.

Then she took off her boots and stuffed them with flowers. She did the same with mine. Her parched voice crackled like flames in my ears. More fires were started. I drank more cider. Rosie told me outrageous fantasies. She liked me, she said, better than Walt, or Ken, Boney Harris, or even the curate. And I admitted to her, in a loud, rough voice, that she was even prettier than Betty Gleed. For a long time we sat with our mouths very close, breathing the same hot air. We kissed, once only, so dry and shy, it was like two leaves colliding in air.

At last the cuckoos stopped singing and slid into the woods. The mowers went home and left us. I heard Jack calling as he went down the lane, calling my name till I heard him no more. And still we lay in our wagon of grass tugging at each other's hands, while her husky, perilous whisper drugged me and the cider beat gongs in my head. . . .

Cider with Rosie by Laurie Lee

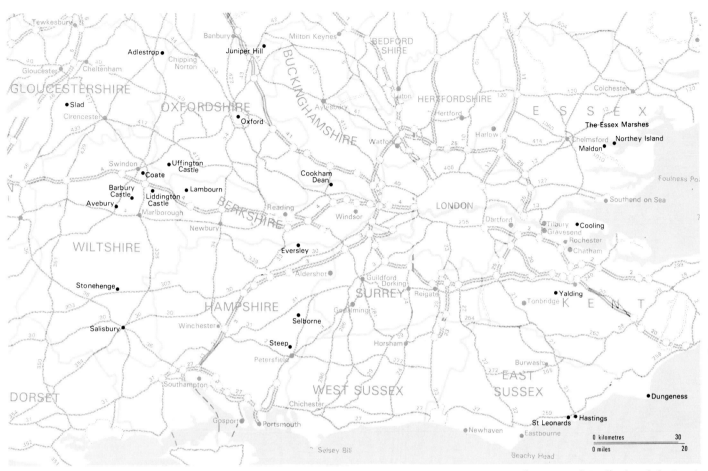

The Heart of England and the South East, see pages 90 to 118.

BERKSHIRE

Cookham Dean
Thames Valley village, just south of Marlow, off the A404.

'I like your clothes awfully, old chap,' he remarked after some half hour or so had passed. 'I'm going to get a black velvet smoking suit myself some day, as soon as I can afford it.' 'I beg your pardon,' said the Mole, pulling himself together with an effort. 'You must think me very rude; but all this is so new to me. So – this – is – a – River!'

'*The* River,' corrected the Rat.

'And you really live by the river? What a jolly life!'

'By it and with it and on it and in it,' said the Rat. 'It's brother and sister to me, and aunts, and company, and food and drink and (naturally) washing. It's my world, and I don't want any other. What it hasn't got is not worth having, and what it doesn't know is not worth knowing. Lord! the times we've had together! Whether in winter or summer, spring or autumn, it's always got its fun and its excitements. When the floods are on in February, and my cellars and basement are brimming

The Thames at Cookham Dean, near Mapledurham.

with drink that's no good to me, and the brown water runs by my best bedroom window; or again when it all drops away and shows patches of mud that smell like plum-cake, and the rushes and weed clog the channels, and I can potter about dry-shod over most of the bed of it and find fresh food to eat, and things careless people have dropped out of boats!'

'But isn't it a bit dull at times?' the Mole ventured to ask. 'Just you and the river, and no one else to pass a word with?'

As everyone knows, *The Wind in the Willows* was begun by Kenneth Grahame as a bedtime story to his son, Alistair, known as Mouse, but it was not a story that simply sprang by chance out of thin air. Rat and Mole's world was already part of its author's imagination, for Kenneth came to it before he was five, grieving for his mother who had died of scarlet fever, when he and his two elder siblings, Helen and Willie, were taken in by their grandmother at her house in Cookham Dean on the banks of the stripling Thames. Henceforth Kenneth's happiest days would be spent playing about on the river, sometimes messing about in boats, though more often on foot. At first it was as new an experience as it was for Mole, for he was a city boy, from Edinburgh, but soon he came to know the life of the river banks intimately. When he grew up and took an important job at the Bank of England, Kenneth continued to come back whenever he could, and the 'remote and dragon-fly' haunted reaches became his spiritual home. What he saw at the core of its beauty, the real spirit of the Thames, as it winds through this part of its course, he gave to Mole and Rat to discover in 'The Piper at the Gates of Dawn'.

A bird piped suddenly, and was still; and a light breeze sprang up and set the reeds and bulrushes rustling. Rat, who was in the stern of the boat, while Mole sculled, sat up suddenly and listened with a passionate intentness. Mole, who with

'"That? O, that's just the Wild Wood," said the Rat shortly. "We don't go there very much, we river-bankers."'

gentle strokes was just keeping the boat moving while he scanned the banks with care, looked at him with curiosity.

'This is the place of my song-dream, the place the music played to me,' whispered the Rat, as if in a trance. 'Here, in this holy place, here if anywhere, surely we shall find Him!'

Then suddenly the Mole felt a great Awe fall upon him, an awe that turned his muscles to water, bowed his head, and rooted his feet to the ground. It was no panic terror – indeed he felt wonderfully at peace and happy – but it was an awe that smote and held him and, without seeing, he knew it could only mean that some august Presence was very, very near. With difficulty he turned to look for his friend, and saw him at his side, cowed, stricken, and trembling violently. And still there was utter silence in the populous bird-haunted branches around them; and still the light grew and grew.

'Rat!' he found breath to whisper, shaking. 'Are you afraid?'

'Afraid?' murmured the Rat, his eyes shining with unutterable love. 'Afraid! Of *Him*. O, never, never! And yet – and yet – O, Mole, I am afraid!'

Then the two animals, crouching to the earth, bowed their heads and did worship.

Sudden and magnificent, the sun's broad golden disc showed itself over the horizon facing them; and the first rays, shooting across the level water-meadows, took the animals full in the eyes and dazzled them. When they were able to look once more, the Vision had vanished, and the air was full of the carol of birds that hailed the dawn.

Mapledurham House, likely model for Toad Hall.

'When they were able to look once more, the Vision had vanished, and the air was full of the carol of birds that hailed the dawn.'

Lambourn

Village on the Lambourn Downs, just north of the M4 around J14, that has been spoken of as the model for Adam Thorpe's novel Ulverton.

I well remember the carriage mounting that last hill north of Ulverton, cresting the bare, nibbled flanks of Frum Down, and giving us all of a sudden that enchanted view of the verdant river, the clustering trees, the black thatch of ancient roofs and the simple grey stone of the church, that bespoke all our exiled dreams, and seemed to embody all our fairest fancies!

Ulverton by Adam Thorpe

Ulverton is the archetypal English village, a palimpsest of personal histories that Adam Thorpe, the author, strips away layer by layer, between 1650 to 1953, ingeniously to anatomise its spirit through people and events and in the style of each consecutive era that has gone to make up its history.

LONDON

According to Geoffrey of Monmouth's *Historia Regum Britanniae* (c1136), London was founded by Brutus, great-grandson of the Trojan Aeneas after he had landed in Britain in the twelfth century before Christ.

Once he had divided up his kingdom, Brutus decided to build a capital. In pursuit of this plan, he visited every part of the land in search of a suitable spot. He came at length to the River Thames, walked up and down its banks and so chose a site suited to his purpose. There then he built his city and called it Troia Nova. It was known by this name for long ages after, but finally by a corruption of the word it came to be called Trinovantum.

Brutus is the first of the kings in Geoffrey's *History of the Kings of Britain*, but Geoffrey's is not the earliest written reference to the city. That is contained in

London before the Starry Heavens had fled from the mighty limbs of Albion. Primrose Hill, a watercolour by John Linnell.

Tacitus's *Annals* (AD61), where it is called Londinium, a place notable for its 'concourse of merchants', and quite clearly, from the start, its position favoured its development as a centre of materialism and power.

William Blake (1757-1827) in many of his writings (for example, *Marriage of Heaven and Hell*) explicitly equates cities with sinfulness, representing as they do industrialism, capitalism, 'Anti-Nature'. In this he is no different to succeeding Romantics. But in a sense London was also the Blakean Ideal - his Creative aesthetic and emphasis upon Will and Power was in many ways embodied in the seething productivity and burgeoning activity of city life. In *Jerusalem*, he makes London the centre of his ideal New England, i.e. Albion, and as far as one can make 'sense' of his vision, what he seems to be attempting is a Transformation of London, a cure for the generalised sickness at work in society. He takes us back to the source of the city, long before Tacitus's 'concourse of merchants' had begun the rot, to a time before the Starry Heavens had 'fled from the mighty limbs of Albion', and literally transforms the city into a 'spirit of place'.

Jerusalem the Emanation of the Giant Albion! Can it be? Is it a Truth that the Learned have explored? Was Britain the Primitive Seat of the Patriarchal Religion? It is true, my title-page is also True, that Jerusalem was & is the Emination of the Giant Albion. It is True and cannot be controverted. Ye are united, O ye Inhabitants of Earth, in One Religion, The Religion of Jesus, the most Ancient, the Eternal & the Everlasting Gospel. The Wicked will turn it to Wickedness, the Righteous to Righteousness. Amen! Huzza! Selah! 'All things Begin & End in Albion's Ancient Druid Rocky Shore.'

Albion was the Parent of the Druids, & in his Chaotic State of Sleep, Satan & Adam & the whole World was Created by the Elohim.

The fields from Islington to Marybone,
To Primrose Hill and St John's Wood,
  Were builded over with pillars of gold,
And there Jerusalem's pillars stood.

Her Little-ones ran on the fields,
The Lamb of God among them seen,
  And fair Jerusalem his Bride,
Among the little meadows green. . .

The Romantic view that London is un-natural, that capitalism rears and kills the city, is prevalent. Richard

Jefferies' novel *After London* (1885) is of a savage future for the metropolis, a poisonous swamp inhabited by cruel dwarfs. And something of this idea persists, we have this sense of London if not exactly in opposition to the mountains and valleys, at least as their man-made alternative, so that Norbert Lynton, the distinguished Art Historian, can legitimately be surprised that London has any connection at all with nature:

I was in my teens when I stood in Bedford Square and was struck by the fact that London is built on earth. Those trees and the patch of green stuff in the middle are not a large saucerful of nature brought into London but nature, London's bed and base.

And Leo Tolstoy, in *Resurrection* (1899), points to the survival of nature in the city in spite of our best efforts:

Though hundreds of thousands had done their very best to disfigure the small piece of land on which they were crowded together . . . still spring was spring, even in the town.

In Martin Amis's novel, *London Fields*, the trees of Maida Vale go 'topless and ashamed' and the birds croak 'in pity or defiance' under the powerful rays of the sun, creator of all life. These are images of a fallen world. And in a way that is a common vision - London is what we left the Garden of Eden to get on with. There are plenty of Londoners who find the city distinctly preferable to the country, find it impossible to sleep in its quietness for example, or find the noises of the country more intrusive (because of the pervading quietude) than city sounds against the continuous background roar of the city.

Typically, the country boy, William Wordsworth needed the quiet of the early morning of September 3rd, 1802, before London was awake, in order to appreciate its beauty:

Earth has not anything to show more fair:
Dull would he be of soul who could pass by
A sight so touching in its majesty:
This City now doth, like a garment, wear
The beauty of the morning; silent, bare,
Ships, towers, domes, theatres, and temples lie
Open unto the fields, and to the sky;
All bright and glittering in the smokeless air.
Never did sun more beautifully steep

In his first splendour, valley, rock, or hill;
Ne're saw I, never felt, a calm so deep!
The river glideth at his own sweet will:
Dear God! the very houses seem asleep;
And all that mighty heart is lying still.

'Westminster Bridge'

Just as characteristically, Charles Lamb wrote to Wordsworth that he had enough in London 'without your mountains . . . My attachments are all local, purely local. I have no passion for groves and valleys . . . The rooms where I was born, the furniture which has been before my eyes all my life, my bookcase . . . old chairs, old tables, streets, squares, where I have sunned myself, my old school – these are my mistresses.'

Of course travel out of the city was far less common in those days, but it is an attitude bred in the bone of established Londoners, and many see no need to have their 'un-natural' spirits revived by visits to the country. On the contrary, like Samuel Johnson (see Glen Moriston, Highlands, Scotland) they often find nature in the raw rather offensive, and would much rather stay at home.

Nevertheless, earlier, there seems to have been a sense of guilt at the lack of restraint, not to say egomania, in developing this cultural alternative to the Garden of Eden.

The apocalyptic tone of Thomas Dekker's *The Wonderful Yeare* (1603) is unmistakable. From the Bible onwards – since the Lord rained sulphur and fire upon Sodom and Gomorroh – cities as centres of vice and corruption have been seen as ripe for Divine Intervention in the form of plague or all-consuming fire, and London of course suffered both:

A stiff and freezing horror sucks up the rivers of my blood. My hair stands on end with the panting of my brains. Mine eye-balls are ready to start out, being beaten with the billows of my tears. Out of my weeping pen does the ink mournfully and more bitterly than gall drop on the pale-faced paper even when I do but think how the bowels of my sick country have been torn. Apollo therefore, and you bewitching silver-tongued Muses, get you gone: I invoke none of your names. Sorrow and Truth, sit you on each side of me whilst I am delivered of this deadly burden: prompt me that I may utter ruthful and passionate condolement; arm my trembling hand that it may boldly rip up and anatomize the ulcerous body of this anthropophagized plague; lend me art,

without any counterfeit shadowing to paint and delineate to the life the whole story of this mortal and pestiferous battle. And you the ghosts of those more by many than 40,000 that with the virulent poison of infection have been driven out of your earthly dwellings, you desolate hand-wringing widows that beat your bosoms over your departing husbands, you woefully distracted mothers that with dishevelled hair are fallen into swoons whilst you lie kissing the insensible cold lips of your breathless infants . . . join all your hands together and with your bodies cast a ring about me; let me behold your ghastly visages, that my paper may receive their true pictures; echo forth the groans through the hollow trunk of my pen . . .

The horrific symptoms of plague, the randomness of its strike, and the sheer number of its victims must have seemed to Dekker's contemporaries beyond rational explanation, Sixty years on came the Great Plague of 1664/5, and apparently another first-hand record:

I went all the first part of the time freely about the streets, though not so freely as to run myself into apparent danger, except when the dug the great pit in the churchyard of our parish of Aldgate. A terrible pit it was, and I could not resist my curiosity to go and see it. As near as I may judge, it was about forty feet in length, and about fifteen or sixteen feet broad, and at the time I first looked at it, about nine feet deep; but it was said they dug it near twenty feet deep afterwards in one part of it, till they could go no deeper for the water; for they had, it seems, dug several large pits before this. for though the plage was long a-coming to our parish, yet, when it did come, there was no parish in or about London where it raged with such violence as in the two parishes of Aldgate and Whitechapel . . .

Into these pits they had put perhaps fifty or sixty bodies each; then they made larger holes wherein they buried all that the cart bought in a week, which, by the middle to the end of August, came from 200 to 400 a week; and they could not well dig them larger, because of the order of the magistrates confining them to leave no bodies within six feet of the surface; and the water coming on at about seventeen or eighteen feet, they could not well, I say, put more in one pit.

In fact, Daniel Defoe's *A Journal of the Plague Year* was written in 1722, and Defoe was born only four years before the plague he describes so vividly. It purports to be written from first-hand experience, but the

London, unpeopled, in the quiet of the dawn: 'The beauty of the morning, silent, bare.'

account is a fiction – not in the sense that his research is suspect but because Defoe is conjuring with his material like a novelist.

One of the typical 18th-century storylines was that of the Rake's Progress – young innocent comes up to London to seek their fortune only to be led astray by an assortment of degenerate characters, ending up in poverty or the madhouse or dead. In A Journal, Defoe transforms this plot. Londoners are seen to undergo a parallel form of success-driven corruption, their bodies putrifying before their very eyes. From Defoe

on, plague is no longer an infectious disease that comes into London from outside, in literary terms it is part of the very nature of the place. 'It was really a wonder,' he wrote, '[that] the whole body of the people did not rise as one man and abandon their dwellings, leaving the place as a space of ground designed by Heaven for an Akeldama, doomed to be destroyed from the face of the earth.'

London as Akeldama, Waste Land, Wilderness – the theme was expounded by London's greatest writer from personal experience: 'Wilderness! Yes it is, it is. Good. It *is* a wilderness – I have never forgotten it. Thank God!' says Cheeryble in *Nicholas Nickleby* (Charles Dickens).

''Tis strange,' wrote Dickens, 'how little notice, good, bad, or indifferent, a man may live and die in London. He awakens no sympathy in the breast of any single person; his existence is a matter of interest to no one save himself; and he cannot be said to be forgotten when he dies, for no one remembered him when he was alive.'

In John Cowper Powys's novel that takes the name of its hero, Wolf Solent . . .

recalled the figure of a man he had seen on the steps outside Waterloo Station. The inert despair upon the face that this figure had turned towards him . . . was of such a character that Wolf knew at once that no conceivable social readjustments or ameleriorative revolutions could ever atone for it – could ever make up for the simple irremediable fact that it had been as it had been!

All Dickens' novels stem from his earliest experiences in the city. As soon as he arrived, aged nine, he is lost, cast adrift in the wilderness. He had been taken by a friend of the family to see the statue of the lion that held sway over Northumberland House, and somehow, 'in the act of looking up with mingled awe and admiration at the famous animal,' the boy became separated from his guardian. 'The child's unreasoning terror of being lost, comes as freshly on me now as it did then . . . I could not have been more horrified.'

Three years later, his father's inability to make money and honour his debts took him to prison, and the twelve-year-old was left to fend for himself.

I know I do not exaggerate, unconsciously and unintentionally, the scantiness of my resources and the difficulties of my life. I know that if a shilling or so were given me by anyone, I spent it in a dinner or a tea. I know that I worked [at Warren's shoe blacking factory in the Strand] from morning to night, with common men and boys, a shabby child . . . I know that I have lounged about the streets, insufficiently and unsatisfactorily fed. I know that, but for the mercy of God, I might easily have been, for any care that was taken of me, a little robber or a little vagabond . . .

David Copperfield is Dickens' most obvious auto-novel, but the experience of being lost as a nine-year-

old he gave to Florence Dombey in *Dombey and Son*, who loses her guardian and is swept up in the seamy side of the city's underworld.

Before long, the boy Dickens became more adventurous. Like a child drawn to a flame he knows he mustn't touch, he begins to be attracted to what at first so horrified him. He goes to visit an uncle in Soho, and pushes on into Seven Dials – 'What wild visions of prodigies of wickedness, want and beggary, arose in my mind out of that place! Covent Garden is soon a regular haunt during tea-breaks from Warren's. He

Seven Dials: the busy face of the dark neighbourhood of St Giles.

hangs around, identifying with the orphan poor, peering down dark alleys and courts, noting the strange characters he sees, and at last gives his imagination full rein:

It was a chill, damp, windy night, when the Jew, buttoning his great-coat tight round his shrivelled body, and pulling the coat up over his ears so as completely to obscure the lower part of his face, emerged from his den. He paused on the step as the door was locked and chained behind him; and having listened while the boys made all secure, and until their returning footsteps were no longer audible, slunk down the street as quickly as he could.

The house to which Oliver had been conveyed, was in the neighbourhood of Whitechapel. The Jew stopped for an instant at the corner of the street; and, glancing suspiciously round, crossed the road, and struck off in the direction of Spitalfields.

The mud lay thick upon the stones, and a black mist hung

over the streets; the rain fell sluggishly down, and everything feld cold and clammy to the touch. It seemed just the night when it befitted such a being as the Jew to be abroad. As he glided stealthily along, creeping beneath the shelter of the walls and doorways, the hideous old man seemed like some loathsome reptile, engendered in the slime and darkness through which he moved: crawling forth, by night, in search of some rich offal for a meal.

He kept on his course through many winding and narrow ways, until he reached Bethnal Green; then, turning suddenly off to the left, he soon became involved in a maze of the mean and dirty streets which abound in that close and densely-populated quarter.

The Jew was evidently too familiar with the ground he traversed to be at all bewildered, either by the darkness of the night, or the intricacies of the way. He hurried through several alleys and streets and at length turned into one, lightened only by a single lamp at the farther end. At the door of a house in this street he knocked; having exchanged a few muttered words with the person who opened it, he walked upstairs.

A dog growled as he touched the handle of a room-door; and a man's voice demanded who was there.

'Only me, Bill; only me, my dear,' said the Jew, looking in.

Oliver Twist

Dickens' London was an extension of his personal phantasmagoria, the child of his imagination, his theatre, constructed out of necessity. Dickens loved the theatre. During his time at Doctors Commons, energetic but disillusioned with his mundane work as a clerk and journalist, he actually offered himself to the theatre as having 'a strong perception of character and oddity, and a natural power of reproducing'. But on the day of the audition he had a bad cold and 'terrible inflammation of the face' and did not go. Nevertheless, what he loved about the theatre he could love about London once he had turned it into theatre –

It was Covent Garden Theatre that I chose . . . the mingled reality and mystery of the show, the influence upon me of the poetry, the lights, the music, the company, the smooth, stupendous changes of glittering and brilliant scenery . . . When I came out into the rainy street, at twelve o'clock at night, I felt as if I had come out of the clouds, where I had been leading a romantic life for ages, to a bawling, splashing, link-lighted, umbrella-struggling, hackney-coach-jostling, patten-clinking, muddy, miserable world. *David Copperfield*

The city took on the shape of Dickens' fears, and he transformed it out of necessity.

A friend once noted that Dickens found in ordinary people material for entertainment equal to that of any play – 'He could imitate, in a manner that I have never heard equalled the low population of the streets of London in all their varieties, whether mere loafers or sellers of fruit, vegetables, or anything else.' Dickens' London as street theatre – this is how others like to think of London too:

The Italian organ-grinder, a martyr to gastric troubles, who regularly appeared every Thursday afternoon; the crossing-sweeper in Ladbroke Grove whose function the internal combustion engine was even then rapidly rendering as decorative . . . the muffin man, the lamplighter and the old gentleman who came out on winter evenings to play the harp by the foggy radiance of the street lamp – Dickensian figures who have obviously no role to play in the Welfare State and have left no successors.

All Done from Memory by Osbert Lancaster

The territory in which I grew up was Bloomsbury and Fitzrovia, where Prince Monolulu . . . a West Indian racing tout with a taste for the exotic, wandered about in garish robes and a head-dress of multi-coloured feathers, shouting 'I got a hoss! I got a hoss!'. At the age of seven I wasn't one for the track, but we were friends and fell into each other's arms whenever our paths crossed.

Jenny Diski in the *Independent on Sunday*

Of course Dickens was not simply out to make London larger than life. There was the social purpose too. He was at his very best when he mingled the 'reality and mystery of the show', as in Jo, the crossing-sweeper who lived at Tom-All-Alone's, a slum in the shadow of Southwark Cathedral, an impoverished illiterate living on the edge of fast-changing Victorian London:

It must be strange to be like Jo! To shuffle through the streets, unfamiliar with the shapes and in utter darkness as to the meaning, of those mysterious symbols, so abundant over the shops, and the corner of streets, and on the doors, and in the windows! To see people read, and to see people write, and to see the postman deliver letters, and not to have the least idea of all that language . . . to see the good company going to church on Sundays, with their books in their hands and to think (for perhaps Jo *does* think, at odd times) what does it all mean, and if it means anything to anybody, how comes it that it means nothing to me? To be hustled, and jostled, and moved on; and really to feel that . . . I have no business here, or there, or anywhere; and yet to be perplexed by the consideration that I am here somehow.

Bleak House

His theatrical vision of London could be a powerful weapon lampooning the thin veneer of New Victorian society, too – 'Mr and Mrs Veneering were bran-new people in a bran-new house in a bran-new quarter of London. Everything about the Veneerings was spick and span and new . . .' (*Our Mutual Friend*). The fact was that Victorian London got the best out of Dickens

and Dickens got the best out of it. The timing was perfect. Never before had there been so many different layers in society available for such treatment, nor in terms of the poverty and riches, the disease and appalling social ills, had there appeared such a need.

Dickens re-wrote London for Londoners in his time, and we still see Victorian London through his eyes. He did not avoid the reality, on the contrary he did really transform it, literally re-wrote it, for the benefit of its social health and not simply for entertainment.

Perhaps London only exists in imagination. Whatever happened to Dickens' London, to Colin Macinnes's '60s' City of Spades? To Dan Farson's or Jeffrey Bernard's Soho? To the Literary London of the Bloomsbury Group that met in the spirit of G E Moore's Principia Ethica, in the belief that the 'rational ultimate end of social progress' lies in the 'pleasures of human intercourse and the enjoyment of beautiful objects'? Were they ever real? Or are they simply 'layers of ideas, images, feelings [that] have fallen upon your brain soft as light.'

De Quincey (1785-1859) gave us the model in *Suspira de Profundis*. The concept of London as a palimpsest, a manuscript on which each successive culture writes its own text – each successive generation transforming the landscape of the city: adding, destroying, modifying, re-writing – is a powerful one because it fits – the London that we walk through today is a living ideological and architectural archive of the past. 'Each succession has seemed to bury all that went before. And yet in reality not one has been extinguished . . .'

In his recent anthology, *The Faber Book of London*, A N Wilson tells us that Tom-All-Alone's (Jo's place in Bleak House) became a cemetry and then a public garden, and how he had seen it being dug up – 'The shock was not merely visual, though. I felt that the bulldozers were interfering with our memories, and that was why the sight caused pain.'

Once we see London in this way the temptation is to burrow around and soil our hands in its more primaeval history.

Recently, there have been a few literary archaeologists that have left us with the notion that if London really is such a repository it may be given to occasional seismic upheaval, reiterations of the past, 'All perils, specially malignant,' wrote De Quincey, 'are recurrent.'

In *Hawksmoor*, Peter Ackroyd weaves a detective story set in the 20th Century, into a tale of architectural satanism set in Defoe's time, which threatens to scrape the palimpsest clean, its 18th-century plot hinging on the work of the architect, Sir Nicholas Hawksmoor – specifically his London churches, each of which as Iain Sinclair explains, occupies a significant site:

The old maps present a sky-line dominated by church towers . . . Eight churches give us the enclosure, the shape of the fear.

Hawksmoor the Surveyor examined and selected the sights, walked over the ground, drew up the plans, made wooden models, rapidly turned out a sequence of sketches, possible structures to contain some portion of his amazing polyglot energies. He had that frenzy, the Coleridge notebook speed to rewrite the city . . .

Nicholas Hawksmoor, His Churches by Iain Sinclair

Sinclair shows that Hawksmoor's plotting of the churches on the map was deliberately designed to form significant geometric shapes:

A triangle is formed between Christ Church, St George-in-the-east, and St Anne, Limehouse. These are centres of power for those territories: sentenial, sphinx-form, slack dynamos abandoned as the culture they supported goes into retreat. The power remains latent, the frustration mounts on a current of animal magnetism, and victims are still claimed.

St George, Bloomsbury, and St Alfege, Greenwich, make up the major pentacle-star. The five card, from the Lesser Arcana, is reversed, beggars in snow pass under the lit church window; the judgement is 'disorder, chaos, ruin, discord, profligacy'.

These churches guard or mark, rest upon, two major sources of occult power: the British Museum and Greenwich Observatory. The locked cellar of words, the labyrinth of all recorded knowledge, the repository of stolen fires and symbols, excavated godforms – and measurement, star-knowledge, time calculations, Maze Hill, the bank of light that faces the Isle of Dogs.

Sinclair describes Hawksmoor's grid in terms of its necromantic potential, 'an active place', a focus of occult power, allowing two descriptions in time. Here past and present could co-exist.

I spoke of the unacknowledged magnetism and control-

Christ Church Spitalfields, one of Sir Nicholas Hawksmoor's 'centres of power'.

power, built-in code force, of these places, I would now specify . . . the ritual slaying of Marie Jeanette Kelly in the ground floor room of Miller's Court, Dorset Street, directly opposite Christ Church . . . the Ratcliffe Highway slaughter of 1811, with the supposed-murder, stake through heart, trampled into the pit where 4 roads cross to the north of St George-in-the-east . . . the battering to death of Mr Abraham Cohen, summer 1974, on Cannon Street Road, '110,000 in old bank-notes in the kiosk behind him, stuffed into cocoa tins and cigarettes packets; 3 ritualistic coins laid at his feet, as they were in 1888 at the feet of Mary Ann Nicholls, the first Ripper victim.

In Peter Ackroyd's *Hawksmoor* these centres of power are 'activated' by ritual observances, poetically (by the author's extraordinary evocation of the spirit of place) and by primitive sacrifice, bodies buried in the churches' foundations. And it is the 'inevitable' recurrence of these murders 200 years later which is the subject of the 20th-century detective story.

One remarkable sideshow of this successful literary enterprise was its apparently groundless prediction that Hawksmoor had built Christ Church 'near a Pitte and there are so vast a Number of Corses that the Pews will alwaies be Rotten and Damp.' If there ever had been any doubt in readers' minds that Ackroyd had really dabbled in the past it was dispelled when archaeologists excavating the crypt of Christ Church at time of publication uncovered a labyrinth of tunnels and chambers packed tight with the coffins and decaying remains of 1,000 Spitalfields parishioners deposited there from 1729. The Guardian reported that the team 'read Ackroyd's book with horror'.

The prophetic nature of Peter Ackroyd's Hawksmoor*, horrified the archaeologists who excavated the crypt of Christ Church Spitalfields and found the 'Pitte', as he had described.*

Defoe's plague city, its dark unconscious, had literally been exhumed.

Dickens also had a strong sense of London's dark unconscious, giving it symbolically to the River Thames. The river was of course the city's raison d'etre, the main conduit of trade, even the poorest citizens used it to make money, by scouring it for dead bodies. The river was also a main source of frightening epidemics which occurred at this time. Half the population received its water from the Thames, which in turn received the effluence from hundreds of sewers. It was both mother of the city and angel of death, and Dickens came nearest to understanding it in the first few pages of *Our Mutual Friend*:

In these times of ours, though concerning the exact year

there is no need to be precise, a boat of dirty and disreputable appearance, with two figures in it, floated on the Thames, between Southwark Bridge which is of iron, and London Bridge which is of stone, as an autumn evening was closing in.

The figures in this boat were those of a strong man with ragged grizzled hair and a sun-browned face, and a girl of nineteen or twenty, sufficiently like him to be recognizable as his daughter. The girl rowed, pulling a pair of skulls very easily; the man, with the rudder-lines slack in his hands, and his hands loose in his waistband, kept an eager look out. He had no net, hook, or line, and he could not be a fisherman; his boat had no cushion for a sitter, no paint, no inscription, no appliance beyond a rusty boathook and a coil of rope, and he could not be a waterman; his boat was too cazy and too small to take in cargo for delivery, and he could not be a lighterman or river-carrier; there was no clue to what he looked for, but he looked for something, with a most intent and searching gaze. The tide, which had turned an hour before, was running down, and his eyes watched every little race and eddy in its broad sweep, as the boat made slight head-way against it, or drove stern foremost before it, according as he directed his daughter by a movement of his head. She watched his face as earnestly as he watched the driver. But, in the intensity of her look there was a touch of dread or horror.

Allied to the bottom of the river rather than the surface, by reason of the slime and ooze with which it was covered, and its sodden state, this boat and the two figures in it obviously were doing something that they often did, and were seeking what they often sought. Half savage as the man showed, with no covering on his matted head, his brown arms bare to between the elbow and the shoulder, with the loose knot of a looser kerchief lying low on his bare breast in a wilderness of beard and whisker, with such dress as he wore seeming to be made out of the mud that begrimed his boat, still there was businesss-like usage in his steady gaze. So with every lithe action of the girl, with every turn of her wrist, perhaps most of all with her look of dread or horror; they were things of usage.

'Keep her out, Lizzie. Tide runs strong here. Keep her well afore the sweep of it.'

Trusting to the girl's skill and making no use of the rudder, he eyed the coming tide with an absorbed attention. So the girl eyed him. But, it happened now, that the slant of the light from the setting sun glanced into the bottom of the boat, and, touching a rotten stain there which bore some resemblance to the outline of a muffled human form, coloured it as though with diluted blood. This caught the

The Thames between Southwark Bridge and London Bridge 'as an autumn evening was closing in.'

girl's eye and she shivered.

'What ails you?' said the man, immediately aware of it, though so intent on the advancing waters; 'I see nothing afloat.'

The red light was gone, the shudder was gone, and his gaze, which had come back to the boat for a moment, travelled away again. Wheresoever the strong tide met with an impediment, his gaze paused for an instant. At every mooring-chain and rope, and at every stationary boat or barge that split the current into a broad-arrowhead, at the offsets of the piers of Southwark Bridge, at the paddles of the river steamboats as they beat the filthy water, at the floating logs of timber lashed together lying off certain wharves, his shining eyes darted a hungry look. After a darkening hour or so, suddenly the rudder-lines tightened in his hold, and he steered hard towards the Surrey shore.

Always watching his face, the girl instantly answered to the action in her sculling; presently the boat swung round, quivered as from a sudden jerk, and the upper half of the man was stretched out over the stern.

The girl pulled the hood of the cloak she wore, over her head and over her face, and, looking backward so that the front folds of this hood were turned down the river, kept the boat in that direction going before the tide. Until now the boat had barely held her own, and had hovered about one spot; but now, the banks changed swiftly, and the deepening shadows and the kindling lights of London Bridge were passed, and the tiers of shipping lay on either hand.

It was not until now that the upper half of the man came back into the boat. His arms were wet and dirty, and he washed them over the side. In his right hand he held something, and he washed that in the river too. It was money. He clinked it once, and he blew upon it once, and he spat upon it once . . .

In Iain Sinclair's novel *Downriver* there is also a sense of London's darker side, a sense that the soul of

Rotherhithe Tunnel. 'Traffic scrapes so narrowly past: the drivers are mean-faced and locked into sadistic fantasies . . . You feel the brain-stem ineluctably dying, releasing, at its margins, dim and flaccid hallucinations . . . The tunnel covertly opens a vein between two distinct systems, two descriptions of time.' Downriver by Iain Sinclair

the city is not good yet magnetically attractive. His narrator descends Rotherhithe Tunnel beneath the Thames 'to sample the worst London can offer', and not only in his time. Again, Conan Doyle, whose London is again a two-tier world, the underworld and the day-to-day, feels the same compulsion as Sinclair to visit this otherworld, to sample the darker side. In order to make sense of the city Holmes, its hero, must frequently assume disguises of underworld characters, and more than this, sometimes become part of the criminal world he despises, even to the point of living a Jekyll and Hyde existence. Watson, on the other hand – the rational, the everyday – lives on the surface of life and is quite baffled by Holmes's intuitional propensity.

In *The Man With The Twisted Lip* Holmes transforms himself from the brilliant detective into the drug-taking bohemian. Doctor Watson has been asked to go to an opium den to rescue a friend, whose addiction is 'an object of mingled horror and pity to his friends':

Upper Swandam Lane is a vile alley lurking behind the high wharves which line the north side of the river to the east of London Bridge. Between a slop-shop and a gin-shop, approached by a steep flight of steps leading down to a black gap like the mouth of a cave. I found the den of which I was in search. Ordering my cab to wait, I passed down the steps, worn hollow in the centre by the ceaseless tread of drunken feet, and by the light of a flickering oil-lamp above the door I found the latch and made my way into a long, low room, thick and heavy with the brown opium smoke, and terraced with wooden berths, like the forecastle of an emigrant ship.

Through the gloom one could dimly catch the glimpse of bodies lying in strange fantastic poses, bowed shoulders, bent knees, heads thrown back, and chins pointing upwards, with here and there a dark, lack-lustre eye turned upon the newcomer. Out of the black shadows there glimmered little red circles of light, now bright, now faint, as the burning poison waxed or waned in the bowls of the metal pipes. The most lay silent, but some muttered to themselves, and others talked together in a strange, low, monotonous voice, their conversation coming in gushes, and then suddenly tailing off into silence, each mumbling out his own thoughts and paying little heed to the words of his neighbour. At the farther end was a small brazier of burning charcoal, beside which on a three-legged wooden stool there sat a tall, thin old man, with his jaw resting upon his two fists, and his elbows upon his knees, staring into the fire.

As I entered, a sallow Malay attendant had hurried up with a pipe for me and a supply of the drug, beckoning me to an empty berth.

'Thank you. I have not come to stay,' said I. 'There is a friend of mine here, Mr Isa Whitney, and I wish to speak with him.'

There was a movement and an exclamation from my right, and peering through the gloom I saw Whitney, pale, haggered, and unkempt, staring out at me.

'My God! It's Watson,' said he. He was in a pitiable state of reaction, with every nerve in a twitter. 'I say, Watson, what o'clock is it?'

'Nearly eleven.'

'Of what day?'

'Of Friday, June 19th.'

'Good heavens! I thought it was Wednesday. It is Wednesday. What d'you want to frighten the chap for?' He sank his face onto his arms and began to sob in a high treble key.

'I tell you that it is Friday, man. Your wife has been waiting this two days for you. You should be ashamed of yourself!'

'So I am. But you've got mixed, Watson, for I have only been here a few hours, three pipes, four pipes – I forget how many. But I'll go home with you. I wouldn't frighten Kate – poor little Kate. Give me your hand! Have you a cab?'

'Yes, I have one waiting.'

'Then I shall go in it. But I must owe something. Find what I owe, Watson. I am all off colour. I can do nothing for myself.'

I walked down the narrow passage between the double row of sleepers, holding my breath to keep out the vile, stupefying fumes of the drug, and looking about for the manager. As I passed the tall man who sat by the brazier I felt a sudden pluck at my skirt, and a low voice whispered, 'Walk past me, and then look back at me.' The words fell quite distinctly upon my ear. I glanced down. They could only have come from the old man at my side, yet he sat now as absorbed as ever, very thin, very wrinkled, bent with age, an opium pipe dangling down from between his knees, as though it had dropped in sheer lassitude from his fingers. I took two steps forward and looked back. It took all my self-control to prevent me from breaking out into a cry of astonishment. He had turned his back so that none could see him but I. His form had filled out, his wrinkles were gone, the dull eyes had regained their fire, and there, sitting by the fire and grinning at my surprise, was none other than Sherlock Holmes. He made a slight motion to me to approach him, and instantly, as he turned his face half round to the company once more, subsided into a doddering loose-lipped senility.

'Holmes!' I whispered, 'what on earth are you doing in this den?'

For many the attraction of London is in the present. The past is all around us but there is too much going on to read between the fractured lines of the literary palimpsest. We don't look beyond the 'bellow and the uproar'; London is our London, whatever London we want it to be, as it surely is too for the 'miseries on the doorsteps'. Then again, for some, as for these writers, the veil does lift, and we are made aware of the primaeval earth beneath.

In Virginia Woolf's novel, *Mrs Dalloway*, Clarissa senses the significance of 'the moment' before the striking of Big Ben – 'a particular hush, or solemnity; an indescribable pause; a suspense . . . before Big Ben strikes. There! Out it boomed. First a warning, musical; then the hour, irrevocable. The leaden circles dissolved in the air.' Living in London is about making 'the moment' happen, 'making it up, building it round one, tumbling it, creating it every moment afresh', and 'the most dejected of miseries sitting on doorsteps . . . do the same; can't be dealt with . . . by Acts of Parliament for that very reason: they love life. In people's eyes, in the swing, tramp, and trudge; in the bellow and the uproar; the carriages, motor cars, omnibuses, vans, sandwich men shuffling and swinging; brass bands; barrel organs; in the triumph and the jingle and the strange high singing of some aeroplane overhead was what she loved; life; London; this moment in June.'

Northey Island, Essex scene of the Battle of Maldon.

ESSEX

The Great Essex Marsh
The marshland round and about the area of the Blackwater and Mersea Island.

The great marsh lies on the Essex coast between the village of Chelmbury and the ancient Saxon oyster-fishing hamlet of Wickaeldroth. It is one of the last of the wild places of England, a low, far-reaching expanse of grass and reeds and half-submerged meadowlands ending in the great saltings and mud flats and tidal pools near the restless sea.

Tidal creeks and estuaries and the crooked, meandering arms of many little rivers whose mouths lap at the edge of the ocean cut through the sodden land that seems to rise and fall and breathe with the recurrence of the daily tides. It is desolate, utterly lonely, and made lonelier by the calls and cries of the wildfowl that make their homes in the marsh-lands and saltings – the wild geese and the gulls, the teal and widgeon, the redshanks and curlews that pick their way through the tidal pools. Of human habitants there are none, and none are seen, with the occasional exception of a wild-fowler or native oyster-fishermen, who still ply a trade already ancient when the Normans came to Hastings.

Greys and blues and soft greens are the colours, for when the skies are dark in the long winters, the many waters of the beaches and marshes reflect the cold and sombre colour. But sometimes, with sunrise and sunset, sky and land are aflame with red and golden fire. . . .

At low water the blackened and ruptured stones of the ruins of an abandoned lighthouse show above the surface, with here and there, like buoy markers, the top of a sagging fence-post.

Lately it served again as a human habitation. In it there lived a lonely man. His body was warped, but his heart was filled with love for wild and hunted things. He was ugly to look upon, but he created great beauty. It is about him, and a child who came to know him and see beyond the grotesque form that housed him to what lay within, that this story is told.

The Snow Goose by Paul Gallico

Maldon

On the Blackwater estuary, 10m east of Chelmsford.

In this year [991AD] Olaf came with 93 ships to Folkestone, and ravaged round about it, and then from there went on to Sandwich, and so from there to Ipswich, and overran it, and so to Maldon. And Ealdorman Byrhtnoth came against him there with his army and fought against him; and they killed the ealdorman there and had control of the field . . .

The Anglo-Saxon Chronicle

'The Battle of Maldon' is a 325-line poem written very soon after this crucial battle between the Danes, who are camped on Northey Island in the Blackwater Estuary, and the English under Byrhtnoth, ealdorman of Essex since 956, who are ranged on the opposite shore. The Panta of the poem is the Blackwater.

> The time had come for all the doomed men
> to fall in the fight. The clamour began;
> the ravens wheeled and the eagle circled overhead,
> craving for carrion; there was shouting on earth.
> They sent their spears, hard as files,
> and darts, ground sharp, flying from their hands.

From 'The Battle of Maldon' (c1000), anon.

What we have here is not dry history, but a battle fought a thousand years ago, reported as if it were yesterday. We have in Byrhtnoth, a pure example of the heroic Germanic code that came with the Saxons to Britain. We see the Danes manipulating him by challenging his loyalty to the code, and Byrhtnoth falling for the challenge and allowing the Danes access to a ford. We also see the heroic death of Byrhtnoth himself, the cowardice of a section of his men, and the supreme loyalty of the rest after their leader is dead.

The scars of the battle are long gone from the banks of the Blackwater, but the picture of the scene, thanks to this poem, will always be part of them – those who have read it cannot fail to pour into the sand the tumult and clamour of battle. As the poet Edward Thomas wrote – 'the relics of every age, skull and weapon and shroudpin and coin and carven stone, are spread out upon the clean, untrodden sand, and the learned, the imaginative, the fanciful, the utterly un-historic and merely human man exercises his spirit upon them and responds, if only for a moment.'

KENT

Cooling

Village off the A228, 6m north east of Rochester.

Dickens knew that in the churchyard at Cooling there were 13 small brothers and sisters of the same family buried in a neat row. He would often walk from his home at Gad's Hill and look at them. It is suggested that he included only 5 of them in *Great Expectations* (1860) so as not to test credibility. The place, grim and dreary, situated between the Thames Estuary and the mouth of the Medway, quite simply fulfilled itself in the first few pages of Dickens' novel.

My father's family name being Pirrip, and my christian name Philip, my infant tongue could make of both names nothing longer or more explicit than Pip. So, I called myself Pip, and came to be called Pip.

I give Pirrip as my father's family name, on the authority of his tombstone and my sister – Mrs Joe Gargery, who married the blacksmith. As I never saw my father or my mother, and never saw any likeness of either of them (for their days were long before the days of photographs), my first fancies regarding what they were like, were un-reasonably derived from their tombstones. The shape of the letters on my father's, gave me an odd idea that he was a square, stout, dark man, with curly black hair. From the character and turn of the inscription, '*Also Georgiana Wife of the Above,*' I drew a childish conclusion that my mother was freckled and sickly. To five little stone lozenges, each about a foot and a half long, which were arranged in a neat row beside their grave, and were sacred to the memory of five little brothers of mine – who gave up trying to get a living, exceedingly early in that universal struggle – I am indebted for a belief I religiously entertained that they had all been born on their backs with their hands in their trousers-pockets, and had never taken them out in this state of existence.

Ours was the marsh country, down by the river, within, as the river wound, twenty miles of the sea. My first most vivid and broad impression of the identity of things, seems to me to have been gained on a memorable raw afternoon towards evening. At such a time I found out for certain, that this bleak place overgrown with nettles was the churchyard; and that Philip Pirrip, late of this parish, and also Georgiana wife of the above, were dead and buried; and that Alexander,

Bartholomew, Abraham, Tobias, and Roger, infant children of the aforesaid, were also dead and buried; and that the dark flat wilderness beyond the churchyard, intersected with dykes and mounds and gates, with scattered cattle feeding on it, was the marshes; and that the low leaden line beyond, was the river; and that the distant savage lair from which the wind was rushing, was the sea; and that the small bundle of shivers growing afraid of it all and beginning to cry, was Pip.

'Hold your noise!' cried a terrible voice, as a man started up from among the graves at the side of the church porch. 'Keep still, you little devil, or I'll cut your throat!'

A fearful man, all in coarse grey, with a great iron on his leg. A man with no hat, and with broken shoes, and with an old rag tied round his head. A man who had been soaked in water, and smothered in mud, and lamed by stones, and cut by flints, and stung by nettles, and torn by briars; who limped, and shivered, and glared and growled; and whose teeth chattered in his head as he seized me by the chin.

'O! Don't cut my throat, sir,' I pleaded in terror. 'Pray don't do it, sir.'

'Tell us your name!' said the man. 'Quick!'

'Pip, sir.'

'Once more,' said the man, staring at me. 'Give it mouth!'

'Pip. Pip, sir.'

'Show us where you live,' said the man. 'Pint out the place!'

I pointed to where our village lay, on the flat in-shore among the alder-trees and pollards, a mile or more from the church.

The man, after looking at me for a moment, turned me upside down, and emptied my pockets. There was nothing in them but a piece of bread. When the church came to itself – for he was so sudden and strong that he made it go head over heels before me, and I saw the steeple under my feet – when the church came to itself, I say, I was seated on a high tombstone, trembling, while he ate the bread ravenously.

'You young dog,' said the man, licking his lips, 'what fat cheeks you ha' got.'

I believe they were fat, though I was at that time undersized for my years, and not strong.

'Darn Me if I couldn't eat em,' said the man, with a threatening shake of his head, 'and if I han't half a mind to't!'

I earnestly expressed my hope that he wouldn't, and held tighter to the tombstone on which he had put me; partly, to keep myself upon it; partly, to keep myself from crying.

'Now lookee here!' said the man. 'Where's your mother?'

'There, sir!' said I.

He started, made a short run, and stopped and looked over his shoulder.

'There, sir!' I timidly explained. 'Also Georgiana. That's my mother.'

'Oh!' said he, coming back. 'And is that your father alonger your mother?'

'Yes, sir,' said I; 'him too; late of this parish.'

'Ha!' he muttered then, considering. 'Who d'ye live with – supposin' you're kindly let to live, which I han't made up my mind about?'

'My sister, sir – Mrs Joe Gargery – wife of Joe Gargery, the blacksmith, sir.'

'Blacksmith, eh?' said he. And looked down at his leg.

After darkly looking at his leg and me several times, he came closer to my tombstone, took me by both arms, and tilted me back as far as he could hold me; so that his eyes looked most powerfully down into mine, and mine looked most helplessly up into his.

'Now lookee here,' he said, 'the question being whether you're to be let to live. You know what a file is?'

'Yes, sir.'

'And you know what wittles is?'

'Yes, sir.'

After each question he tilted me over a little more, so as to give me a greater sense of helplessness and danger.

'You get me a file.' He tilted me again. 'And you get me wittles.' He tilted me again. 'You bring 'em both to me.' He tilted me again. 'Or I'll have your heart and liver out.' He tilted me again.

I was dreadfully frightened, and so giddy that I clung to him with both hands, and said, 'If you would kindly please to let me keep upright, sir, perhaps I shouldn't be sick, and perhaps I could attend more.'

He gave me a most tremendous dip and roll, so that the church jumped over its own weather-cock. Then, he held me by the arms, in an upright position on the top of the stone, and went on in these fearful terms:

'You bring me, to-morrow morning early, that file and them wittles. You bring the lot to me, at that old Battery over yonder. You do it, and you never dare to say a word or dare to make a sign concerning your having seen such a person as me, or any person sumever, and you shall be let to live. You fail, or you go from my words in any partickler, no matter how small it is, and your heart and your liver shall be tore out, roasted and ate. Now, I ain't alone, as you may think I am. There's a young man hid with me, in comparison with which young man I am a Angel. That young man hears the words I speak. That young man has a secret way pecooliar to himself, of getting at a boy, and at his heart, and at his liver. It is in wain for a boy to attempt to hide himself from that young man. A boy may lock his door, may be

Dreary Cooling graveyard, between the Thames Estuary and the mouth of the Medway, no more than seven miles from Dickens' home at Gad's Hill and close to Rochester, almost certainly the cathedral town where Miss Haversham lived.

warm in bed, may tuck himself up, may draw the clothes over his head, may think himself comfortable and safe, but that young man will softly creep and creep his way to him and tear him open. I am a keeping that young man from harming of you at the present moment, with great difficulty. I find it wery hard to hold that young man off of your inside. Now, what do you say?'

I said that I would get him the file, and I would get him what broken bits of food I could, and I would come to him at the Battery, early in the morning.

'Say Lord strike you dead if you don't!' said the man.

I said so, and he took me down.

'Now,' he pursued, 'you remember what you've undertook, and you remember that young man, and you get home!'

'Goo-good night, sir,' I faltered.

'Much of that!' said he, glancing about him over the cold wet flat. 'I wish I was a frog. Or a eel!'

At the same time, he hugged his shuddering body in both his arms – clasping himself, as if to hold himself together – and limped towards the low church wall. As I saw him go, picking his way among the nettles, and among the brambles that bound the green mounds, he looked in my young eyes as if he were eluding the hands of the dead people, stretching up cautiously out of their graves, to get a twist upon his ankle and pull him in.

When he came to the low church wall, he got over it, like a man whose legs were numbed and stiff, and then turned round to look for me. When I saw him turning, I set my face towards home, and made the best use of my legs. But presently I looked over my shoulder, and saw him going on again towards the river, still hugging himself in both arms, and picking his way with his sore feet among the great stones dropped into the marshes here and there, for stepping-places when the rains were heavy, or the tide was in.

The marshes were just a long black horizontal line then, as I stopped to look after him; and the river was just another horizontal line, not nearly so broad nor yet so black; and the sky was just a row of long angry red lines and dense black lines intermixed. On the edge of the river I could faintly make out the only two black things in all the prospect that seemed to be standing upright; one of these was the beacon by which the sailors steered – like an un-hooped cask upon a pole – an ugly thing when you were near it; the other a gibbet, with some chains hanging to it which had once held a pirate. The man was limping on towards this latter, as if he were the pirate come to life, and come down, and going back to hook himself up again. It gave me a terrible turn when I thought so; and as I saw the cattle lifting their heads to gaze after him, I wondered whether they thought so too. I looked all round for the horrible young man, and could see no signs of him. But, now I was frightened again, and ran home without stopping.

Yalding
Village on the B2162, 5m south west of Maidstone.

After the First War, Edmund Blunden, one of England's most gifted poets, seeing perhaps the cultural and spiritual consequences for the nation of unnaturally accelerated fundamental change, and at the same time trying to make sense of his own terrible war-time experiences in the trenches, sought to bring to mind – to ours, to his – what at root he felt really mattered in English life. Unsurprisingly, he turned to his pre-war vision of the village of Yalding in the heart of hop-growing country. His parents taught at the local school, and his father was organist and choirmaster at the church. Edmund had become Senior Classics Scholar at Queens College, Oxford.

The crows flapped lazily over the molehilly pastures, where the boy who minded the cow had gone to sleep below the chestnut-trees.

Slow? You might accuse us of being so, but we should have been puzzled and obstinate. Excitement is to be measured by individual standard, and the circling year brought enough for the desires of that microcosm on the somnolent Medway.

A thing was none the worse there for being old.

Curious as it may appear in a few years' time, the village church was the centre and source of many notable events.

Folks were proud of that church, in the pews of which were prayer books that had not been moved many yards since the spacious days of George the Third, in the tower of which were six bells commemorating ancient churchwardens still represented in the parish by their posterity. It was a sizable church, but the evening service often filled it, and harvest thanksgiving packed the aisles as well as the pews with pleased labourers and tradesmen.

Perhaps the greatest chapter in those calmly unfolding volumes of kindly time was that headed The New Organ. . . . When at last the miraculous new organ was ready for opening, a gorgeous ceremony was held; quite a staff of clergymen shared the service, one of whom preached on 'Church Music' with such eloquence that the choir-boys stopped eating black currant lozenges; the organist himself struck out inimitable chords at those passages of the Psalms which referred to thunder, lightning, dragons and so on, and a still more agile performer from a college chapel supplemented such glories with a recital that seemed to make the purple of the painted windows turn pale.

Other high days which Mother Church gave us could readily be recounted; even funerals used to be considered one of life's advantages (more or less); but recollection hurries on to secular blessings.

That village had a cricket ground almost as smooth and level as a billiard table, and two teams supported our reputation, the first consisting of the aristocrats, as farmers, brewers, doctors, the clergy, and 'visitors'; the second enlisting such humbler sportsmen, as the village schoolmaster, butcher, farm bailifs, railway clerks, footmen, and simple Hodge. The excitement of all matches in which these teams (but particularly the second) took part almost takes my breath away even at this time. The chorus which used to reverberate through the lanes as they drove home in white-blossomed twilight from far-away matches had a genuine jollity worthy of Mr Pickwick's notebook.

As summer grew middle-aged and a little grey, the season of hop-picking arrived with unfailing activity and excitement, in the local sense of the word. Our meadows and copses, even some of the sacred lairs of our redoubtable anglers, were then invaded by the annual tribes from the East End or the slums of Brighton; no place was too venerable for these joyful and blasphemous marauders. However, the actual business of hop-picking, which occupies almost all of daylight, kept them from taking us, and our damsons, entirely by storm. They came in families, and alliances of families, to 'take on' as last year with the farmer whose mien and pay pleased best. It must be a wonderful holiday, hop-picking, for those who ordinarily have to fight for a little sun and air in mean streets, and there used to be many a smile as the measurer and the book-keeper moved among the bins of those hop-pickers. ''Ere, there's ahr little bookie. Hi Bookie.' 'I remember you, sir, that I do – lawst year I 'ad to stay 'ome, but I remember you' – such cries of recognition cheered the opening day of hop-picking. The same old fellows as ever in football jerseys and patchwork trousers appeared opposite the village stores to do a roaring trade in dried fish, clothing, gaudy sweets, bottled mysteries; the same brawls took place outside the Two Brewers – 'She called our 'op-'ouse a stinkin' monkey-'ouse.' 'An' you 'it young Ike' (produced, holding hand to jaw), 'on the chops, yer coward.' Besides these personal differences, occasionally the pickers at some of the farms would strike, but how gently! A few hours, and all was proceeding as before, nor would any graver disturbance usually interrupt the ingathering of the hops, until at length the special train with cushionless seats carried back the Londoners to their homes, singing:

> 'Oppin' is all over,
> Money is all spent,
> Don't I wish I'd never
> Come 'oppin dahn in Kent –
> Wiv a tee-ay-ay, tee-ay-ay, tee-ay-ee-ay-O!

These were not our only visitors. At regular seasons the circus folk arrived, and the puffing engines which pulled their great wagons along scarcely puffed more than the small boys and girls who darted to the line of march. The usual process of roundabouts, swingboats, coco-nut shies, sword-swallowers and 'try your strength' apparatus soon brought unearthly bliss to our midst, except where parents were too 'respectable' or disciplinary. I, for instance, was

Yalding village, its hops fields beyond.

invariably forbidden to possess, carry, or use a water-pistol, and have been sharply criticized for entering the tent of 'Howitzer George. Has Won Upward of Sixty Belts in the West Country.' And one of our lads, always despised for ponderous inability in cricket, dared step into the ring (often looking out of it to his comrades, whose confidence was wonderful). Well might we all join mightily in the psalm the following Sunday night, 'The mountains skipped like rams.'

Such soothing remembrances one owes to the rural community in the days of Edward the Seventh.

The Hop Leaf by Edmund Blunden

SUSSEX

Hastings
South coast resort on the A21/A259.

The development of the seaside resort in the 19th century reflected a whole new recreational attitude towards the coast, the sea hitherto a place reserved for industry – fishing, mercantile trade, etc – and held in reverence and awe. Mr Parker's enthusiasm for a resort in *Sanditon* (Jane Austen's novel written in 1817, but unfinished owing to her death), is believed

to have been influenced by a scheme for one at St Leonards, a town west of Hastings along the coast, though Austen (through Mr Parker) places it, in true picturesque fashion, nearer Eastbourne:

'The finest, purest sea breeze on the coast – acknowledged to be so – excellent bathing – fine hard sand – deep water ten yards from the shore – no mud – no weeds – no slimey rocks – Never was there a place more palpably designed by nature for the resort of the invalid – the very spot which thousands seemed in need of. – The most desirable distance from London! One complete, measured mile nearer than Eastbourne. Only conceive sir, the advantage of saving a whole mile, in a long journey.'

Not everyone agrees with Mr Parker. 'Every five years, one hears of some new place or other starting up by the sea, and growing the fashion,' observes Mr Heywood. 'Bad things for a country; – sure to raise

'In general, it was a thorough pause of company, it was emptiness and tranquillity on the Terrace, the cliffs and the sands.'

the price of provisions and make the poor good for nothing . . . '

In 'Gala Day' (*Private Parts*, 1987), Fiona Pitt-Kethley brings the spirit of English seaside holidays up to date and shows it spreading up the line:

'Gala Day' on the Hastings-Tonbridge line
was all 'special attractions and displays . . .
50p per person (Adult or Child)'.
They'd painted stations right along the way
and hung out plastic flags – red-white and blue.
The programme had a picture on the back –
The Wrotham White Star Sword Dance Team at work –
six knickerbockered blokes with left legs raised;
the youngest had bagpipes under one arm;
the fattest held a pentacle of swords;
they all had beards, bow-ties and cummerbunds.

A harassed beauty queen came round the train
with pencils, beer-mats, biros, stickers, bags
and 'twirly hats'. I got a bag and pen.
The trains were packed with Mums and Dads and kids.
('Look Dad, you can get in half-price with this
to Hastings Castle and the Caves.' Dad sat
on Mummy's lap and said, 'They'd have to pay
to get ME to go round that lot.') . . .

Burwash
Village on the A265, 10m south east of Tunbridge Wells.

Of all the trees that grow so fair,
  Old England to adorn,
Greater are none beneath the Sun,
  Than Oak, and Ash, and Thorn,
Sing Oak, and Ash, and Thorn, good Sirs
  (All of a Midsummer morn)!
Surely we sing no little thing,
  In Oak, and Ash, and Thorn!

Rudyard Kipling

Born in Bombay, in 1865, Kipling finally settled here in 1902. Of the house that he chose, Bateman's, he declared that he felt its 'Spirit – her Feng Shui – to be good,' and celebrated the quintessentially English spirit of the hill that he could see from it, in classical fashion:

The children were at the Theatre, acting to Three Cows as much as they could remember of *Midsummer Night's Dream*.

Their play went beautifully. Dan remembered all his parts – Puck, Bottom, and the three Fairies – and Una never forgot a word of Titania – not even the difficult piece where she tells the Fairies how to feed Bottom with 'apricocks, ripe figs, and dewberries', and all the lines end in 'ies'. They were both so pleased that they acted it three times over from beginning to end before they sat down in the unthistly centre of the Ring to eat eggs and Bath Olivers. This was when they heard a whistle among the alders on the bank, and they jumped.

The bushes parted. In the very spot where Dan had stood as Puck they saw a small, brown, broad-shouldered, pointy-eared person with a snub nose, slanting blue eyes, and a grin that ran right across his freckled face. He shaded his fore-head as though he were watching Quince, Snout, Bottom, and the others rehearsing *Pyramis and Thisbe*, and in a voice as deep as Three Cows asking to be milked, he began:

'What hempen homespuns have we swaggering here,
  So near the cradle of our fairy Queen?'

He stopped, hollowed one hand round his ear, and with a wicked twinkle in his eye, went on . . .
'What on Human Earth made you act *Midsummer Night's Dream* three times over, *on* Midsummer Eve, *in* the middle of a Ring, and under – right *under* one of my oldest hills in Old England? Pook's Hill – Puck's Hill – Puck's Hill – Pook's Hill! It's as plain as the nose on my face.'

He pointed to the bare, fern-covered slope of Pook's Hill that runs up from the far side of the mill-stream to a dark wood. Beyond that wood the ground rises and rises for five hundred feet, till at last you climb out on the bare top of Beacon Hill, to look over the Pevensey Levels and the Channel and half the naked South Downs.

'By Oak, Ash, and Thorn!' he cried, still laughing. 'If this had happened a few hundred years ago you'd have had all the People of the Hills out like bees in June!'

'We didn't know it was wrong,' said Dan.

'Wrong!' The little fellow shook with laughter. 'Indeed, it isn't wrong. You've done something that Kings and Knights and Scholars in old days would have given their crowns and spurs and books to find out. If Merlin himself had helped you, you couldn't have managed better! You've broken the Hills – you've broken the Hills! It hasn't happened in a thousand years.'

Puck of Pook's Hill by Rudyard Kipling

OXFORDSHIRE

Juniper Hill
Just north of Cottisford, off the B4031, 17m north east of Oxford.

The hamlet stood on a gentle rise in the flat, wheat-growing north-east corner of Oxfordshire. We will call it Lark Rise because of the great number of skylarks which made the surrounding fields their springboard and nested on the bare earth between the rows of green corn.

All around, from every quarter, the stiff, clayey soil of the arable fields crept up; bare, brown and windswept for eight months out of the twelve. Spring brought a flush of green wheat and there were violets under the hedges and pussy-willows out beside the brook at the bottom of the 'Hundred Acres'; but only for a few weeks in later summer had the landscape real beauty. Then the ripened cornfields rippled up to the doorsteps of the cottages and the hamlet became an island in a sea of dark gold. . . .

Harvest time at Juniper hill, 'a natural holiday', but 'a hemmed hard-worked 'n.'

Harvest time was a natural holiday. 'A hemmed hard-worked 'n' the men would have said; but they all enjoyed the stir and excitement of getting in the crops and their own importance as skilled and trusted workers, with extra beer at the farmer's expense and extra harvest money to follow.

The 'eighties brought a succession of hot summers and, day after day, as harvest time approached, the children at the end house would wake to the dewy, pearly pink of a fine summer dawn and the *swizzh, swizzh* of the early morning breeze

Below: *A cottage at Juniper Hill today. The larks still hover above the* Rise (right), *chattering and squealing in the early morning as they play in the wind currents over the little hamlet.* 'All times are times of transition,' *Flora Thompson wrote, but the skylarks sing a song of continuity, too.*

rustling through the ripe corn beyond their doorstep.

Then, very early one morning, the men would come out of their houses, pulling on coats and lighting pipes as they hurried and calling to each other with skyward glances: 'Think weather's a-gooin' to hold?' For three weeks or more during the harvest the hamlet was astir before dawn and the homely odours of bacon frying, wood fires and tobacco smoke over-powered the pure, damp, earthy scent of the fields. It would be school holidays then and the children at the end house always wanted to get up hours before their time.

Awed, yet uplifted by the silence and clean-washed loveliness of the dawn, the children would pass along the narrow field paths with rustling wheat on each side. Or Laura would make little dashes into the corn for poppies, or pull trails of the lesser bindweed with its pink-striped trumpets, like clean cotton frocks, to trim her hat and girdle her waist, while Edmund would stump on, red-faced with indignation at her carelessness in making trails in the standing corn.

In the fields where the harvest had begun all was bustle and activity. The scythe still did most of the work and they did not dream it would ever be superseded.

After the mowing and reaping and binding came the carrying, the busiest time of all. Every man and boy put his best foot forward then, for, when the corn was cut and dried it was imperative to get it stacked and thatched before the weather broke. All day and far into the twilight the yellow-and-blue painted farm wagons passed and repassed along the roads between the field and the stack-yard. Big cart-horses returning with an empty wagon were made to gallop like two-year-olds. Straws hung on the roadside hedges and many a gate-post was knocked down through hasty driving. In the fields men pitch-forked the sheaves to the one who was building the load on the wagon, and the air resounded with *Hold tights*, and *Wert ups*, and *Who-o-oas*. The Hold tight! was no empty cry; sometimes, in the past, the man on top of the load had not held tight or not tight enough. There were tales of fathers and grandfathers whose necks or backs had been broken by a fall from a load, and of other fatal accidents afield, bad cuts from scythes, pitch-forks passing through feet, to be followed by lockjaw, and of sunstroke; but, happily, nothing of this kind happened on that particular farm in the 'eighties. At last, in the cool dusk of an August evening, the last load was brought in, with a nest of merry boys' faces among the sheaves on the top, and the men walking alongside with pitch-forks on shoulders. As they past along the roads they shouted:

>Harvest home! Harvest home!
>Merry, merry, merry harvest home!

and women came to their cottage gates and waved, and the few passers-by looked up and smiled their congratulations. The joy and pleasure of the labourers in their task well done was pathetic, considering their very small share in the gain.

Lark Rise to Candleford by Flora Thompson

Oxford
University city 50m north west of London. M40.

'that sweet city with her dreaming spires.' Matthew Arnold

Clearly it was vain to seek distraction in my old College. I floated out into the untenanted meadows. Over them was the usual coverlet of white vapour, trailed from the Isis right up to Merton Wall. The scent of these meadows' moisture is the scent of Oxford. Even in hottest noon, one feels that the sun has not dried *them*. Always there is moisture drifting across them, drifting into the Colleges. It, one suspects, must have had much to do with the evocation of what is called the Oxford spirit – that gentlest spirit, so lingering and searching, so dear to them who as youths were brought into ken of it, so exasperating to them who were not.

And on that moonlit night, when I floated among the vapours of these meadows, myself less than a vapour, I knew and loved Oxford as never before, as never since. Yonder, in the Colleges, was the fume and fret of tragedy – Love as Death's decoy, and Youth following her. What then? Not Oxford was menaced. Come what might, not a stone of Oxford's walls would be loosened, not a wreath of her vapours be undone, nor lost a breath of her sacred spirit.

I floated up into the higher drier air, that I might, for once, see the total body of that spirit.

There lay Oxford far beneath me, like a map in grey and black and silver. All that I had known only as great single things I saw now outspread in apposition, and tiny; tiny symbols, as it were, of themselves, greatly symbolising their oneness. There they lay, these multitudinous and disparate quadrangles, all their rivalries merged in the making of a great catholic pattern. And the roofs of the buildings around them seemed level with their lawns. No higher the roofs of the very towers. Up from their tiny segment of the earth's spinning surface they stood negligible beneath infinity. And new, too, quite new, in eternity; transient upstarts. I saw Oxford as a place that had no more past and no more future than a mining-camp. I smiled down. O hoary and unassailable mushroom! . . . But if a man carry his sense of proportion far enough, lo! he is back at the point from which he started. He knows that eternity, as conceived by him, is but an instant in eternity, and infinity but a speck in infinity. How should they belittle the things near to him? . . . Oxford was venerable and magical, after all, and enduring.

Zuleika Dobson (1911) by Max Beerbohm

Left: '*It was Eights Week – submerged now and obliterated, irrecoverable as Lyonesse . . . (but) still a city of aquatint.*' Brideshead Revisited *(1945) by Evelyn Waugh.*
Below: *Oxford is Christminster, and the church of St Mary the Virgin 'the church with the Italian Porch', in Thomas Hardy's Jude the Obscure.*

Heart of England and East Anglia

WARWICKSHIRE

....

Nuneaton
Town 7m north of Coventry on the A444.

A human life should be well rooted in some spot of a native land . . . a spot where the definiteness of early memories may be inwrought with affection.

From *Daniel Deronda* (1874)

In all the years I have lived I remember nothing that is much earlier than the knowledge that I had a brother Robert, and I have always thought of him, throughout the years we have been separated, as one whose heart had on every opportunity shown its ready kindness towards me.

From *Letters*

Nature repairs her ravages – but not all. The uptorn trees are not rooted again – the parted hills are left scarred: if there is a new growth, the trees are not the same as the old, and the hills underneath their green vesture bear the marks of the past rending. To the eyes that have dwelt on the past, there is no thorough repair.

From 'Conclusion', *The Mill on the Floss* (1860)

George Eliot (Mary Ann Evans) was born on November 22nd 1819, at

Gryff House, where George Eliot lived for 21 years. It is now a hotel.

Arbury Farm, now South Farm on the Arbury Estate, where Eliot was born.

Arbury Farm (now South Farm) on the Arbury Estate which lies within the parish of Chilvers Cotton, Nuneaton. Her father became land agent for Arbury Hall, the Warwickshire seat of the Newdegate family, now the home of Viscount Daventry, and the inspiration for Cheverel Manor in *Mr. Gilfil's Love Story* (1857):

And a charming picture Cheverel Manor would have made that evening, if some English Watteau had been there to paint it: the castellated house of grey-tinted stone, with the flickering sunbeams sending dashes of golden light across the many-shaped panes in the mullioned windows, and a great beech leaning athwart one of the flanking towers, and breaking, with its dark flattened boughs, the too formal symmetry of the front . . .

Here, on the Arbury Estate, riding in a gig between the knees of her father on estate business, the seeds not only of later landscapes but of rural characters that peopled her landscapes were sown –

Little details give each field a particular physiognomy, dear to the eyes that have looked on them from childhood: the pool in the corner where the grasses were dank and trees leaned whisperingly; the great oak shadowing a bare place in mid-pasture; the high bank where the ash-trees grew; the sudden slope of the old marl-pit making a red background for the burdock; the huddled roofs and ricks of the homestead without a traceable way of approach; the grey gate and fences against the depths of the bordering wood; and the stray hovel, its old, old thatch full of mossy hills and valleys with wondrous modulations of light and shadow such as we travel far to see in later life, and see larger, but not more beautiful. These are the things that make the gamut of joy in landscape to midland-bred souls – the things

Arbury Hall, the 'castellated house of grey-tinted stone', Eliot's Cheveral Manor. Left: the lake on the Estate.

they toddled among, or perhaps learned by heart standing between their father's knees while he drove leisurely.

Middlemarch

Like so many great writers the nature of the talent, which had to have been born anyway, was child of circumstance. Eliot was cut off from her roots. she had begun to live with a married man, the actor and writer G H Lewes, and when she told her brother Isaac that she had taken Lewes's name, he broke off relations with her and forbade her sister Chrissie to communicate. As a result, in her work, Eliot recalled her home and childhood with a longing, and need for detail, exacerbated by enforced alienation.

After South Farm the family had moved to Griff House (now a hotel, on the corner of the A444 Bedworth By-pass and Arbury Lane, about a mile from Chilvers Coton Church). Eliot had lived there for 21 years, and although in the quote above it is her brother Robert whom she recalls so warmly, it was Isaac, just three years her senior with whom she would go fishing in the Round Pool (still visible in the hotel grounds) and with whom she had been specially close:

The brown canal of the autobiographical sonnets, Brother and Sister, 'My present Past, my root of piety'.

So ended the sorrows of this day, and the next morning Maggie was trotting with her own fishing-rod in one hand, and a handle of the basket in the other, stepping always by a peculiar gift in the muddiest places and looking darkly radiant from under her beaver-bonnet because Tom was good to her. She had told Tom, however, that she should like him to put the worms on the hook for her, although she accepted his word when he assured her that worms couldn't feel (it was Tom's private opinion that it didn't much matter if they did). He knew all about worms and fish and those things; and what birds were mischievous and how padlocks opened, and which way the handles of the gates were to be lifted. Maggie thought this sort of knowledge was very wonderful – much more difficult than remembering what was in the books; and she was rather in awe of Tom's superiority, for he was the only person who called her knowledge 'stuff' and did not feel surprised at her cleverness. Tom, indeed, was of opinion that Maggie was a silly little thing: all girls were silly – they couldn't throw a stone so as to hit anything, couldn't do anything with a pocket-knife, and were frightened at frogs. Still, he was very fond of his sister, and meant always to take care of her, make her his housekeeper, and punish her when she did wrong.

They were on their way to the Round Pool – that wonderful pool, which the floods had made a long while ago: no one knew how deep it was; and it was mysterious too that it should be almost a perfect round, framed in with willows and tall reeds, so that the water was only to be seen when you got close to the brink.

She was looking dreamily at the glassy water, when Tom said, in a loud whisper, 'Look, look, Maggie!' and came running to prevent her from snatching her line away.

Maggie was frightened lest she had been doing something wrong, as usual, but presently Tom drew out her line and brought a large tench bouncing on the grass.

Tom was excited.

'O Magsie! you little duck! Empty the basket.'

Maggie was not conscious of unusual merit, but it was enough that Tom called her Magsie, and was pleased with her. There was nothing to mar her delight in the whispers and the dreamy silences, when she listened to the light dipping sounds of the rising fish and the gentle rustling, as if the willows and the reeds and the water had their happy whisperings also. Maggie thought it would make a very nice heaven to sit by the pool in that way, and never be scolded. She never knew she had a bite till Tom told her, but she liked fishing very much.

It was one of their happy mornings.

'We could never have loved the earth so well if we had had no childhood in it . . . What novelty is worth that sweet monotony where everything is known and loved because it is known?'
George Eliot

Long years have left their writing on my brow,
But yet the freshness and the few-fed beam
Of those young mornings are about me now,
When we two wandered toward the far-off stream

With rod and line. Our basket held a store
Baked for us only, and I thought with joy
That I should have my share, though he had more,
Because he was the elder and a boy.

The firmaments of daisies since to me
Have had those mornings in their opening eyes,
The bunchèd cowslip's pale transparency
Carries that sunshine of sweet memories,

And wild-rose branches take their finest scent
From those blest hours of infantine content . . .

From 'Brother and Sister' by George Eliot

Life did change for Tom and Maggie; and yet they were not wrong in believing that the thoughts and loves of these first years would always make part of their lives. We could never have loved the earth so well if we had had no childhood in it, – if it were not the earth where the same flowers come up again every spring that we used to gather with our tiny fingers as we sat lisping to ourselves on the grass – the same hips and haws on the autumn hedgerows – the same redbreasts that we used to call 'God's birds' because they did no harm to the precious crops. What novelty is worth that sweet monotony where everything is known and *loved* because it is known?

The wood I walk in on this mild May day, with the young yellow-brown foliage of the oaks between me and the blue sky, the white star-flowers and the blue-eyed speedwell and the ground ivy at my feet – what grove of tropic palms, what strange ferns or splendid broad-petalled blossoms, could ever thrill such deep and delicate fibres within me as this home-scene? These familiar flowers, these well-remembered bird-notes, this sky with its fitful brightness, these furrowed and grassy fields, each with a sort of personality given to it by the capricious hedgerows – such things as these are the mother tongue of our imagination, the language that is laden with all the subtle inextricable associations the fleeting hours of our childhood left behind them. Our delight in the sunshine on the deep bladed grass today, might be no more than the faint perception of wearied souls, if it were not for the sunshine and the grass in the far-off years, which still live in us and transform our perception into love.

The Mill on the Floss by George Eliot

Dorlcote Mill was modelled in her mind's eye on Arbury Mill, but the environment she wanted for the novel she found in the tidal Trent at Gainsborough (below).

Attaching the spirit of the countryside to a precious love between sister and brother enables Eliot to comment in heart-rending style on a 19th-century landscape in change. She resolves the novel and her own trauma in the flood of the tidal Floss, when Maggie and Tom die in each other's arms. 'Nature repairs her ravages,' she wrote, 'but not all . . . the parted hills are left scarred.'

CAMBRIDGESHIRE

Helpston
Village 5m north west of Peterborough, off the A15.

John Clare was born in Helpston in 1793. His father was a flail thresher and wrestler; both parents were illiterate. His childhood was spent, often alone, wandering Emmonsales, the heathland just outside the village, and later he wrote about it in prose deliberately unrestrained by grammar and punctuation.

> I felt the most happy to be alone – with such merry company
> I heard the black and brown beetle sing their evening song
> with rapture & lovd to see the black snail steal out upon the
> dewy baulks
> I saw the nimble horse bee at noon spinning on wanton I
> lovd to meet the woodman whistling away to his toils & to
> see the shepherd bending over his hook on the thistly greens
> chattering love storys to the listening milkmaid while she
> milkd her brindld cow
>   The first primrose in spring was as delightful as if seen
> for the first time & how the copper colord clouds of the
> morning was watchd

He also wrote poetry. When first published in 1820, success was immediate. He continued to focus his work on the landscape of his childhood, finding in the great change wrought by the Enclosure system (the taming of nature's wilderness) an illuminating parallel with what he believed to be the fruitless taming of childhood freedoms – the enslavement of nature's child by man:

Helpston village.

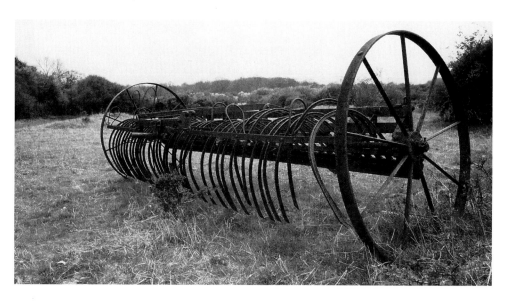

The heathland, Emmonsales.

Helpston fields. 'I love to walk the fields they are to me a legacy no evil can destroy.'

Thou far fled pasture, long evanish'd scene!
Where nature's freedom spread the flow'ry green,
Where golden kingcups open'd into view,
Where silver daisies in profusion grew;

But now, alas! those scenes exist no more;
The pride of life with thee, like mine, is o'er . . .

From 'Helpstone'

Clare's cottage.

Oh, I never thought that joys would run away from boys,
Or that boys would change their minds and forsake such
    summer joys . . .

From 'Remembrances'

Sadly, at last, hypnotising himself with the melancholy of childhood loss, even identifying his Muse with a childhood sweetheart, Mary Joyce, now, like all his childhood joys, unattainable, Clare's work becomes more lyrical than descriptive and his mind drifts away from reality.

In 1837 he was admitted to the insane asylum at High Beach, Epping. Four years later, with help from a gypsy and the idea of reuniting with Mary, he escaped and walked the 90 miles home, reduced at one stage to eating the grass by the road.

The Fens

The fen country incorporates areas of Norfolk, Cambridgeshire and Lincolnshire around the Wash.

When you work with water, you have to know and respect it. When you labour to subdue it, you have to understand that one day it may rise up and turn all your labours to nothing. For what is water, children, which seeks to make all things level, which has no taste or colour of its own, but a liquid form of Nothing? And what are the Fens, which so imitate in their levelness the natural disposition of water, but a landscape which, of all landscapes, most approximates to Nothing? Every Fenman secretly concedes this; every Fenman suffers now and then the illusion that the land he walks over is *not there*, is floating . . . And every Fen-child, who is given picture-books to read in which the sun bounces over mountain tops and the road of life winds through heaps of green cushions, and is taught nursery rhymes in which persons go up and down hills, is apt to demand of its elders: Why are the Fens flat?

. . .Flat, with an unrelieved and monotonous flatness, enough of itself, some might say, to drive a man to unquiet and sleep-defeating thoughts. From the raised banks of the Leem, it stretched away to the horizon, its uniform colour, peat-black, varied only by the crops that grew upon it – grey-green potato leaves, blue-green beet leaves, yellow-green wheat; its uniform levelness broken only by the furrowed and dead-straight lines of ditches and drains, which, depending on the state of the sky and the angle of the sun, ran like silver, copper or golden wires across the fields and which, when you stood and looked at them, made you shut one eye and fall prey to fruitless meditations on the laws of perspective.

'My ancestors were water people.' Graham Swift in Waterland

And yet this land, so regular, so prostrate, so tamed and cultivated, would transform itself, in my five- or six-year-old mind, into an empty wilderness. On those nights when my mother would be forced to tell me stories, it would seem that in our lock-keeper's cottage we were in the middle of nowhere; and the noise of the trains passing on the lines to King's Lynn, Gildsey and Ely was like the baying of a monster closing in on us in our isolation.

A fairy-tale land, after all.

The story of Graham Swift's *Waterland,* of all the novels set in this flat, artificial, but strangely appealing country, seems to be formed from the cultural ether of the place, not necessarily because it is 'an exact fit', but because his prose sings true. He makes you believe that his imaginings were sourced beneath the flat stillness of the fens a long time ago.

. . .My ancestors were water people. They speared fish and netted ducks. When I was small I possessed a living image of my ancestors in the form of Bill Clay, a shrunken, leathery carcase of a man, whose age was unknown but was never put at less than eighty, a one-time punt-gunner and turf-cutter, who had witnessed in his lifetime the passing of all but the dregs of the old wild fens in our area; who stank, even with his livelihood half gone, of goose fat and fish slime, mud and peat smoke; who wore an otter-skin cap, eel-skin gaiters and whose brain was permanently crazed by the poppy-head tea

The yet unacademic stream?
Is dawn a secret shy and cold
Anadyomene, silver gold?
And sunset still a golden sea
From Haslingfield to Madingley?
And after, ere the night is born,
Do hares come out about the corn?
Oh, is the water sweet and cool
Gentle brown, above the pool?
And laughs the immortal river still
Under the mill, under the mill?
Say, is there beauty yet to find?
And certainty? and Quiet kind?
Deep meadows yet, for to forget
The lies, and truths, and pain? . . . oh! yet
Stands the Church clock at ten to three?
And is there honey still for tea?

Little Gidding
West off the A1 at Sawtry, 6m north west of Huntingdon.

he drank to ward off winter agues. Old Bill lived with his wife Martha in a damp, crack-walled cottage not far from the Ouse and on the edge of the shrinking, reed-filled marsh known, after the watery expanse it had once been, as Wash Fen Mere. But some said that Martha Clay, who was some twenty years younger than Bill, was never Bill's wife at all. Some said that Martha Clay was a witch . . .

Grantchester
A mile or so south of Cambridge, off the A1309.

The Old Vicarage at Grantchester inspired possibly the most quintessentially English poetic expression of nostalgia for England's unspoiled rural scene. Its appearance in print shortly before the First War would have struck a particular chord in the minds of the English about to go to war and sensing the end of an already fading rural culture. 'The Old Vicarage, Grantchester' was written by Rupert Brooke in 1912.

Say, do the elm-clumps greatly stand,
Still guardians of that holy land?
The chestnuts shade, in reverend dream,

Between 1625 and 1646, Nicholas Ferrar, upon his retirement as a Member of Parliament and business-man, founded an Anglican community at Little Gidding, an estate belonging to his mother. The community, which worshipped three times a day in the little chapel, was dispersed by Parliamentary forces during the Civil War.

In the fourth of his *Four Quartets* T S Eliot fixed Little Gidding on the spiritual map of Britain.

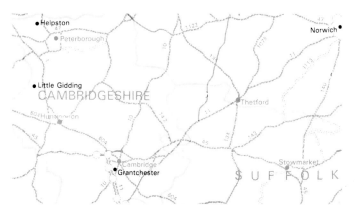

It is now a place of pilgrimage for poets as well as Christians:

In one hand Eliot, in the other Pevsner:
And yet we have arrived here unprepared.

From 'At Little Gidding' by Neil Powell

This is a place of departure
Not of arrival. Even the signpost
Saying Little Gidding, a shock
To any poetry-lover, seems
Meant to be read retrospectively
By tourists on their way back.

From 'A Visit to Little Gidding' by Patricia Beer

NORFOLK

The Broads
A group of lakes connected by a network of rivers, east of Norwich.

The sun had gone down. The tide was on the point of turning, and up-river a calm green-and-golden glow filled the sky and was reflected on the scarcely moving water. A heron came flying downstream with long slow flaps of his great wings. Only twenty yards away he lifted easily over the tall reeds and settled with a noisy disturbance of twigs on the top of a tree in a little wood at the edge of the marshes.

This is the area that inspired *The Coot Club* and *The Big Six*, Arthur Ransome's tales of adventure for children. As with the Coniston based stories (see Nibthwaite, Cumbria), he wrote them from first-hand experience.

It was growing dark now. Nobody but Tom was moving on the river, and the only noise was the loud singing of the birds on both banks and over the marshes, whistling black-birds, throaty thrushes, starlings copying first one and then the other, a snipe drumming overhead. Everything was all right with everybody. And then a pale barn owl swayed across the river like a great moth, and with her, furiously chattering, a little crowd of small birds, for whom the owl was nothing but an enemy. And suddenly into Tom's head came a picture of the *Margoletta* as a hostile owl, mobbed by a lot of small birds, the Death and Glories and himself.

The Coot Club by Arthur Ransome

SUFFOLK

Aldeburgh
Coastal village on the A1094, north east of Ipswich.

With ceaseless motion comes and goes the tide,
Flowing, it fills the channel vast and wide;
Then back to sea, with strong majestic sweep
It rolls, in ebb yet terrible and deep . . .

From 'The Borough' by George Crabbe
– Aldeburgh, 1810

David Matthews, the composer and sometime amanuensis of Benjamin Britten, writes that Frank Bridge's suite 'The Sea' was the first orchestral piece that Britten heard as a boy. 'In his own words, he was "knocked sideways" by it.' Much later, the sea was the view from Britten's seaside house at Aldeburgh, and Britten 'went on to produce a series of definitive

'My imaginative life and my inner self would have been very different . . . if I had not been so over-whelmingly affected by Britten . . . but it was not until twelve years later that I finally made my first pilgrimage to the small seaside town of Aldeburgh.' Susan Hill

English seascapes in music in his opera Peter Grimes . . . The sea is evoked in all its moods, from the sullen calm of a grey winter dawn to the sparkling waves on a bright, sunny morning, the moon reflected glints on the sea at night, or the pent-up violence of a storm.' It is an inspiring piece.

'At once, I fell under its spell both as it was in reality, and as that other Aldeburgh, whose spirit permeates the music.'

The debt writers owe to their sources of inspiration cannot always be acknowledged, simply because it is not always possible to trace back to that source. But the debt I owe to the work of Benjamin Britten is crystal clear to me, and clearest of all in the case of *The Albatross*. Without the dramatic impact upon me of Britten's music, as well as his personality and the place in which he worked, together with some of the books and ideas that had in their turn inspired him, I would not have written the book at all – and that holds good for at least another two of my novels, *Strange Meeting* and *The Bird of Night*. My imaginative life and my inner self would have been very different and greatly impoverished if I had not been so over-whelmingly affected by Britten.

I first heard his music the 'Sea Interludes' from the opera *Peter Grimes* when I was still at school, and it made a startling impact upon me, as few other things in my life have done, so that I still remember in vivid detail the room in which I was sitting, even the design on the cover of the file on my knee. In part, the music reminded me of the bleak North Sea coast beside which I was born and where I had lived until a few months before – and which, in my Midlands city sixth form, I desperately missed. But the impact went much deeper, and I became completely obsessed by the music and the story behind *Peter Grimes* – and so, gradually, by the rest of Britten's life and work.

But it was not until twelve years later that I finally made my first pilgrimage to the small Suffolk seaside town of Aldeburgh, where Britten lived and worked and which pervaded his imaginative life. At once, I fell under its spell both as it was in

reality, and as that other Aldeburgh, whose spirit permeates the music.

Once there, it was only a matter of time before I wrote about it and before the real and the imaginary Aldeburgh merged in my own work. So, the Heype of *The Albatross* is Aldeburgh; that coast is the Suffolk coast – and yet, of course, because the book is my fiction the two are entirely different.

I do not know, otherwise, where the story and the characters of *The Albatross* came from; I know only that the book wrote itself. All the best writing does that – and by 'the best' I mean that which comes from the deepest depths of the self and speaks the truth and could be in no way other than it is. I began to make a few notes while I was staying in Suffolk that first winter, and when I started writing (on a train, going between London and Warwickshire!) the story unwound itself from me like a thread and knitted itself together into paragraphs before my astonished eyes. I felt as if I were having no part of it, as if I were taking down dictation from some inner voice. That has happened just a few times in the course of my writing life. It is an awesome experience.

What *The Albatross* is about is pretty plain; it is about the misfit, the odd, the simple, the strange one in the midst of the rest of ordinary humanity, and about the power of love and pure goodness, shining through all manner of human exteriors. It is about possessiveness and cruelty and oppression, about fear and pride. Duncan is one of God's fools. Old Beatty is one of His saints. Yet both are in some way outside of and outcasts from society. Hilda Pike's wrongs are understandable, though not excusable.

Beyond the people, the story is about a place – a place which has as strong a character as any of the human figures – about the coast, the sea and its power and the little fishing town that has grown up at its edge in subservience to it, about the narrow dark lanes and the wide East Anglian skies, the boats, the raging elements – all those things that I found in Aldeburgh which had been so intimate a part of my childhood and which I had rediscovered again imaginatively through Britten's music.

Susan Hill

Duncan Pike wants to break free, free from the clutches of his mother, Hilda, free from his own feebleness. Here, Duncan is given the opportunity to take his chances. There is him, the 'heroic' Ted Flint and the sea, but the struggle is within himself.

Ted Flint paused for a second and then turned and began to get ready, hailing to one of the other men to help him, taking the rust-stained fishing hooks up from where they lay on the beach, and the lines, and luminous orange floats, loosening the cable. Without warning he began to give Duncan orders, as Cragg did: do this, move that, lift it, let it go, hold it, and Duncan obeyed, transfixed, desperate to please. The other man left them, to walk slowly beside the waterline, smoking his pipe.

The boat was down and ready, the motor running. Ted Flint was standing up in it, towering above Duncan, tall as a king.

'Get in then, if you're coming.'

Why should he take me out there, Duncan thought. *Why*? I've never been, I don't know anything, he doesn't speak to me, why should he ask me to go? Though he could sense no animosity in Ted Flint, no threat of danger. He was entirely puzzled.

A wave gathered, battleship-grey and seething along its crest, and then crashed over. The boat lifted and rocked.

'Hey?'

There was a moment when Duncan was ready to spring forwards and up, when he could already feel himself going out to sea, imagine the movement of it beneath him, they were pushing ahead. 'Want to come out in the boat then?' With Ted Flint. *I could go.*

And then another wave began to gather, and suddenly, he saw them coming at him, one after the next, rising up higher and higher, ready to break about his head and drag him down into them, and he knew that once they had pushed the boat out, then there would be no escape for him, and he would be alone with Ted Flint, towering above him, in the middle of the endless sky and heaving sea, and he was seized with choking panic, he turned and began to run, pounding off down the beach to get away from the menace of the waves and wind, and the chugging of the boat, out of the reach of Ted Flint, he would have done anything rather than go on that sea.

The Albatross by Susan Hill

'From parted clouds the moon her
  radiance throws
On the wild waves, and all the
  danger shows;
But shows them beaming in her
  shining vest,
Terrific splendour! gloom in glory
  dressed!
This for a moment, and then clouds
  again
Hide every beam, and fear and
  darkness reign.'

From 'The Borough' by George Crabbe

Scotland

GRAMPIAN

The Howe of the Mearns
Coastal agricultural district, west of Arbuthnott and the A94, 20m south of Aberdeen.

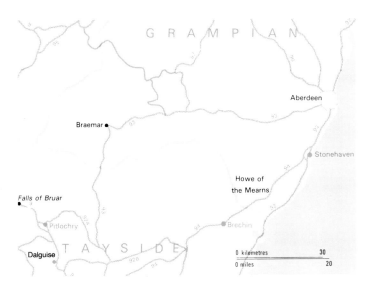

And out she went, though it wasn't near kye-time yet, and wandered away over the fields; it was a cold and louring day, the sound of the sea came plain to her, as though heard in a shell, Kinraddie wilted under the greyness . . .

And then a queer thought came to her there in the drooked fields, that nothing endured at all, nothing but the land she passed across, tossed and turned and perpetually changed below the hands of the crofter folk since the oldest of them had set the Standing Stones by the loch of Blawearie and climbed there on their holy days and saw their terraced crops ride brave in the wind and sun. Sea and sky and the folk who wrote and fought and were learnèd, teaching and saying and praying, they lasted but as a breath, a mist of fog in the hills, but the land was forever, it moved and changed below you, but was forever, you were close to it and it to you, not at a bleak remove it held you and hurted you. And she had thought to leave it all!

From *Sunset Song* (1932), first book in a trilogy, *A Scots Quair*, by Lewis Grassic Gibbon

A Scots Quair is a hapless love song that grows out of the soil of Gibbon's native North-east Lowlands and the culture of 'the old farmtoun folk, that itinerant society of wandering cottars moving on with each Mayterm day from one tied cottage to the next, of footloose bothy lads, crofters and small farmers . . . They were dour, awkward, argumentative, malicious and foulmouthed folk . . . a society caught finally in that long farming depression that followed from the growing influx of imports . . . they were figures trapped in a landscape of unrelenting toil, locked in a love-hate

The red earth of the Howe of the Mearns

relationship with the soil and frequently with each other.' (David Kerr Cameron)

TAYSIDE

Dalguise
Off the B898, 15m north of Perth via the A9.

The favourite holiday retreat of the Potter family when Beatrix was a child. Dalguise had the greatest influence on Beatrix Potter's imagination, both as a writer and painter. There –

Everything was romantic in my imagination. The Woods were peopled by the mysterious good folk. The Lords and Ladies of the last century walked with me along the overgrown paths, and picked the old-fashioned flowers among the box and rose hedges of the garden. Half believing the picturesque superstitions of the district, seeing my own fancies so clearly that they became true to me, I lived in a separate world.

Dalguise, the greatest influence on Beatrix Potter's imagination.

In 1893, at Eastwood, a dower house at nearby Dunkeld, she decided to share one of her stories with Noel Moore, the son of her erstwhile governness, Annie Moore. It became one of the most famous letters ever, and it began like this -

Her imagination was stirred but fantasy was not part of the art. The anthropomorphism was in vogue, through Randolph Caldecott. As John Millais put it, 'you have observation.' Even the lowliest cottage on the estate would figure (as Mrs Tiggywinkle's abode).

My deal Noel,
  I don't know what to write to you so I shall tell you a story about four little rabbits whose names were –

Flopsy
Mopsy,
Cotton-tail,

and Peter . . .

HIGHLAND

Ardnamurchan
Peninsula of the far West Highlands north of Mull, approached by the B8007.

On waking this morning,
with the dew on the woods,
on this very bright morning,
in a shady wee hollow
I heard then the chanter
with elegance played,
and the rocks' Echo sounded
their sweet-sad reply.

The fine-scented birch-tree,
new-branched over the cairn,
wet with tender warm May-dew
warm with sun's kindly shining,
exudes foliage from twiglets
in this lovely month, May:
month of dappled calves folded,
month for mating and milk.

Each grove, close and secret,
has its mantle of green,
the wood-sap is rising
from the roots at the bottom,
through arteries twisting
to swell out the growth;
thrush and cuckoo at evening
sing their litany above.

From 'Song of Summer' by Alasdair MacMhaighstir Alasdair

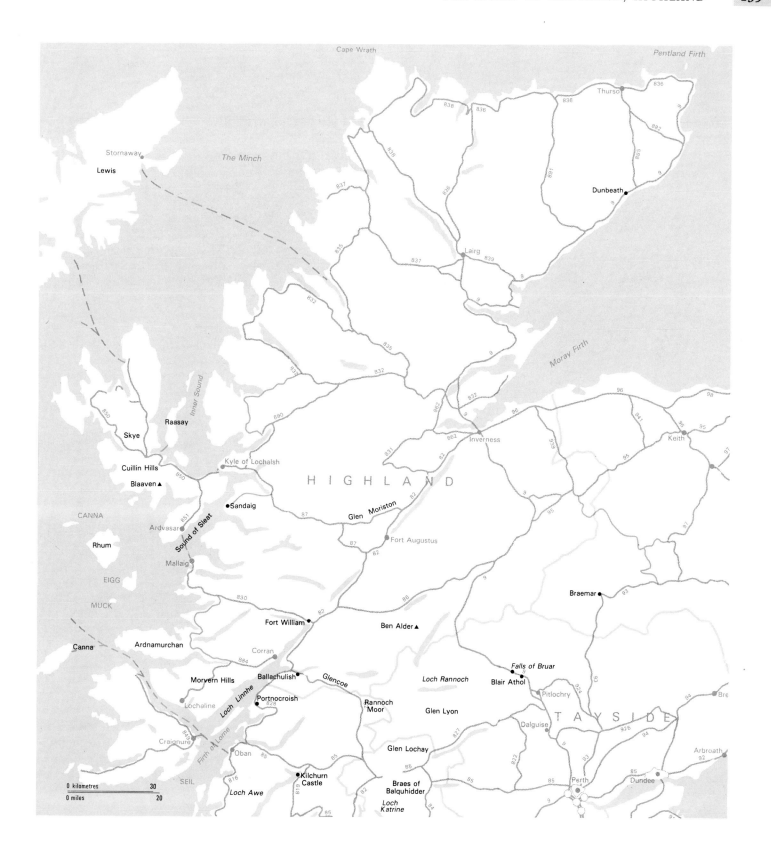

Cape Wrath

Pentland Firth

The Minch

Stornaway

Lewis

Thurso

Dunbeath

Lairg

Moray Firth

Inverness

Keith

H I G H L A N D

Skye

Raasay

Cuillin Hills

Kyle of Lochalsh

Blaaven ▲

Sandaig

Glen Moriston

CANNA

Ardvasar

Sound of Sleat

Fort Augustus

Rhum

Mallaig

EIGG

MUCK

Braemar

Canna

Ardnamurchan

Fort William

Ben Alder ▲

Corran

Falls of Bruar

Morvern Hills

Ballachulish

Glencoe

Loch Rannoch

Blair Athol

Pitlochry

Lochaline

Portnocroish

Loch Linnhe

Rannoch Moor

Glen Lyon

T A Y S I D E

Dalguise

Craignure

Firth of Lorne

Oban

Glen Lochay

Arbroath

Loch Awe

Kilchurn Castle

SEIL

Braes of Balquhidder

Perth

Dundee

Loch Katrine

0 kilometres   30

0 miles   20

Ben Alder

A mountain, 3,757 feet high, which sprawls along the west bank of Loch Ericht, approximately 20m east of Fort William as the crow flies.

Ben Alder is the pivot of Robert Louis Stevenson's *Kidnapped*, the novel that celebrated his vision of the Highlands as the Scotland of 'huts and peat smoke and brown swirling rivers and wet clothes and whisky, and the romance of the past, and the indescribable bite of the whole thing at a man's heart which is, or rather lies, at the bottom of a story.'

Stevenson's love of the Highlands was born out of boyhood holidays spent at the Bridge of Allen, just north of Stirling, near the Highland border. Stirling was the market for the inhabitants of Appin, Lorne and Balquhidder, the birthplace of Rob Roy and a hereditary haunt of Jacobitism. Sherriffmuir had been fought on the hill above Bridge of Allen, and some of Rob Roy's notorious exploits had taken place in the neighbourhood. When Stevenson first went there, the '45 (the last Jacobite rising led by the Young Pretender, Bonnie Prince Charlie, which after initial success had been crushed at Culloden) was little more than a century past and the whole countryside was still full of traditions of that stirring time.

Here Stevenson would have learned much first-hand of the tales of the Stewarts and the Campbells, the Macgregors and the M'Larens. 'I shall never forget the days at the Bridge of Allen,' he wrote later, 'they were one golden dream.'

The freedom and adventure he associated with the Highlands was in stark contrast to the stern realities of a Calvinist upbringing at home in Edinburgh, where, when consumptive coughing fits and sickness kept the boy awake long into the night, his nurse Alison Cunningham would sit up with him and implant an 'extraordinary terror of hell in me . . . I remember repeatedly waking from a dream of Hell, clinging to the horizontal bar of the bed, with my knees and chin together, my soul shaken, my body convulsed with agony.'

'Does not life go down with a better grace foaming in full body over a precipice, than miserably struggling to an end in sandy deltas?'

As an adult, Louis chose to express his hopes in heroic imagery of the Highland landscape: 'Does not life go down with a better grace foaming in full body over a precipice, than miserably struggling to an end in sandy deltas?' Then, in 1881, when he was 31, his father made him a present of a copy of *The Trial of James of the Glens*, that 'blessed little volume', as Louis called it, which provided the perfect real-life story with which to invest all that had been brewing inside him for so long.

In the fictional world of *Kidnapped*, David Balfour, a Lowland teenager, fresh-faced, tall and strong, rigorous in the defence of the strict tenets of Presbyterianism, collides with the real Highland world of James of the Glens, after the boat on which he is being forcibly conveyed to America, founders off the coast of Mull.

The year is 1752, six years after Culloden. David has found his way into Appin country, between Ballachulish and Kentallen, home of the Jacobite clan Stewart, whose land (after the '45 rebellion) is forfeit to King George II, and whose leader, Ardshiel, is in exile abroad, leaving James in charge.

A small party of loyalists led by Colin Roy Campbell, known as the Red Fox, arrives on horseback at precisely the same moment – minutes before

Looking back to Glencoe before entering Rannoch Moor. 'We went down into the waste, and began to make our toilsome and devious travel towards the eastern verge.'

5.30 p.m. on Thursday May 14th. Campbell has a commission from the King to remove certain rent defaulting tenants from their farms.

The weather is hot, the atmosphere tense; there have been rumours of a fresh Jacobite rising; clumps of redcoats are moving around the body of the countryside like sanguine corpuscles in search of disorder and disease. Then, as David watches, the Campbell party passes beneath the hanging wood of Lettermore, by the side of the Linnhe Loch; the still air is rent by the sharp crack of a firelock, and the Red Fox falls dying to the ground.

David chases after the murderer, the redcoats mistake him for the assassin, then David bumps into Alan Breck Stewart taking shelter in the trees. His immediate assumption is that Alan is the assassin.

And what of Alan?

'What of the wind that bloweth where it listeth?' Alan is Stevenson's 'fair-heather cat', 'here and awa', free spirit of the Highlands, alias 'the wild man of Appin', a Jacobite, and now, in the unlikely company of a Presbyterian Lowlander, prime suspect in the conspiracy of Campbell's murder.

Stevenson has set the stage for the 200 mile chase that takes up most of the remainder of the book. But the action is only the half of it.

What undoubtedly appealed to Stevenson about the book, *The Trial of James of the Glens*, was a particular mystery attached to it, the secret, kept by one Highland family for 130 years, as to who really killed the Red Fox. The Campbells had been swift to arrest James for the murder, and post a wanted notice for Alan Breck, who did really exist and did really flee eastwards. James was peremptorily convicted by a Campbell jury in the Campbell city of Inverary without a shread of evidence against him, and hanged on a hillock overlooking the Ballachulish ferry. That James and Alan were innocent there is no doubt. We are told that the real culprit had to be tied to a bed on the day of the hanging to prevent him coming forward. (Clearly there were those more important to the Jacobite cause than poor James.)

Over the centuries the mystery of who killed the Red Fox has inspired a number of literary detectives. For instance, in 1904 Andrew Lang wrote that he had discovered the killer's name but had been sworn to secrecy; twenty years later the Revd T Ratcliffe Barnett claimed 'an old man with the Gaelic tradition in his soul' had confessed it to him; and in 1938 Frank Hersey declared unconvincingly after a gripping yarn that the murderer was 'young Stewart of Ballachulish'.

In the end, the truth is that no name is as intriguing as the tradition of secrecy sustained by that one family – a tradition now 240 years old, because if you go to Appin today the story is still told, that the secret of who killed the Red Fox is passed on the dying lips of one generation to the next. Patently, the keeping of the secret has long been more important than the fact kept hidden. Stevenson appreciated this. What drew him in was not a desire to find out who fired the fatal shot, but the secret behind the secret, the reason why Highland lore insists that the murderer's name remains a mystery. That is what sparked the chase in *Kidnapped*, which was nothing less than a quest for the tartan fleece, the Highland ideal that suffures all the various legends and has moulded the intransigent character of the Highlander for thousands of years.

The key, he held, must lie in the landscape, the heroic Highland landscape in complete collusion with myth, itself the lifeblood of the Highland people.

Always Stevenson comes back to place. As a boy he had an intuition of 'a fitness in events and places . . . It is thus that tracts of young fir, and low rocks that reach into deep soundings, particularly torture and delight me . . . Some places speak distinctly. Certain dank gardens cry aloud for a murder; certain old houses demand to be haunted; certain coasts are set apart for shipwreck.'

Immediately following the shooting, David is thrown into the thick of it – 'We're in the Hielands, David,' says Alan, 'and when I tell ye to run, take my word and run . . . '

'I'll chance it, Alan,' David replies. 'I'll go with you.'

'But mind you,' says Alan, 'it's no small thing. Ye maun lie bare and hard, and brook many an empty belly. Your bed shall be the moorcock's, and your life shall be like the hunted deer's, and ye shall sleep with your hand upon your weapons. Ay, man, ye shall taigle many a weary foot, or we get clear! I tell ye this at the start, for it's a life that I ken well. But if ye ask

There is 'a fitness in events and places . . . Some places speak distinctly. Certain dank gardens cry aloud for a murder; certain old houses demand to be haunted; certain coasts are set apart for shipwreck.'

what other chance ye have, I answer: Nane. Either take to the heather with me, or else hang.'

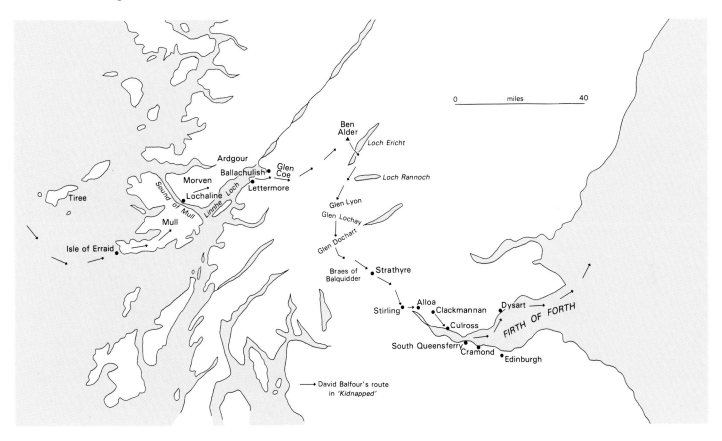

Now we ran among the birches; now stopping behind low humps upon the mountain side; now crawling on all fours among the heather. The pace was deadly; my heart seemed bursting against my ribs; and I had neither time to think nor breath to speak with. Only I remember seeing with wonder, that Alan every now and then would straighten himself to his full height and look back; and every time he did so, there came a great far-away cheering and crying of the soldiers.

From Lettermore they go to Glencoe, 'a prodigious valley, strewn with rocks and where ran a foaming river. Wild mountains stood around it . . .'

Sometimes we walked, sometimes ran; and as it drew on to morning, walked ever the less and ran the more. Though, upon its face, that country appeared to be a desert, yet there were huts and houses of the people, of which we must have passed more than twenty, hidden in quiet places of the hills. When we came to one of these, Alan would leave me in the way, and go himself and rap upon the side of the house and speak a while at the window with some sleeper awakened. This was to pass the news; which, in that country, was so much of a duty that Alan must pause to attend to it even while fleeing for his life; and so well attended to by

The route taken by David Balfour and Alan Breck Stewart – the Kidnapped trail.

Sunset over Blackwater from Rannoch Moor.

others, that in more than half of the houses where we called they heard already of the murder. In the others, as well as I could make out (standing back at a distance and hearing a strange tongue), the news was received with more of consternation than surprise.

For all our hurry, day began to come in while we were still far from any shelter. It found us in a prodigious valley, strewn with rocks and where ran a foaming river. Wild mountains stood around it; there grew there neither grass nor trees; and I have sometimes thought since then, that it may have been the valley called Glencoe, where the massacre was in the time of King William. But for the details of our itinerary, I am all to seek; our way lying now by short cuts, now by great detours; our pace being so hurried, our time of journeying usually by night; and the names of such places as I asked, and heard, being in the Gaelic tongue and the more easily forgotten.

and from Glencoe to Rannoch Moor.

More than eleven hours of incessant, hard travelling bought us early in the morning to the end of a range of mountains. In front of us there lay a piece of low, broken, desert land, which we must now cross. The sun was not long up, and shone straight in our eyes; a little thin mist went up from the face of the moorland like a smoke; so that (as Alan said) there might have been twenty squadron of dragoons there and we none the wiser . . .

The mist rose and died away, and showed us that country lying as waste as the sea; only the moorfowl and the peewees crying upon it, and far over to the east, a herd of deer, moving like dots. Much of it was red with heather; much of the rest broken up with bogs and hags and peaty pools; some had been burnt black in a heath fire; and in another place there was quite a forest of dead firs, standing like skeletons. A wearier-looking desert man never saw; but at least it was clear of troops, which was our point.

The site of the Cage.

Stevenson could not resist bringing David and Alan to Ben Alder, even though in reality, after Rannoch Moor, Alan had continued eastwards to the coast and thence to France. For Ben Alder lies at the heart of Highland myth.

From 5th to 13th September, 1746, while on the run after Culloden, Bonnie Prince Charlie hid out in a 'cage' made of trees and brushwood by fugitive clan leader Ewen Macpherson of Cluny. The Prince's adventures during this time and the blind loyalty with which Highlanders protected him are what turned Culloden from military defeat into mythic victory. 'During his wanderings,' wrote Sir Walter Scott, 'the secret of his concealment was entrusted to hundreds of every sex, age, and condition; but no individual was found, in high or low situation, who thought for an instant of obtaining opulence at the expense of treachery to the proscribed and miserable fugitive.'

In Ben Alder's bold, brooding, immoveable presence Stevenson found a clear expression of the intransigence of the Highland character, and carried into its endlessly cratered depths by Cluny's men, a sense of Highland secrets harboured still.

We came at last to the foot of an exceeding steep wood, which scrambled up a craggy hill-side, and was crowned by a naked precipice.

'It's here,' said one of the guides, and we struck up hill.

The trees clung upon the slope, like sailors on the shrouds of a ship; and their trunks were like the rounds of a ladder, by which we mounted.

Quite at the top, and just before the rocky face of the cliff sprang above the foliage, we found that strange house which was known in the country as Cluny's Cage.

Here, in the cage, Stevenson hatches the quarrel between Alan and David that is the moral crux of the book. David falls unconscious as a result of the rigours of the journey. Alan falls to cards with Cluny, drunkenly gambling away first his, then David's money. When David recovers he is furious, and Alan, now sober, is contrite. It is conceivable at this stage that all will be worked out happily and they will continue on their journey. What throws a spanner in the works is Cluny's generous assurance that he will

'Do ye see yon mountain? . . . Its name is Ben Alder; it is a wild desert mountain full of hills and hollows, and if we can win it by morn, we may do yet.'

'For the best part of three nights we travelled on eerie mountains and among the well-heads of rivers; often buried in mist, almost continually blown and rained upon, and not once cheered by any glimpse of sunshine.'

hand back the money.

David acknowledges Cluny's generosity but cannot accept it. His Presbyterian ethic tells him gambling and drunkenness is wrong, but the same code forbids him from taking back the money – 'My friend has fairly lost his money, after having fairly gained a far greater sum of yours; can I accept it back again? Would that be the right part for me to play?'

The quarrel that develops turns on the difference between what is right and wrong according to David's dogma, and what is Good or Evil according to 'natural' Highland Law. It is Cluny who tells David where his repressive moral code will lead: 'Ye give me very much the look of a man that has entrapped poor people to their hurt,' he says, iterating Stevenson's indictment elsewhere of the self-righteous Victorian law enforcer happy, say, to heap misery on a petty criminal bent only on survival.

Clansmen would come from miles around to have Cluny settle their differences. There on Ben Alder, looking out over the majestic landscape of Loch Ericht, the chief of the clan Vourich would dispense nature's justice. As the great mountain breathed Beauty and Brooding Gloom over his shoulder and 'his gillies trembled and crouched away from him like children before a hasty father', absolute values of Good and Evil were weighed in the balance.

David and Alan's quarrel, acted out against the stern majestic backdrop of Ben Alder, turns into a Pilgrim's Progress for David across the next sixty miles of 'the most dismal deserts of Scotland', and somehow you know that the Lowlander is going to lose.

For the best part of three nights travelled on eerie mountains and among the well-heads of wild rivers; often buried in mist, almost continually blown and rained upon, and not once cheered by any glimpse of sunshine. By day, we lay and slept in the drenching heather; by night, incessantly clambered upon breakneck hills and among rude crags. We often wandered; we were often so involved in fog, that we must lie quiet till it lightened. A fire was never to be thought of. Our only food was drammach and a portion of cold meat that we had carried from the Cage; and as for drink, Heaven knows we had no want of water.

This was a dreadful time, rendered the more dreadful by the gloom of the weather and the country. I was never warm; my teeth chattered in my head; I was troubled with a very sore throat, such as I had on the isle; I had a painful stitch in my side, which never left me; and when I slept in my wet bed, with the rain beating above and the mud oozing below me, it was to live over again in fancy the worst part of my adventures – to see the tower of Shaws lit by lightning, Ransome carried below on the men's backs, Shuan dying on the round-house floor, or Colin Campbell grasping at the bosom of his coat. From such broken slumbers I would be aroused in the gloaming, to sit up in the same puddle where I had slept, and sup cold drammach; the rain driving sharp in my face or running down my back in icy trickles; the mist enfolding us like as in a gloomy chamber – or, perhaps, if the wind blew, falling suddenly apart and showing us the gulf of some dark valley where the streams were crying loud.

The sound of an infinite number of rivers came up from all round. In this steady rain the springs of the mountains were broken up; every glen gushed water like a cistern; every stream was in high spate, and had filled and overflowed its channel. During our night tramps, it was solemn to hear the voice of them below in the valleys, now booming like thunder, now with an angry cry. I could well understand the story of the Water Kelpie, that demon of the streams, who is fabled to keep wailing and roaring at the ford until the coming of the doomed traveller. Alan I saw believed it, or half believed it; and when the cry of the river rose more than usually sharp, I was little surprised (though, of course, I would still be shocked) to see him cross himself in the manner of the Catholics.

During all these horrid wanderings we had no familiarity, scarcely even that of speech. . . .

'Every glen gushed water like a cistern; every stream was in high spate . . . it was solemn to hear the voice of them below in the valleys, now booming like thunder, now with an angry cry.'

In the end the wilderness closes in and shames David's blinkered Protestant ethic into submission. He and Alan embrace in a heroic spirit that transcends their differences, and the landscape softens into the romantic idyll of the Braes of Balquhidder.

What Stevenson felt he had found up there among the rushing well-heads of life was a root in the Absolute, a semblance of utter reality, values that the gods themselves were made of. The hounding of Jacobite clansmen from their mountain abodes amounted to an attempt by the English to pull the plug on the Highland myth, a deliberate process of alienation from the spirit of the land, brewed in fear. For Stevenson, the Appin murder had it all. Repression by the English, revenge by the Jacobite Highlander, martyrdom, mystery, and the secrecy that has ensured its safe passage into folklore.

While mountains like Ben Alder continue to exist, secrets like who killed the Red Fox? are what keep the Highland myth alive. Why do they bother? Tourism apart, there are still those who will tell you that nature is not known to forgo her revenge.

Dunbeath

Coastal village on the A9, south of Wick, on the extreme north east of Scotland.

Fathoms away, there was a gleam from a solid silver bar, and amid the swirls of light that glowed and died it remained constant. It came with the net, came up out of the sea, in a silver dance, and passed down into the hold . . . Slowly and carefully, now, steadily. Here they come! And they came in their companies, fluttering up out of the sea, the silver darlings, dancing in over the gunnel with small thin cries.

The Silver Darlings (above, 1941), a story of herring fishing in the savage North Sea around Moray Firth. *Morning Tide* (1931) and *Highland River* (1937) are also set here – all three novels by Neil Gunn.

Glen Moriston

Area round the A887 in the North West Highlands, near Loch Ness.

When this part of Scotland was first visited and written about, some, like Dr Samuel Johnson, found it difficult to come to terms with the fact that nature does not always conform picturesquely to the Christian idea that it is all beautiful and good.

What is not heath is nakedness, a little diversified by now and then a stream rushing down the steep. An eye accustomed to flowery pastures and waving harvests is astonished and repelled by this wide extent of hopeless sterility. The appearance is that of matter incapable of form or usefulness, dismissed by nature from her care and disinherited of her favours, left in its original elemental state, or quickened only with one sullen power of useless vegetation. . . .

We were in this place at ease and by choice, and had no evils to suffer or to fear; yet the imaginations excited by the view of an unknown and untravelled wilderness are not such as arise in the artificial solitude of parks and gardens, a flattering notion of self-sufficiency, a placid indulgence of voluntary delusions, a secure expansion of the fancy, or a cool concentration of the mental powers. The phantoms which haunt a desert are want, and misery, and danger; the evils of dereliction rush upon the thoughts; man is made unwillingly acquainted with his own weakness, and meditation shews him only how little he can sustain, and how little he can perform. There were no traces of inhabitants, except perhaps a rude pile of clods called a summer hut, in which a herdsman had rested in the favourable seasons.

It is natural, in traversing this gloom of desolation, to inquire, whether something may not be done to give nature a more cheerful face, and whether those hills and moors that afford heath cannot with a little care and labour bear something better? The first thought that occurs is to cover them with trees. . . .

A Journey to the Western Islands of Scotland (1775) by Samuel Johnson.

Sandaig

There are two Sandaigs in the Sound of Sleat on the west of the mainland across the water from Skye. This one is about a mile from a track that is connected eventually to the A87 at Shiel Bridge.

Once more
The yellow iris on the wrack-strewn shore
Blooms in our midsummer
Whose root is in that realm
Where the dead are
Everywhere underfoot
Where the salt of the sea makes sweet the grass of the land.
Among the roots of the turf the fine sea-sand
Of innumerable broken shells
Makes fertile root and flower.
Bright forms return:
Not once, but in multitude is shown
In signature of living gold the mystery
Of immortal joy.

'Kore' by Kathleen Raine

I lived like Psyche in the house of love, alone yet not alone. In the pool of his waterfall I bathed, on his beaches I gathered shells and stones written with the strange language of the sea.

And one day I went to gather rowan-berries, and leaned from a little rocky crag, my head among the branches and leaves; and I saw a blackbird there. It did not move, but remained quiet as if unafraid in its own place; and as at Martindale I had experienced the life of the hyacinth, so – almost – my consciousness seemed one with the bird-thought, the pattern of leaves, the sense of sanctuary where the bird's invisible comings and goings were woven into the tree like a living texture I could sense as some subtle field of vital force; the sense of the bird-soul in the tree, intimate and inviolate sanctuary of the *spiritus mundi*.

I do not know whether such happiness as I then knew is

the rarest or the commonest of earthly things; broadcast as the light, as flowers, as leaves, as common as heather, asphodel, bog-cotton and brown butterflies on a moor; for in such things we find it, give and receive it; but like manna it cannot be kept. At the time it seemed in no way strange to be so happy; and yet in retrospect I wonder how such riches could ever have been mine. I planted herbs at Gavin's door and tended the rose that grew against his wall; made him seats from the kipper-boxes cast up on the shore; left for him to find treasures thrown up by the sea, wave-worn wood, scallop-shells, cowries, and mussle-pearls; and all his gifts to me were of the same kind, gifts beyond price. Such things were a language in which we communicated – or so I imagined, as I scattered everywhere what Blake calls the 'gold of Eden'. hoping that he would gather it. Now I do not know if he ever found that fairy-gold, or if it turned back, as such gold does, to a few withered leaves and worthless pebbles and empty shells.

The Lion's Mouth by Kathleen Raine

The Gavin of Kathleen Raine's autobiography, *The Lion's Mouth* (1977), is of course Gavin Maxwell. She gave the title to his enchanting tale of life here with Mij an otter in whose 'constant and violently affectionate companionship' he crystallised all that was beautiful in his life:

Maxwell came to the cottage at Sandaig when a friend let him have it after his shark oil business on Soay went down, and he had gone to London to earn a living as a portrait painter. 'It's right on the sea and there's no road to it,' his friend told him, 'Camusfearna, it's called.'

It was thus casually, ten years ago, that I was handed the keys of my home, and nowhere in all the West Highlands and islands have I seen any place of so intense or varied a beauty in so small a compass.

I left my car at a fank, a dry-stone enclosure for dipping sheep, close to the burn side, and because I was unfamiliar with the ill-defined footpath that is the more usual route from the road to Camusfeàrna, I began to follow the course of the burn downward. The burn has its source far back in the hills, near to the very summit of the dominant peak; it has worn a fissure in the scarcely sloping mountain wall, and for the first thousand feet of its course it part flows, part falls, chill as snow-water even in summer, between tumbled boulders and small multi-coloured lichens. Up there, where it seems the only moving thing besides the eagles, the deer and the ptarmigan, it is called the Blue Burn, but at the foot of the outcrop, where it passes through a reedy lochan and enters a wide glacial glen it takes the name of its destination – Allt na Feàrna, the Alder Burn. Here in the glen the clear topaz-coloured water rushes and twitters between low oaks, birches and alders, at whose feet the deep-cushioned green moss is stippled with bright toadstools of scarlet and purple and yellow, and in summer swarms of electric-blue dragon-flies flicker and hover in the glades.

After some four miles the burn passes under the road at Druimfiaclach, a stone's-throw from the fank where I had left my car. It was early spring when I came to live at Camusfeàrna for the first time, and the grass at the burn side was gay with thick-clustering primroses and violets, though the snow was still heavy on the high peaks and lay like lace over the lower hills of Skye across the Sound. The air was fresh and sharp, and from east to west and north to south there was not a single cloud upon the cold clear blue; against it, the still-bare birch branches were purple in the sun and the dark-banded stems were as white as the distant snows. On the sunny slopes grazing Highland cattle made a foreground to a landscape whose vivid colours had found no place on Landseer's palette. . . .

Presently the burn became narrower, and afforded no foothold at its steep banks, then it tilted sharply seaward between rock walls, and below me I could hear the roar of a high waterfall. I climbed out from the ravine and found

'He has married me with a ring, a ring of bright water
Whose ripples travel from the heart of the sea.' Kathleen Raine

myself on a bluff of heather and red bracken, looking down upon the sea and upon Camusfeàrna.

The landscape and seascape that lay below me was of such beauty that I had no room for it all at once; my eye flickered from the house to the islands, from the white sands to the flat green pasture round the croft, from the wheeling gulls to the pale satin sea and on to the snow-topped Cuillins of Skye in the distance.

Immediately below me the steep hill-side of heather and ochre mountain grasses fell to a broad green field, almost an island, for the burn flanked it at the right and then curved round seaward in a glittering horseshoe. The sea took up where the burn left off, and its foreshore formed the whole frontage of the field, running up nearest to me into a bay of rocks and sand. At the edge of this bay, a stone's throw from the sea on one side and the burn on the other, the house of Camusfeàrna stood unfenced in green grass among grazing black-faced sheep. The field, except immediately opposite to the house, sloped gently upwards from the sea, and was

divided from it by a ridge of sand dunes grown over with pale marram grass and tussocky sea-bents. There were rabbits scampering on the short turf round the house, and out over the dunes the bullet heads of two seals were black in the tide.

Ring of Bright Water by Gavin Maxwell

Is there a spiritual geography, are there certain places upon the earth which are more, or less, attuned to certain modes of consciousness? And if so, do such qualities belong to the earth itself, to certain qualities of light, or sound, or scent, or rock formation? Is there a natural magic, and elemental spirits who inhabit certain places, or kinds of place? Or do people of a certain cast of mind impart to the land their own qualities?

The Lion's Mouth by Kathleen Raine

Skye

Island off the west of Scotland reached by means of a car ferry from Kyle of Lochalsh (A87) or, summer only, past Galltair across Gleneig Bay, or from Mallaig (A830).

The noise of the world does not touch me. I live too far inland to hear the thunder of the reef. To this place no postman comes; no tax-gatherer. This region never heard the sound of the church-going bell. The land is Pagan as when the yellow-haired Norseman landed a thousand years ago. I almost feel a Pagan myself. Not using a notched stick, I have lost all count of time, and don't know Saturday from Sunday. Civilisation is like a soldier's stock, it makes you carry your head a good deal higher, makes the angels weep a little more at your fantastic tricks, and half suffocates you the while. I have thrown it away, and breathe freely. My bed is the heather, my mirror the stream from the hills, my comb and brush the sea breeze, my watch the sun, my theatre the sunset, and my evening service – not without a rude natural religion in it – watching the pinnacles of the hills of Cuchullin sharpening in intense purple against the pallid orange of the sky, or listening to the melancholy voices of the sea-birds and the tide; that over, I am asleep, till touched by the earliest splendour of the dawn. I am, not without reason, hugely enamoured of my vagabond existence.

Blaavin and the Cuchullin hills are the chief attractions, and I never weary watching them. In the morning they wear a great white caftan of mist; but that lifts away before noon, and they stand with all their scars and passionate torrent-lines bare to the blue heavens, with perhaps a solitary shoulder for a moment gleaming wet to the sunlight. After a while a vapour begins to steam up from their abysses, gathering itself into strange shapes, knotting and twisting itself like smoke; while above, the terrible crests are now lost, now revealed, in a stream of flying rack. In an hour a wall of rain, gray as granite, opaque as iron to the eye, stands up from sea to heaven. The loch is roughening before the wind, and the islets, black dots a second ago, are patches of roaring foam. You hear fierce sound of its coming. Anon, the lashing tempest sweeps over you, and looking behind, up the long inland glen, you can see the birch-woods and over the sides of the hills, driven on the wind, the white smoke of the rain. Though fierce as a charge of Highland bayonets these squalls are seldom of long duration, and you bless them when you creep from your shelter, for out comes the sun, and the birch-woods are twinkling, and more intensely flash the levels of the sea, and at a stroke the clouds are scattered from the wet brow of Blaavin, and to the whole a new element has been added; the voice of the swollen stream as it rushes red over a hundred tiny cataracts, and roars river-broad into the sea, making turbid the azure. Then I have my amusements in this solitary place. The mountains are of course open, and this morning, at dawn, a roe swept past me like the wind, with its nose to the dewy ground – 'tracking', they call it here. Above all, I can wander on the ebbed beach. Hogg speaks of that

Undefined and mingled hum,
Voice of the desert, never dumb.

But far more than the murmuring and insecty air of the moorland does the wet *chirk-chirking* of the living shore give one the idea of crowded and multitudinous life. . . . At ebb of tide wild-looking children, from turf cabins on the hillside, come down to hunt shell-fish. Even now a troop is busy; how their shrill voices go the while! Old Effie I see is out to-day, quite a picturesque object, with her white cap and red shawl. With a tin can in one hand, an old reaping-hook in the other, she goes poking among the tangle. Let us see what sport she has had. She turns round at our salutation – very old, old almost as the worn rocks around. She might have been the wife of Wordsworth's 'Leech-gatherer'. Her can is sprawling with brown crabs; and, opening her apron, she exhibits a large black and blue lobster – a fellow such as she alone can capture. A queer woman is Effie, and an awesome. She is familiar with ghosts and apparitions. She can relate legends that have power over the superstitious blood, and with little coaxing will sing those wild Gaelic songs of hers – of dead lights on the sea, of fishing-boats going down in squalls, of unburied bodies tossing day and night upon the gray peaks of the waves, and of girls that pray God to lay them by the sides of their drowned lovers. . .

A Summer in Skye by Alexander Smith

O great Island, my Island, my love,
many a night I lay stretched
by your side in that slumber
when the mist of twilight swathed you.
My love every leaflet of heather on you
from Rudha Hunish to Loch Slapin,
and every leaflet of bog-myrtle kin
from Stron Bhiornaill to the Garsven,
every tarn, stream and burn a joy
from Romisdale to Brae Eynort,
and even if I came in sight of Paradise,
what price its moon without Blaven?

From 'The Island' by Sorley Maclean

Blaven on Skye: 'and even if I came in sight of Paradise / what price its moon without Blaven?' Sorley Maclean

Raasay
An island between Skye and the mainland.

The window is nailed and boarded
through which I saw the West
and my love is at the Burn of Hallaig,
a birch tree, and she has always been

between Inver and Milk Hollow,
here and there about Baile-chuirn:
she is a birch, a hazel,
a straight, slender young rowan.

In Screapadal of my people
where Norman and Big Hector were,
their daughters and their sons are a wood
going up beside the stream.

Proud tonight the pine cocks
crowing on the top of Cnoc an Ra,
straight their backs in the moonlight –
they are not the wood I love. . . .

From the Burn of Fearns to the raised beach
that is clear in the mystery of the hills,
there is only the congregation of the girls
keeping up the endless walk,

coming back to Hallaig in the evening,
in the dumb living twilight,
filling the steep slopes,

their laughter a mist in my ears,

and their beauty a film on my heart
before the dimness comes on the kyles,
and when the sun goes down behind Dun Cana
a vehement bullet will come from the gun of Love;

and will strike the deer that goes dizzily,
sniffing at the grass-grown ruined homes;
his eye will freeze in the wood,
his blood will not be traced while I live.

From 'Time, the Deer, is in the Wood of Hallaig'
by Sorley Maclean

Hallaig is a deserted township, north of Beinn na Lice, where Sorley Maclean was born in 1911. It was 'cleared' in 1846.

Trees, to the Celtic consciousness, are of great spiritual significance, their ancient alphabet, the Beth-Luis-Nion ('Birch-Rowan-Ash'), being composed of the initial letters of the Celtic names of trees. There is no letter for pine, the tree that has replaced so much indigenous forest. Fearn is the Alder, the tree of Bran (see Harlech, Gwynedd, Wales).

SHETLAND

An archipelago of about 100 islands, of which fewer than 20 are inhabited, off the north coast of Scotland.

I always like to feel – and generally succeed in securing an adequate basis for feeling – that my principal personal characteristics exhibit clearly the great historical directives of my people and dream, of course, always of such a moment in relation to Scotland as, when St Paul wrote to the Galatians, 'universal' history stood over him and dictated his words – a marvellous work of the spirit, to collect the possible in the present, the infinite in the intrinsic of the present, and this as a value, a principle-value, a motive-value.

Lucky Poet by Hugh MacDiarmid

Skye: 'A scene so rude, so wild as this / Yet so sublime in barrenness'
– Walter Scott in 'The Lord of the Isles'

Christopher Murray Grieve (1892-1978) wrote under the pseudonym Hugh MacDiarmid and was a founder of the Scottish National Party. He was as rigorous and immoveable in his own imaginative self-discipline as he was in his loyalty to his ruthlessly unsentimental vision of Scotland. His tombstone reads:

I'll hae'e nae hauf-way hoose, but aye be whaur
Extremes meet – it's the only way I ken
To dodge the curst conceit o' bein' richt
That damns the vast majority of men

He was born in Langholm, Dumfries, and claimed in his autobiography, 'Lucky Poet', that his happy boyhood there influenced his poetry – 'supplied all my subsequent poetry with a tremendous wealth of sensuous satisfaction . . . My earliest impressions are of . . . great forests, of honey-scented hills, and moorlands infinitely rich in little-appreciated beauties of flowering, of animal and insect life, of strange and subtle relationships of water and light'.

Much later he took 'a nice commodious four-roomed cottage standing on a hillside and looking out over a tangled pattern of complicated tideways, voes, and islands with snaggled coasts to the North Shetland mainland and the Atlantic – for 27s per annum!'

The isle of Whalsey in the Shetlands provided him with what he felt he needed to produce anything worthwhile – 'I will have nothing interposed between my sensitiveness and the barren but beautiful reality,' he wrote. Conditions were indeed harsh . . . 'It is not a restful place to write. The cottage is rattling like a 'tin lizzie' in a 90-miles-per-hour wind, and every now and again there is a terrific rattling of hail. We have had well-nigh continuous gales, with heavy snowstorms and great downpours of rain, for the last two months – the worst winter the Shetlands have had within living memory.' But it was a privilege to live among the Shetlands' sparse population of crofters and fishermen: 'These men belong to an age when man's sense of the drama of life was strong and undimmed by the physical ease and psychological difficulty of urban living.'

[Here] one comes to bedrock . . . Is not this our natural element? I have written elsewhere: 'Just as the adventures, the dangers, the thrills of work in these dim Northern waters are best brought out, not by over-statement, but by a calm regard for fact and an intimate knowledge of the subject –

just as the fishermen are engaged in a trade that still demands the qualities of individual judgement, courage and hardihood that tend to disappear both from literature and life elsewhere – the Shetlands call alike in the arts and in affairs for the true creative spirit. Anything pettier would be sadly out of place in these little-known and lonely regions, encompassed about with the strange beauty of the North, the fluctuation of unearthly colours at different levels of the sun, the luminous air, the gleam of distant ice and the awful stillness of Northern fog. Or transfigured with such marvellous spectacles as when 'the stars are almost dimmed by the shaking curtain of aurora, at first a nebulous radiance but gradually changing to clear-cut ribbons of light, quivering and wavering like seaweed fixed to a rock in a strong tide'. As I have put it in one of my Shetland poems ('Raised Beach' in *Stony Limits*, 1934).

It will be ever increasingly necessary to find
In the interests of all mankind
Men capable of rejecting all that all other men
    Think as a stone remains
Essential to the world, inseparable from it,
    And rejects all other life yet.
Great work cannot be combined with surrender to the crowd . . .

MacDiarmid himself epitomised many of the characteristics he recognised and enjoyed in the Celtic character. His most memorable expression of this was contained in his poem, 'A Drunk Man Looks at the Thistle' (1926), wherein the essential qualities of the thistle gradually impinge on the drunk man's consciousness as it confronts him on a hill on the way home, as if altogether they amounted to that 'universal' symbol of Scotland that the poet is seeking:

Haud the slow scaly serpent in respect,
The Gothic thistle, whaur the insect's hum
Soon's fer aff, lifts abune the rock it scorns
Its rigid virtue for the Heavens to see.
The too'ering boulders gaird it. And the bee
Mak's honey frae the roses on its thorns.'

And yet like bindweed through my clay it's run,
And a' my folks' – it's queer to see't unroll.
My ain soul looks me in the face, as 'twere,
And mair than my ain soul – my nation's soul!

Hugh MacDiarmid

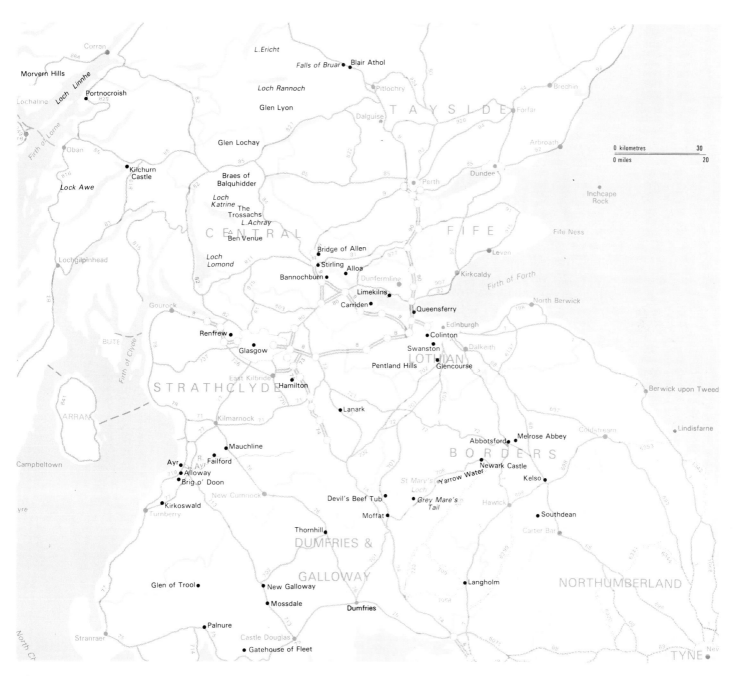

CENTRAL

The Trossachs
*The country between Loch Katrine and Loch Achray, north west of Stirling via the
A84 and 821, north of Glasgow via the A82, 811, 81, and 821.*

Coronach from 'The Lady of the Lake' by Walter Scott

He is gone on the mountain,
　He is lost to the forest,
Like a summer-dried fountain,
　When our need was the sorest.
The font, reappearing,
　From the rain-drops shall borrow,
But to us comes no cheering,
　To Duncan no morrow!
The hand of the reaper
　Takes the ears that are hoary,
But the voice of the weeper
　Wails manhood in glory.
The autumn winds rushing
　Waft the leaves that are searest,
But our flower was in flushing,
　When blighting was nearest.

Fleet foot on the correi,
　Sage counsel in cumber
Red hand in the foray,
　How sound is thy slumber!
Like the dew on the mountain,
　Like the foam on the river,
Like the bubble on the fountain
　Thou art gone, and for ever!

The Trossachs: Loch Katrine and Ellen's Isle

The poem appeared in May and before July the Trossachs had been invaded by a horde of pleasure-travellers. The little inns were filled to overflowing, numerous cottages were turned into taverns. Shepherds and gillies suddenly found themselves able to make what they deemed splendid fortunes, by acting as guides.

The Trossachs, or Bristled Territory, as the word signifies in Gaelic, now form the entrance to one of the chief passes of the Grampians; but formerly it was a barrier to the progress of all, save the most alert and enterprising travellers. Until a comparatively recent time a ladder of branches and roots of trees, suspended over a steep crag, afforded the only means of traversing the defile.

Ellen's Isle, also, blocks the prospect. It is only by a rude scramble over the rocks in the direction of the old road that the point can be reached from which Fitzjames beheld the lake and its islets. Some lower eminences afford a partial view, but it is usually from the little steamer which plies during the season that the magnificent scene is disclosed to the tourist in its full extent. The lake measures about ten miles in length, and two in average breadth, and is of a winding serpentine form. Towards the west its shores are rocky and precipitious, and each side is clothed with dense copse-wood.

Palgrave edition 'The Lady of the Lake' (1897)

Fitzjames, the 'royal wanderer', the king himself, though Ellen does not know, beholds the lake and Ellen's Isle for the first time and sounds his bugle, to which Ellen responds. The romantic scene inspired Scotland's tourist industry – 'There gentlemen and ladies, is where Fitzjames blow'd his bugle, and waited for the light shallop of Ellen Douglas; and here where you landed and came up them steps, is where she brought him to the bower, and the very tree's still there – as you see me tak' hold of it – and over the hill yonder . . . Pencillings in the Way by N P Willis

The broom's tough roots his ladder made,
The hazel saplings lent their aid;
And thus an airy point he won,
Where, gleaming with the setting sun,
One burnish'd sheet of living gold,
Loch Katrine lay beneath him roll'd . . .
High on the south, huge Benvenue
Down to the lake in masses threw
Crags, knolls, and mounds, confusedly hurl'd,
The fragments of an earlier world;
A wildering forest feather'd o'er
His ruin'd sides and summit hoar,
While on the north, through middle air,
Ben-an heaved high his forehead bare.

From the steep promontory gazed
The stranger, raptured and amazed
. . . How blithely might the bugle-horn
Chide, on the lake, the lingering morn!
. . . But scarce again his horn he wound,
When lo! forth starting at the sound,
From underneath an aged oak,
That slanted from the islet rock,
A damsel guider of its way,
A little skiff shot to the bay . . .
With head up-raised, and look intent,
And eye and ear attentive bent,
And locks flung back, and lips apart,
Like monument of Grecian art,
In listening mood, she seem'd to stand,
The guardian Naiad of the strand . . .

The Trossachs are also featured in Scott's novel *Rob Roy* as hiding place of the Jacobite rebel.

The Falls of Ledard
To the west of Loch Ard, near the B829.

In Scott's first novel, *Waverley*, the eponymous hero, a young British officer unwisely falls in love with Flora, the Jacobite daughter of a Highland chief. Edward Waverley's seduction is orchestrated by Flora with help from her attendant, Una, at a spot – one of the most beautiful sites in the country – near her castle home:

Advancing a few yards, and passing under the bridge which he had viewed with so much terror, the path ascended rapidly from the edge of the brook, and the glen widened into a sylvan amphitheatre, waving with birch, young oaks, and hazels, with here and there a scattered yew-tree. The rocks now receded, but still showed their grey and shaggy crests rising among the copse-wood. Still higher, rose eminences and peaks, some bare, some clothed with wood, some round and purple with heath, and others splintered into rocks and crags. At a short turning, the path, which had for some furlongs lost sight of the brook, suddenly placed Waverley in front of a romantic waterfall. It was not so remarkable either for great height or quantity of water, as for the beautiful accompaniments which made the spot interesting. After a broken cataract of about twenty feet, the stream was received in a large natural basin filled to the brim with water, which, when the bubbles of the fall subsided, was so exquisitely clear, that, although it was of great depth, the eye could discern each pebble at the bottom. Eddying round this reservoir, the brook found its way over a broken part of the ledge, and formed a second fall, which seemed to seek the very abyss; then, wheeling out beneath from among the smooth dark rocks, which it had polished for ages, it wandered murmuring down the glen, forming the stream up which Waverley had just ascended. The borders of this romantic reservoir corresponded in beauty; but it was beauty of a stern and commanding cast, as if in the act of expanding into grandeur. Mossy banks of turf were broken and interrupted by huge fragments of rock, and decorated with trees and shrubs, some of which had been planted under the direction of Flora, but so cautiously, that they added to the grace, without diminishing the romantic wildness of the scene.

Here, like one of those lovely forms which decorate the landscapes of Poussin, Waverley found Flora gazing on the waterfall. Two paces further back stood Cathleen, holding a small Scottish harp, the use of which had been taught to Flora by Rory Dall, one of the last harpers of the Western Highlands. The sun, now stooping in the west, gave a rich and varied tinge to all the objects which surrounded Waverley, and seemed to add more than human brilliancy to the full expressive darkness of Flora's eye, exalted the richness and purity of her complexion, and enhanced the dignity and grace of her beautiful form. Edward thought he had never, even in his wildest dreams, imagined a figure of such exquisite and interesting loveliness. The wild beauty of the retreat, bursting upon him as if by magic, augmented the mingled feeling of delight and awe with which he approached her, like a fair enchantress of Boiardo or Ariosto, by whose nod the scenery around seemed to have been created, an Eden in the wilderness.

Probably the first ever to describe such scenery, Scott's piece is remarkably stage set, dressed up with all the picturesque appeal of a '50s Hollywood romantic fantasy.

As Waverley, 'like a knight of romance', is coaxed to rendezvous, he looks up and sees a bridge made of two pine-trees joining two sheer faces of rock above him. Suddenly, while gazing at this 'pass of peril', a distant black line across the small piece of blue sky visible up the sheer rock chimney, Flora and her attendant appear on it, 'like inhabitants of another region, propped, as it were in mid-air, upon this trembling structure. She stopped . . . and with an air of graceful ease waved her handkerchief to him by way of a sign.'

DUMFRIES AND GALLOWAY

The Fleet at Gatehouse of Fleet, where the chase proper begins.

Dumfries
Town at the intersection of the A75, 76, and 701, above Solway Firth.

Dumfries is a point of departure for Richard Hannay in *The Thirty-Nine Steps* (1915), John Buchan's best known and most popular adventure story, and the old county town is a good place to start for anyone wanting to follow in his steps.

Many do. The book is extraordinarily addictive, like a sort of 'al fresco' *Times* crossword puzzle, full of cunning twists and turns through the wide-open country of Dumfries and Galloway, briefly up into the Borders, then down to Berkshire, London, and Ramsgate in Kent.

Like *Kidnapped* for Robert Louis Stevenson (see Ben Alder, Highlands), *The Thirty-Nine Steps* took off first in the mind of a creator beset by illness – 'while pinned to my bed during the first months of war [1914] and compelled to keep my mind off too tragic realities, I gave myself to stories of adventure.' Perhaps that is what makes it go.

It is barely 130 pages in length; in that sense lightweight and of course none of its characters are more than cut-out. But does it matter? Buchan gives all the signposts necessary, we know who his people are – as Graham Greene wrote, 'Each character carries around with him his school, his regiment, his religious beliefs, often touched with Calvinism: memories of grouse-shooting and deer-stalking, of sport at Eton, debates in the House' – the action does the rest.

His approach to landscape is similar, a little description, then let the action speak. Dumfries and Galloway is suited to this, and after reading the novel you cannot go to the wilderness north of Moffat without seeing the fugitive Hannay dodging among the heather with his hunters fanning out on the moor below or swooping down in a monoplane from the air.

Spectacled Roadman country, see map page 158. 'I saw the highroad for maybe ten miles, and far down it something that was moving, and that I took to be a motor-car . . . Away down the slope, a couple of miles away, men were advancing like a row of beaters at a shoot.'

I sat down on the very crest of the pass and took stock of my position.

Behind me was the road climbing through a long cleft in the hills, which was the upper glen of some notable river. In front was a flat space of maybe a mile, all pitted with bog-holes and rough with tussocks, and then beyond it the road fell steeply down another glen to a plain whose blue dimness melted into the distance. To left and right were round-shouldered green hills as smooth as pancakes, but to the south – that is, the left hand – there was a glimpse of high heathery mountains, which I remembered from the map as the big knot of hill which I had chosen for my sanctuary. I was on the central boss of a huge upland country, and could see everything moving for miles. In the meadows below the road half a mile back a cottage smoked, but it was the only sign of human life. Otherwise there was only the calling of plovers and the tinkling of little streams.

It was now about seven o'clock, and as I waited I heard once again that ominous beat in the air. Then I realized that my vantage-ground might be in reality a trap. There was no cover for a tomtit in those bald green places.

I sat quite still and hopeless while the beat grew louder. Then I saw an aeroplane coming up from the east. It was flying high, but as I looked it dropped several

The Galloway hills

The spirit of Buchan Country is the spirit of the chase. The police want Richard Hannay for the Portland Place Murder, as it comes to be known, of Franklin Scudder, whose body has been found in Hannay's flat just around the corner from the BBC (a few houses away from the real Buchan residence, as it happens). The Black Stone Gang who murdered Scudder want him because, if he cracks the code of Scudder's pocketbook, he can spoil their plot to precipitate a pan-European war.

What we like about Buchan is that his heroes are from a formal recognisable set, whose lives, for a while at least, break out of the thin crust of the civilised norm. The part landscape plays is crucial. When Hannay alights from the St Pancras train it is 'a gorgeous spring evening, with every hill showing as clear as a cut amethyst. The air had the queer, rooty smell of bogs, but it was as fresh as mid-ocean, and it had the strangest effect on my spirits. I actually felt light-hearted. I might have been a boy out for a spring holiday tramp, instead of a man of thirty-seven very much wanted by the police.' It is the freedom of the wild untainted hills that Hannay exalts in. He is on their side and they are on his against a hostile, misinformed, so-called civilised urban world. Here in the hills he is at home, not simply because he (or at least Buchan the author) knows them inside out from his youth or that the hills are a useful sanctuary, although they are, but because they offer this escapist alternative.

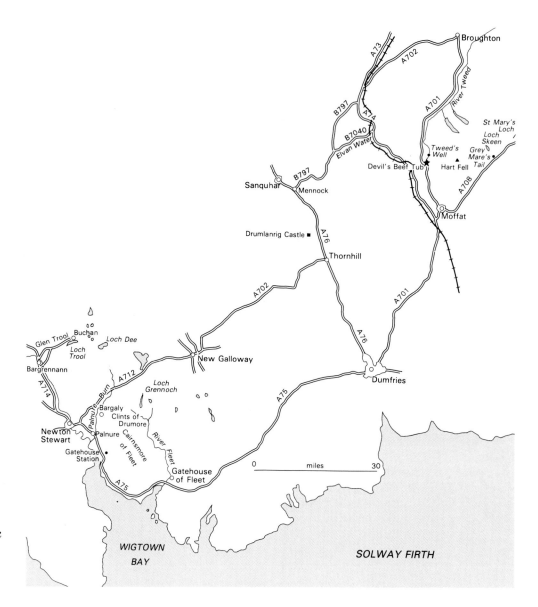

There is a Buchan Centre at the Biggar Museum at the old Free Kirk at Broughton. Central contact number for Biggar Museums 0899 21050.

hundred feet and began to circle round the knot of hill in narrowing circles, just as a hawk wheels before it pounces. Now it was flying very low, and now the observer onboard caught sight of me. I could see one of the two occupants examining me through glasses.

Suddenly it began to rise in swift whorls, and the next I knew it was speeding eastward again till it became a speck in the blue morning.

That made me do some savage thinking. . . .

I have said there was not cover in the whole place to hide a rat. As the day advanced it was flooded with soft fresh light till it had the fragrant sunniness of

The Hannay Trail

1. Leaving Scudder's dead body in his flat in London Hannay takes the train from St Pancras to Dumfries.

2. At Dumfries he changes onto 'the slow Galloway train' (no longer in service).

3. The train drops him at Palnure. He cuts a hazel walking stick and proceeds by 'a bawling stream' (the Palnure Burn) towards Bargaly, where he stays with a shepherd and his wife for the night. The next day he doubles back, skirting the Cairnmore of Fleet – 'nesting curlews were crying everywhere, and the links of green pasture by the streams were dotted with young lambs' – goes south by the Fleet River, espies a train (near Gatehouse of Fleet), takes it, but after catching sight of the police, he sets off (north) for the hills on foot.

4. During his encounter with the Literary Innkeeper, his pursuers catch up. He takes their car and steers 'east by the sun' (along the A702), 'down from the moorlands and traversing the broad haugh of a river [the Nith].' He sees Drumlanrig castle (near the A76), swings 'through little old thatched villages, and over peaceful lowland streams, and past gardens blazing with hawthorn and yellow laburnum.'

5. Thence, north up the A76 to Mennock, right onto the B797, up the valley of Mennock Water, onto the B7040 beside Elvan Water, and across the main Glasgow to London line. From here he travels north, possibly even as far as Broughton, where he meets the well-connected Radical Candidate.

6. Next he moves off to the 'upper waters of the River Tweed', and meets the Spectacled Roadman – stunning country.

7. Then, moving southwards towards the mighty Hart Fell and the Devil's Beef Tub where Walter Scott's Laird of Summertrees leapt to freedom from the hangman's noose in *Redgauntlet*, he is lured by his creator into the house of the Bald Archaeologist, before finally freeing himself with some handy explosive and repairing to the bee-humming quietude of the Berkshire countryside.

The John Buchan Society, Limpsfield, 16 Ranfurly Road, Bridge of Weir, produces a Journal and information on request.

the South African veld. At other times I would have liked the place, but now it seemed to suffocate me. The free moorlands were prison walls, and the keen hill air was the breath of a dungeon.

I tossed a coin – heads right, tails left – and it fell heads, so I turned to the north. In a little I came to the brow of the ridge which was the containing wall of the pass. I saw the highroad for maybe ten miles, and far down it something that was moving, and that I took to be a motor-car. Beyond the ridge I looked on a rolling green moor, which fell away into wooden glens. Now my life on the veld has given me the eyes of a kite, and I can see things for which most men need a telescope

Where Hannay meets the roadman where the road fell 'steeply down another glen whose blue dimness melted into the distance', almost certainly just north of Devil's Beef Tub, which is Walter Scott country too – 'Ye must have seen it as ye cam this way; it looks as if four hills were laying their heads together to shut out the daylight from the dark hollow between them. A d——d deep, black, blackguard-looking abyss of a hole it is.' Redgauntlet

. . . Away down the slope, a couple of miles away, men were advancing like a row of beaters at a shoot.

I dropped out of sight behind the sky-line. That way was shut to me, and I must try the bigger hills to the south beyond the highway. The car I had noticed was getting nearer, but it was still a long way off with some very steep gradients before it. I ran hard, crouching low except in the hollows, and as I ran I kept scanning the brow of the hill before me. Was it imagination, or did I see figures – one, two, perhaps more – moving in a glen beyond the stream?

If you are hemmed in on all sides in a patch of land there is only one chance of escape. You must stay in the patch, and let your enemies search it and not find you. That was good sense, but how on earth was I to escape notice in that table-cloth of a place? I would have buried myself to the neck in mud or lain below water or climbed the tallest tree. But there was not a stick of wood, the bog-holes were little puddles, the stream was a slender trickle. There was nothing but short heather, and bare hill bent, and the white highway.

The Thirty-Nine Steps by John Buchan

The Grey Mare's Tail

North west of the A708 8m north of Moffat, a dramatic 200-foot fall of water from Loch Skeen into Moffat Water.

Anyone who has spent time in the hills among the streams and waterfalls of Scotland, particularly in the Highlands, will know what Scott (and Stevenson and others) mean when they write about the sounds and daemons heard in crashing, beating water. Scott's novel, *Old Mortality* (1816), includes a perfect description of the Grey Mare's Tail, even though he transfers it to Hamilton, where the main action of the rest of the novel occurs. Scott knew the Tail well, as he did all his novels' haunts. As Ruskin said, Scott could describe nothing he had not seen.

They soon came to a decayed thicket, where brambles and thorns supplied the room of the oak and birches of which it had once consisted. Here the guide turned short off the open heath, and by a sheep track conducted Morton to the brook. A hoarse and sullen roar had in part prepared him for the scene which presented itself, yet it was not to be viewed without surprise and even terror. When he emerged from the devious path which conducted him through the thicket, he found himself placed on a ledge of flat rock, projecting over one side of a chasm not less than a hundred feet deep, where the dark mountain-stream made decided and rapid shoot over the precipice, and was swallowed up by a deep, black, yawning gulf. The eye in vain strove to see the bottom of the fall; it could catch but one sheet of foaming uproar and sheer descent, until the view was obstructed by the projecting crags which inclosed the bottom of the water-fall, and hid from sight the dark pool which received its tortured waters; far beneath, at the distance of perhaps a quarter of a mile, the eye caught the winding of the stream as it emerged into a more open course. But for that distance they were lost to sight as much as if a cavern had been arched over them; and indeed the steep and projecting ledges of rock through which they wound their way in darkness were very nearly closing and over-roofing their course.

While Morton gazed at this scene of tumult, which seemed, by the surrounding thickets and the clefts into which the waters descended, to seek to hide itself from every eye, his little attendant, as she stood beside him on the platform of rock which commanded the best view of the fall, pulled him by the sleeve, and said, in a tone which he could not hear without stooping his ear near the speaker, 'Hear till him! Eh! hear till him!'

Morton listened more attentively, and out of the very abyss into which the brook fell, and amidst the tumultuary sounds of the cataract, thought he could distinguish shouts, screams, and even articulate words, as if the tortured demon of the stream had been mingling his complaints with the roar of his broken waters.

Old Mortality by Walter Scott

There eagles scream from isle to shore;
Down all the rocks the torrents roar;
O'er the black waves incessant driven,
Dark mists infect the summer heaven;
Through the rude barriers of the lake,
Away its hurrying waters break,
Faster and whiter dash and curl,
Till down yon dark abyss they hurl.

From 'Marmion' by Walter Scott

LOTHIAN

Edinburgh

Capital city on the south side of the Firth of Forth. Main feed roads, M8, A702, 7, 68, 1.

My Water of Leith runs through a double city;
My city is threaded by a complex stream.
A matter for regret.

       From 'Double Life' by Norman McCaig

Edinburgh has always attracted the attention of writers. William Dunbar critcised 15th-century Edinburgh for its materialism –

Quhy will ye, merchantis of renoun,
Lat Edinburgh, your nobill toun,
For laik of reformatioun
The commone proffeitt tyine and fame?
  Think ye no schame,
that onie uther regioun
Sall with dishonour hurt your name!

Nearly 300 years later, its amusements and dissipations were singled out by Robert Fergusson –

  Whan Feet in dirty Gutters plash,
And Fock to wale their Fitstaps fash;
At night the Macaroni drunk,
In Pools or Gutters aftimes sunk:
Heugh! what a Fright he now appears,
Whan he his Corpse dejected rears!

Scott's novel, *The Heart of Mid-Lothian* (1818), made immortal many of the City's localities, but his eulogy of the city in 'Marmion' (1808), seems oddly forced.

     Stern then, and steel-girt was thy brow,
     Dun-Edin! O, how alter'd now,
     When safe amid thy mountain court
     Thou sit'st, like Empress at her sport,
     And liberal, unconfin'd, and free,
     Flinging thy white arms to the sea,
     For thy dark cloud, with umber'd lower,
     That hung o'er cliff, and lake, and tower,
     Thou gleam'st against the western ray
     Ten thousand lines of brighter day.

     So thou, fair City! disarray'd
     Of battled wall, and rampart's aid,
     As stately seem'st, but lovelier far
     Than in that panoply of war.
     Nor deem that from thy fenceless throne
     Strength and security are flown;
     Still, as of yore, Queen of the North!
     Still canst thou send thy children forth.

From a historical and picturesque point of view, the Old Town is the most interesting part of Edinburgh; and the great street running from Holyrood to the Castle – in

various portions of its length called the Lawnmarket, the High Street, and the Canongate – is the most interesting part of the Old Town. In that street the houses preserve their ancient appearance; they climb up heavenward, story upon story, with outside stairs and wooden panellings, all strangely peaked and gabled. With the exception of the inhabitants, who exist amidst squalor, and filth, and evil smells undeniably modern, everything in this long street breathes of the antique world. If you penetrate the narrow wynds that run at right angles from it, you see traces of ancient gardens. Occasionally the original names are retained, and they touch the visitor pathetically, like the scent of long-withered flowers. Old armorial bearings may yet be traced above the doorways. Two centuries ago fair eyes looked down from yonder window, now in possession of a drunken Irishwoman. If we but knew it, every crazy tenement has its tragic story; every crumbling wall could its tale unfold.

          Alexander Smith (1865)

It was by this time about nine in the morning, and the first fog of the season. A great chocolate-coloured pall lowered over heaven, but the wind was continually charging and routing these embattled vapours; so that as the cab crawled from street to street, Mr Utterson beheld a marvellous number of degrees and hues of twilight; for here it would be dark like the back-end of evening; and there would be a glow of a rich, lurid brown, like the light of some strange conflagration; and here, for a moment, the fog would be quite broken up, and a haggard shaft of daylight would glance in between the swirling wreaths. The dismal quarter ... seen under these changing glimpses, with its muddy ways, and slatternly passengers, and its lamps, which had never been extinguished or had been kindled afresh to combat this mournful reinvasion of darkness, seemed, in the lawyer's eyes, like a district of some city in a nightmare. The thoughts of his mind, besides, were of the gloomiest dye; and when he glanced at the companion of his drive, he was conscious of some touch of that terror of the law and the law's officers which may at times assail the most honest.

As the cab drew up before the address indicated, the fog lifted a little and showed him a dingy street, a gin palace, a low French eating-house, a shop for the retail of penny numbers and two-penny salads, many ragged children huddled in the doorways, and many women of many different nationalities passing out, key in hand, to have a morning glass; and the next moment the fog settled down again upon that part, as brown as umber, and cut him off from his blackguardly surroundings. This was the home of Henry Jekyll's favourite; of a man who was heir to a quarter of a million sterling.

An ivory-faced and silvery-haired old woman opened the door. She had an evil face, smoothed by hypocrisy; but her manners were excellent. Yes, she said, this was My Hyde's, but he was not at home; he had been in that night very late, but had gone away again in less than an hour: there was nothing strange in that; his habits were very irregular, and he was often absent; for instance, it was nearly two months since she had seen him till yesterday.

'Very well then, we wish to see his rooms,' said the lawyer; and when the woman began to declare it was impossible, 'I had better tell you who this person is,' he added. 'This is Inspector Newcomen of Scotland Yard.'

A flash of odious joy appeared upon the woman's face, 'Ah!' said she, 'he is in trouble! What has he done?'

'The Strange Case of Dr Jekyll and Mr Hyde' (1886)
by Robert Louis Stevenson

The sheer atmosphere of *Jekyll and Hyde* is of course one of its most memorable qualities. The setting is London. But the ambience is without a doubt Edinburgh, the Edinburgh of the Old Town's dark wynds and closes, where the turn of a corner could, in Stevenson's day and even now, abruptly leave behind the world of surface respectability, and the lingering shades of Burke and Hare, the grave-robbers, and Deacon Brodie, cabinet maker by day, criminal by night, still flavoured the atmosphere. Stevenson had absorbed the Deacon Brodie story in his infancy – in fact there was in his own room in his parents' dignified Georgian residence a cabinet Deacon Brodie had himself made. He was an irresistible symbol of the duality that entered Stevenson's consciousness as a very young child, when he would terrify himself with thoughts of the devil, and reprove himself for the possibility of sin.

Jenni Calder (1979)

From the 16th and 17th centuries Edinburgh developed its 'double life', its material evils and dissipations (Dunbar, Fergusson, and their many modern imitators), its protestations of loveliness, history, strength and security (Scott et al), and its guilty secrets (Stevenson, McGaig), under the heavy cloak of Calvin.

In 'Jekyll and Hyde' Stevenson's message is that the 'hard law of religion' which shapes respectable men's lives, is also 'one of the most plentiful springs of distress'. It drives the Devil underground, better to do his work. Stevenson, born in the city, knew what about the repressive nature of Calvinism from personal experience.

Arthur's Seat above Edinburgh, James Hogg's 'rocky precipice' (p. 164)

I had an extraordinary terror of hell implanted in me by my good nurse, which used to haunt me terribly on stormy nights. . . . It is to my nurse that my high-strung religious ecstasies and terrors – I would not only lie awake and weep for Jesus, which I have done many a time, but I would fear to trust myself to slumber lest I was not accepted or should slip ere I awoke into eternal ruin . . . I suffered at other times from the most hideous nightmares, which would wake me screaming and in the extremist frenzy of terror. On such occasions none could pacify my nerves but my good father . . . One that I remember, I dreamed I was to swallow the world: and the terror of the fancy arose from the complete conception I had of the hugeness and populaceness of our sphere. Disproportion and a peculiar shade of brown, something like that of seelskin, haunted me particularly during these visitations.

Stevenson was not, however the first to express the duality of the spirit of the city in terms of the schizoid personality and doppelganger effect:

. . . One morning, chancing to waken very early, he arose [and] seated himself on the pinnacle of the rocky precipice, a little within the top of the hill to the westward, and, with a light and buoyant heart, viewed the beauties of the morning, and inhaled its salubrious breeze. 'Here,' thought he, 'I can converse with nature without disturbance, and without being intruded on by any appalling or obnoxious visitor.' The idea of his brother's dark and malevolent looks coming at that moment across his mind, he turned his eyes instinctively to the right, to the point where that unwelcome quest was wont to make his appearance. Gracious Heaven! What an apparition was there presented to his view! He saw, delineated in the cloud, the shoulders, arms, and features of a human being of the most dreadful aspect. The face was the face of his brother, but dilated to twenty times the natural size. Its dark eyes gleamed on him through the mist, while every furrow of its hideous brow frowned deep as the ravines on the brow of the hill. George started, and his hair stood up in bristles as he gazed on this horrible monster. He saw every feature and every line of the face distinctly as it gazed on him with an intensity that was hardly brookable. Its eyes were fixed on him, in the same manner as those of some carnivorous animal fixed on its prey; and yet there was fear and trembling in these unearthly features, as plainly depicted as murderous malice. The giant apparition seemed sometimes to be cowering down as in terror, so that nothing but his brow and eyes were seen . . .

George conceived it to be a spirit. He could conceive it to be nothing else; and he took it for some horrid demon by which he was haunted, that had assumed the features of his brother in every lineament, but, in taking on itself the human form, had miscalculated dreadfully on the size, and presented itself thus to him in a blow-up, dilated frame of embodied air, exhaled from the caverns of death or the regions of devouring fire. He was further confirmed in the belief that it was a malignant spirit on perceiving that it approached him across the front of a precipice, where there was not footing for thing of mortal frame. Still, what with terror and astonishment, he continued riveted to the spot, till it approached, as he deemed, to within two yards of him; and then, perceiving that it was setting itself to make a violent spring on him, he started to his feet and fled distractedly in the opposite direction, keeping his eye cast behind him lest he had been seized in that dangerous place. But the very first bolt that he made in his flight he came in contact with a *real* body of flesh and blood, and that with such violence that both went down among some scragged rocks, and George rolled over the other. The being called out, 'Murder'; and, rising, fled precipitately. George then perceived that it was his brother . . .

James Hogg's highly original *Private Memoirs and Confessions of a Justified Sinner* (1824) is set in Calvinist Edinburgh of the late 17th, early 18th centuries. The hero believes, according to the Calvinist tradition of predestination, that he is one of the 'saved', but that he is under the 'evil eye' of a stranger, in fact his alter ego or doppelganger, responsible for killing his half-brother.

In the second part of the book, the hero's memoir, discovered after he has committed suicide, reveals that he has also killed his mother, a girl, and a preacher, believing their murder to have been God's will. When his body is exhumed his skull is found to have horn-like protrudences.

Another Edinburgh novel, published 150 years later makes a connection between the Calvinist doctrine of predestination and the rise of the Nazi party in Germany. In Muriel Spark's *The Prime of Miss Jean Brodie* (1961), Brodie, the schoolmistress with her 'creme de la creme', her chosen few, her 'set' of 16-year-olds whose minds she manipulates, is betrayed by one of the girls, Sandy Stewart, appropriately while Brodie is away touring Hitler's Germany in the summer of '38.

The Pentland Hills
Range of hills stretching south west of the City of Edinburgh.

Kirk Yetton forms the north-eastern angle of the range; thence, the Pentlands trend off south and west. From the summit you look over a great expanse of champaign sloping to the sea and behold a large variety of distant hills. There are the hills of Fife, the hills of Peebles, the Lammermoors and the Ochils, more or less mountainous in outline, more or less blue with distance. Of the Pentlands themselves, you see a field of wild heathery peaks with a pond gleaming in the midst . . .

Edinburgh: Picturesque Notes (1878) by R L Stevenson

Wherever Stevenson travelled in later years, his imagination continually inhabited this 'cold, old huddle of hills from which we came.' They were the setting for *St Ives* (1897, unfinished novel completed by Quiller Couch – see Cornwall) and *Weir of Hermiston* (1896). The family took a holiday cottage for many years at Swanston in the shadow of Kirk Yetton, a few miles away from Glencourse churchyard, the location of his horror story, 'The Body Snatcher' and of chapter 6 of *Weir of Hermiston*, and the garden of the Manse at nearby Colinton, where his uncle George Balfour was Minister, inspired *A Child's Garden of Verses*, today as innocently fresh and evocative as when it was first published in 1885.

The Manse garden at Colinton, overgrown and still haunted with Stevenson's verses.

I have not space to tell of my pleasures at the manse. I have been happier since; for I think most people exaggerate the capacity for happiness of a child; but I have never again been happy in the same way. For indeed it was scarce a happiness of this world, as we conceive it when we are grown up, and was more akin to that of animal than to that of a man. The sense of sunshine, of green leaves, and the singing of birds, seems never to have been so strong in me as in that place. The deodar upon the lawn, the laurel thickets, the mills, the river, the church bell, the sight of people ploughing, the Indian curiosities with which my uncles had stocked the house, the sharp contrast between this place and the city where I spent the other portion of my time, all these took hold of me, and still remain upon my memory, with a peculiar sparkle and sensuous excitement . . .

'Out through the breach in the wall of the garden / Down by the banks of the river we go.'

> Dear Uncle Jim, this garden ground
> That now you smoke your pipe around
> Has seen immortal actions done
> And valiant battles lost and won.
>
> Here we had best on tip-toe tread,
> While I for safety march ahead,
> For this is that enchanted ground
> Where all who loiter slumber sound.
>
> Here is the sea, here is the sand,
> Here is the simple Shepherd's Land,
> Here are the fairy hollyhocks,
> And there are Ali Baba's rocks.

But yonder, see! apart and high,
Frozen Siberia lies; where I,
With Robert Bruce and William Tell,
Was bound by an enchanter's spell.

There, then, awhile in chains we lay,
In wintry dungeons, far from day;
But ris'n at length, with might and main,
Our iron fetters burst in twain,

Then all the horns were blown in town;
And, to the ramparts clanging down,
All the giants leaped to horse
And charged behind us through the gorse.

On we rode, the others and I,
Over the mountains blue, and by
The Silent River, the sounding sea,
And the robber woods of Tartary.

A thousand miles we galloped fast,
And down the witches' lane we passed,
And rode amain, with brandished sword,
Up to the middle, through the ford.

Last we drew rein – a weary three –
Upon the lawn, in time for tea,
And from our steeds alighted down
Before the gates of Babylon.

STRATHCLYDE

Glasgow
Industrial city on the River Clyde.

I am so far happy as to have seen Glasgow, which, to the best of my recollection and judgment, is one of the prettiest towns in Europe; and, without all doubt, it is one of the most flourishing in Great Britain. In short, it is a perfect bee-hive in point of industry. It stands partly on a gentle declivity; but the greatest part of it is in a plain, watered by the river Clyde. The streets are straight, open, airy, and well paved; and the houses lofty and well built of hewn stone. At the upper end of the town, there is a venerable cathedral, that may be compared with York-minster or Westminster; and, about the middle of the descent from this to the Cross, is the

college, a respectable pile of building, with all manner of accommodation for the professors and students, including an elegant library, and an observatory well provided with astronomical instruments. The number of inhabitants is said to amount to thirty thousand; and marks of opulence and independency appear in every quarter of this commercial city, which, however, is not without its inconveniences and defects. The water of their public pumps is generally hard and brackish, an imperfection the less excusable, as the river Clyde runs by their doors, in the lower part of the town; and there are rivulets and springs above the cathedral, sufficient to fill a large reservoir with excellent water, which might be thence distributed to all the different parts of the city. It is of more consequence to consult the health of the inhabitants in this article, than to employ so much attention in beautifying their town with new streets, squares, and churches.

The Expedition of Humphrey Clinker, Tobias Smollet (1771)

The idea of Glasgow in the ordinary British mind is probably something like the following:– 'Glasgow, believed by the natives to be the second city of the empire, is covered by a smoky canopy through which rain penetrates, but which is impervious to sunbeam. It is celebrated for every kind of industrial activity: it is fervent in business six days of the

week, and spends the seventh in hearing sermon and drinking toddy. Its population consists of a great variety of classes. The "operative", quiet and orderly enough while plentifully supplied with provisions, becomes a Chartist when hungry, and extracts great satisfaction in listening to orators – mainly from the Emerald Isle – declaiming against a bloated aristocracy. The "merchant prince", known to all ends of the earth, and subject sometimes to strange vagaries; at one moment he is glittering away cheerily in the commercial heaven, the next he has disappeared, like the lost Pleiad, swallowed up of night for ever. The history of Glasgow may be summed up in one word – cotton; its deity, gold; its river, besung by poets, a sewer; its environs, dust and ashes; the *gamin* of its wynds and closes less tinctured by education that a Bosjesman; a creature that has never heard a lark sing save perhaps in a cage outside a window in the sixth story, where a consumptive seamstress is rehearsing the "Song of the Shirt", "the swallows with their sunny backs" omitted.' Now this idea of Glasgow is entirely wrong.

Glasgow is the pride of Scotland, and, indeed, it might very well pass for an elegant and flourishing city in any part of Christendom. There we had the good fortune to be received into the house of Mr Moore, an eminent surgeon, to whom we were recommended by one of our friends at Edinburgh; and, truly, he could not have done us more essential service – Mr Moore is a merry facetious companion, sensible and shrewd, with a considerable fund of humour; and his wife an agreeable woman, well bred, kind, and obliging – Kindness, which I take to be the essence of good-nature and humanity, is the distinguishing characteristic of the Scotch ladies in their own country — Our landlord shewed us every thing, and introduced us to all the world at Glasgow; where, through his recommendation, we were complimented with the freedom of the town. . . .

A Summer in Skye, Alexander Smith (1865)

Everything had changed. You could walk for as long as you liked in this city. It wouldn't know you. You could call every part of it by name. But it wouldn't answer. St. George's Cross was only cars, inventing destinations for the people in them. The cars controlled the people. Sauchiehall Street was a graveyard of illuminated tombstones. Buchanan Street was an escalator bearing strangers.

George Square. You should have known it. How many times had you waited for one of the buses that ran all through the night? The Square rejected you. Your past meant nothing. Even the black man on the black horse was from another country, a different time. Sir John Moore.

'Shipyard cranes have come down again / To drink at the river . From 'Landscape with One Finger' by Douglas Dunn

'They buried him darkly at dead of night.' Who told you his name? An English teacher who was always tired. Yawner Johnson. He told you interesting things between yawns. But he hadn't told you the truth. Nobody had. This was the truth.

Laidlaw, William McIlvanney (1977)

'Sauchiehall Street was a graveyard of illuminated tombstones.'

Ayr
Coastal town off the A77, approximately 30m south west of Glasgow.

> The simple Bard, rough at the rustic plough,
>   Learning his tuneful trade from ev'ry bough;
> The chanting linnet, or the mellow thrush,
> Hailing the setting sun, sweet, in the green thorn bush,
> The soaring lark, the perching red-breast shrill,
> Or deep-ton'd plovers, grey, wild-whistling o'er the hill . . .

From 'The Brigs of Ayr' by Robert Burns

Burns was born in 1759 near Alloway. His father, a cotter, a man labouring in exchange for a cottage and land, saw that he was well-educated, but the boy's spare time was spent on the farm, and when his father died, in 1784, Burns and his brother continued farming, at Mossgiel in Mauchline, which figures time and again in his poetry.

Burns was a patriot, he loved his country and he knew it not only through the soil he tilled but through its folk culture – its folklore and songs.

Up until Burns, most folklore had been passed on by word of mouth, but about 1750 a popular vernacular literature began to spread through the countryside written down and peddled around – superstition and fantasy were essential parts of it, and the stories would very often be attached to particular sites.

The tradition had always been there but suddenly there was a demand for it in written form, and the fund of subject matter was as enormous as ever – every place had a story to tell. As Robert Louis Stevenson declared a century later – 'The names, shapes of woodlands, the courses of roads and rivers, the mills and the ruins, the ponds and the ferries, perhaps even the Standing Stones or the Druids' Circle on the heath . . . Here is an inexhaustible fund of interest for anyone with eyes to see or twopenny-worth of imagination.'

In Burns' time spirits were literally in everything, even in bridges, so that his 'Brigs of Ayr' (1786) can speak to the reader quite credibly of their history and argue about their respective merits, and the ordinary peasant would have had no difficulty in relating to a sprite, fully clothed and crowned, emerging from the beck beneath them:

> The Genius of the Stream in front appears,
> A venerable Chief advanc'd in years;
> His hoary head with water-lilies crown'd,
> His manly leg with garter tangle bound.
> Next came the loveliest pair in all the ring,
> Sweet Female Beauty hand in hand with Spring . . .

In August 1787 Burns made a tour around the Highlands and Borders imbibing the culture and history of Scotland that he sensed lived thus in

The cottage where Burns was born.

Still a popular tourist call, the Brig o' Doone at Alloway. Burns fixed it in the public imagination as a piece of folk art with his finest work, 'Tam o' Shanter'.

the spirit of the place. At Bannockburn, where, in 1314, the Scots had freed their land from English domination, he wrote, 'Here no Scot can pass uninterested. I fancy to myself I see my gallant, heroic countrymen coming o'er the hill and down upon the plunderers of their country. I see my countrymen meet on the victorious field exulting in their heroic leader [King Robert the Bruce] and rescued liberty.' But for Burns it wasn't only the history that reverberated in the countryside, it was the song-in-Scotland, the music in the hills and in the streams.

> Flow gently, sweet Afton, among thy green braes,
> Flow gently, I'll sing thee a song in thy praise;
> My Mary's asleep by thy murmuring stream,
> Flow gently, sweet Afton, disturb not her dream.
>
> Thou stock dove whose echo resounds thro' the glen,
> Ye wild whistling blackbirds in yon thorny den,
> Thou green crested lapwing thy screaming forbear,
> I charge you disturb not my slumbering Fair.
>
> How lofty, sweet Afton, thy neighbouring hills,
> Far mark'd with the courses of clear, winding rills;
> There daily I wander as noon rises high,
> My flocks and my Mary's sweet Cot in my eye.

How pleasant thy banks and green vallies below,
Where wild in the woodlands the primroses blow;
There oft as mild ev'ning weeps over the lea,
The sweet scented birk shades my Mary and me.

Thy chrystal stream, Afton, how lovely it glides,
And winds by the cot where my Mary resides;
How wanton thy waters her snowy feet lave,
As gathering sweet flowerets she stems thy clear wave.

Flow gently, sweet Afton, among thy green braes,
Flow gently, sweet River, the theme of my lays;
My Mary's asleep by thy murmuring stream,
Flow gently, sweet Afton, disturb not her dream.

In that same year, 1787, he agreed to help the engraver James Johnson with his *Scots Musical Museum*, a collection of rural songs, and went on to collect them for the rest of his life. Altogether Burns collected, edited and wrote around 250 songs, including 'Auld Lang Syne', 'O my Luve's like a red, red rose', and the battle song 'Scots wha hae'. For all his work, for Johnson and another publisher called Thomson, he took not a penny. He saw it as his patriotic duty, and found no weight in the obligation.

Besides being a poet, peasant and patriot, Burns was physically attractive, amorous, and a bit of a lad. But about at least one of his romantic conquests he was wholly serious. He met Mary Campbell in 1786 when she was working, possibly as a dairymaid, at Coilsfield House near Ayr. They planned to marry and emigrate to the West Indies, but she died of typhus just before they could go. Their final parting occurred near Failford, where the Fail mingles with the Ayr, and Burns wrote 'Highland Mary' in memory of it. These are the first two stanzas – the 'castle o' Montgomery' refers to the house where Mary worked:

There is a memorial to Robert Burns and Mary Campbell near where the Ayr and the Fail rivers meet to mark the spot where the lovers parted for the last time.

Ye banks, and braes, and streams around
   The castle o' Montgomery,
Green be your woods, and fair your flowers,
   Your waters never drumlie!
There Simmer first unfald her robes,
   And there the langest tarry:
For there I took the last Fareweel
   O' my sweet Highland Mary.

How sweetly bloom'd the gay, green birk,
   How rich the hawthorn's blossom;
As underneath their fragrant shade,
   I clasp'd her to my bosom!
The golden Hours, on angel wings,

Flew o'er me and my Dearie;
For dear to me as light and life
    Was my sweet Highland Mary.

His last major poem – and only narrative poem – he wrote from his farm at Ellisland in Dumfries, where he died in 1796. 'Tam o' Shanter' Walter Scott believed to be Burns's finest work, and it does have almost everything that marked Burns out: 1. superstition and folklore – the story of warlocks and witches that befell Douglas Graham and John Davidson on whom Burns modelled Tam and his 'ancient drouthy cronie', was well known, indeed the two were buried in nearby Kirkoswald churchyard; 2. spirit of actual place – Alloway Kirk and Ayr Marketplace feature as does the old Alloway Brig' o' Doon, where Tam oustrips the warlock and her hags, the ride ending at Souter Johnnie's cottage at Kirkoswald; and finally 3. there is a strong sense of an uproarious Burns night out.

It is Market Day at Ayr, and Tam spends the evening at the alehouse, setting off for home in amorous and drunken mood. Passing Alloway Kirk he sees a light and looks inside to find warlocks and witches engaged in some sort of devilish dance. Tam espies a 'winsome wench' and shouts to her, whereupon the lights go out and the whole company turns on him. Scared out of his wits Tam spurs his nag, Meg, into action and makes for the Brig' o' Doon just outside Alloway, knowing that the horde will not cross water. But the girl has managed to catch hold of Meg's tail . . .

Ah, Tam! ah, Tam! thou'll get thy fairin'!   *unearthly deserts*
In hell they'll roast thee like a herrin'!
In vain thy Kate awaits thy comin'!
Kate soon will be a woefu' woman!
Now do thy speedy utmost, Meg,
And win the key-stane of the brig:
There at them thou thy tail may toss,
A running stream they darena cross!
But ere the key-stane she could make,
The fient a tail she had to shake;   *devil*
For Nannie, far before the rest,
Hard upon noble Maggie prest,
And flew at Tam wi' furious ettle;   *intent*
But little wist she Maggie's mettle!
Ae spring brought off her master hale,
But left behind her ain grey tail:
The carlin claught her by the rump,   *clutched*
And left poor Maggie scarce a stump.
    Now, wha this tale o' truth shall read,
Ilk man and mother's son, take heed;
Whene'er to drink you are inclin'd,
Or cutty-sarks run in your mind,
Think! ye may buy the joys o'er dear:
Remember Tam o' Shanter's mare.

Burns brought popular folklore stories into print often for the first time. Before, they were passed round by word of mouth, everyone was involved in the preservation and continuation of the local culture of a place. A decade or so earlier than Burns a man called Dugal Graham, 'a hump-backed dwarf with pigeon-breast and Punch-like nose, resplendent in long scarlet cloak, blue breeches and a cocket hat' was a familiar purveyor of such literature on a rather different level.

BORDERS

O Caledonia! stern and wild,
Meet nurse for a poetic child!
Land of brown heath and shaggy wood,
Land of the mountain and the flood,
Land of my sires! what mortal hand
Can e'er untie the filial band,
That knits me to thy rugged strand!
Still, as I view each well-known scene,
Think what is now, and what hath been,
Seems as, to me, of all bereft,
Sole friends thy woods and streams were left;
And thus I love them better still,
Even in extremity of ill.
By Yarrow's streams still let me stray,
Though none should guide my feeble way;
Still feel the breeze down Ettrick break,
Although it chill my wither'd check;
Still lay my head by Teviot Stone,
Though there, forgotten and alone,
The Bard may draw his parting groan.

From 'The Lay of the Last Minstrel' by Walter Scott

The Borders belong to Scott. His 'first consciousness of existence', he tells us, dated from Sandy Knowe; as a young man his exploration of the landscape was enthusiastically thorough; in 1802-3 his deep interest in Border culture was celebrated uniquely in his 3-volume *Minstrelsy of the Scottish Border*, a compilation of ballads that he hoped would 'contribute somewhat to the history of my native country, the peculiar features of whose manners and character are daily melting and dissolving into those of her sister and ally'; from 1812 he lived here, at Abbotsford House by the Tweed, south east of Galashiels off the A1/A6091; and finally, everywhere one goes in the Borders, there spring up castles and landscapes that inspired his first original work, 'The Lay of the Last Minstrel' (1805), a 16th-century romance, itself based upon an old Border legend of the goblin Gilpin Homer.

Melrose Abbey
Just north of the A6091 that connects the A1 and A68, south east of Galashiels.

Founded in 1136 for Cistercian monks from the monastery at Rievaulx, near Helmsley, Yorkshire, it features in Scott's novels *The Monastery* (1820) and *The Abbot* (1820), and famously in 'The Lay of the Last Minstrel' as the site of the tomb of the wizard, whose magic book is to help the lady of Branksome Hall avenge the killing of her husband –

If thou would'st view fair Melrose aright,
Go visit it by the pale moonlight;
For the gay beams of lightsome day,
Gild, but to flout, the ruins grey.

Yarrow Water

The river rises in St Mary's Loch and joins the Tweed a few miles north east of Selkirk.

'Lone St Mary's silent lake' was immortalised by Scott in 'Marmion: A Tale of Flodden Field' (1808).

Yarrow Water, St Mary's 'child', runs east through Ettrick Forest. On their way back from a tour of Scotland in 1803 William and Dorothy Wordsworth, by dint of a decision to go with Scott to Melrose, missed seeing the Yarrow which had so inspired other poets. The result was his poem 'Yarrow Unvisited'.

Eleven years later, on his return from a second Scottish tour, William was taken to St Mary's Loch, by James Hogg, the so-called Ettrick Shepherd, a poet who had been encouraged in his writing by Scott after they had corresponded over the Minstrelsy (see also Edinburgh, Lothian). Following this excursion Wordsworth wrote 'Yarrow Visited', which turned out to be partly a Romantic dissertation on the relationship between nature and the poetic imagination.

At first, the poet is disappointed – the river in his imagination (in 'Yarrow Unvisited') had been far more impressive.

And is this – Yarrow? – THIS the Stream
Of which my fancy cherished,
So faithfully, a waking dream?

The argument he develops goes further than that 'imagination almost always transcends reality', however, seeming to place the burden of poetic inspiration equally on the spirit in nature and the poet's imagination. The relationship, like a love affair, requires not simply the presence of each party, but their participation. The landscape has everything in place, yet nothing occurs.

Wordsworth's third poem, 'Yarrow Revisited', was written during a stay with Scott at Abbotsford in 1831.

It was, recalled Wordsworth, 'a day of happy hours', their last, as it happened, for Scott died the following year.

This is also the landscape of James Thomson (1700–48), who was born at nearby Ednam (off the A698, south east of Kelso) and can lay claim to being the first poet to make the British landscape his subject. *The*

Seasons (1726–1730) is a stunning, often dramatic, poetic painting, and 'Winter' is especially redolent of the spirit of the landscape of Thomson's birth:

At last the roused-up river pours along:
Resistless, roaring, dreadful, down it comes,
From the rude mountain and the mossy wild,
Tumbling through rocks abrupt, and sounding far;
Then o'er the sanded valley floating spreads,
Calm, sluggish, silent; till again, constrained
Between two meeting hills, it bursts a way
Where rocks and woods o'erhang the turbid stream;
There, gathering triple force, rapid and deep,
It boils, and wheels, and foams, and thunders through.

Nature! great Parent! whose unceasing hand
Rolls around the Seasons of the changeful year,
How mighty, how majestic are thy works!
With what a pleasing dread they swell the soul,
That sees astonished, and astonished sings!
Ye too, ye winds! that now begin to blow
With boisterous sweep, I raise my voice to you.
Where are your stores, ye powerful beings! say,
Where your aerial magazines reserved
To swell the brooding terrors of the storm?
In what far-distant region of the sky,
Hushed in deep silence, sleep you when 'tis calm?

THE NORTH OF ENGLAND

Map 1

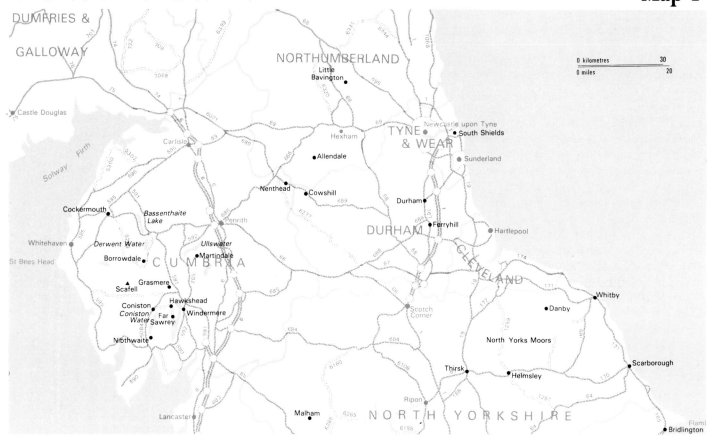

CUMBRIA

....

Borrowdale
Via the B5289, south of Buttermere.

'And so, David, we are passing into the perilous country where the savages live, where there is only hay to eat, and dirty water to drink, where it rains for a hundred days . . .'

For what had he come here? He only knew that already the place was working into his veins – the silence, the air with an offscent of ice in it, the hills that were perhaps only little hills and yet had so strong a power – witchcraft hills, hiding in their corners and wrinkles magic and spells. As he rode on, the outside world was beginning to slip ever farther and farther away from him.

Rogue Herries, the first novel (1930) in Hugh Walpole's *Herries Chronicle* – *Judith Paris* followed in 1931, *The Fortress* in 1932, and *Vanessa* in 1933 – establishes a real and unsettling picture of Borrowdale 250 years ago. His pedlar for example, an itinerant servant of the Devil, is in perfect sympathy with the superstitions of the people that seem to grow out of this wild farflung landscape. Here is the walk from Seathwaite to Grange undertaken one 'grey, overhanging, autumn day' by old Mrs Wilson, who is suspected of being a witch.

She walked as she had lived, in a half-dream. Sometimes it seemed to her that figures were walking with her, sometimes that she was alone. When she reached the river she muttered a little with pleasure, as though she were blessing it. Perhaps she was. This river, the Derwent, had been part of her from birth.

She walked on, resolutely, her stick striking the path, her head in its high black hat, and very far away, beyond Grasmere maybe, the thunder dimly rumbled. She gathered confidence as she went: a silly old woman she had been to stay in that dark house letting fear gather upon her. She would not wonder now but it was that devil Herries that had put those thoughts into her head. It was himself that the people hated, and she had taken his contempt for her own. Just because, forsooth, some boys had thrown stones after her and a labourer cast a word at her, she had hidden away and missed her proper company. It would be good to see Hannah once more. Hannah was dying, they said, but she would be able enough to remind her of the old days when they had both been young and happy together. One kindly look from Hannah's eyes would be a fine thing, and she would walk all the way back to Herries again and show the village that she was no witch, but an old woman who liked company and chatter and friendly faces in candlelight.

As she walked, strength seemed to increase in her. She had no ache nor pain in all her body. She was still good for life. Death had not got her yet. She breathed the air, even though it were close and packed with thunder, and as the hill grew steeper by the Bowder Stone, she set her knees to it and braced her back and climbed bravely to the turning of the road. Then, at the sight of the Grange cottages across the river, again her courage failed her. She was passing Cumma Catta Wood, a place that she had always feared because, when she was a girl, young Broadley had drowned himself in the pool there below the wood. It was a pretty place, a little hill thick with trees hanging over a broad pool, where the river gathered itself together for a while and stayed tranquilly reflecting the sky. But they said that young Broadley haunted it, and that, in ancient days, there had been pagan sacrifices there. You could see the two projecting stones where the sacrifices had been.

The old woman moved on. She paused before she crossed the bridge that raised itself up like a cat's back over the divided strands of the river. The Grange cottages, huddled on the other side, seemed to be waiting, watching for her . . .

Death was nothing odd to Mrs Wilson, yet peering half blindly over the bed she shivered. She would not be greeted by Hannah, then; her journey had been fruitless. Suddenly she felt a deep sorrow for herself. Hannah was gone, the only one who in all these years had sent for her. Nobody now wanted her at all. To pass from this dead house to the dead house Herries was all the same.

Then something made her prick up her ears: she did not know what it was, but it was something that caused her altogether to forget the dead woman on the bed. Fear leapt into her body. Her legs were trembling, so that she caught the post of the bed. She had a sense of being trapped, and yet when she listened again there was no sound, only the careless running of the river. Nevertheless, she knew that

' . . . from the very beginning there had been something about her that set her apart . . . Had it not been for that odd sense of power that sometimes came to her she would have left it alone. But there had been hours when she felt that she held all the valley in her hand to do with as she would.'

The house at Seathwaite.

Cumma Catta Wood.

there was reason for her fear. She looked about the room, at the looking-glass, the wooden box painted with red hearts, a chair with a thin curved back. She listened, her head bent forward, her hat a little crooked. There was a sound behind the soundlessness; the still air was full of it, and the odour of musty decay in the room grew with every second stronger. She must get out, get away, get to Herries.

She pulled back the door, peered out on to the ragged garden, and beyond it the grey smooth running water, and beyond that the field rising to Cumma Catta Wood. Then, although no sound reached her, she turned and stared, across the cobbled path, into a group of faces.

Men and women, close together as though for protection, were gathered at the end of the cobbled path. They stood, huddled together, not speaking, staring at her. Although she could not see well and was so deeply frightened that it was as though her heart were beating in her eyes, yet certain faces were very distinct to her. One belonged to a large stout man in a brown wig and green coat and breeches. His face was red as a tomato and his eyes wide and staring. There was the smooth white face of a young woman; a face with a black beard; there was a young girl's face, very fresh and rosy, with a mole on one cheek.

She looked back behind her; there was no way out there, only a thick rough-stone wall. They could easily stop her if she ran in front of the river.

She walked forward towards them, leaning on her stick because her knees trembled so badly, and at her movement a hoarse whisper broke the thick air: 'T'witch . . . t'witch . . . t'witch.' . . .

Three women ran forward. They bent down over her; shouting they tore her clothes from her. They threw her clothes over their heads into the crowd. They tore her flesh as they dragged her things away. One stood up, tugging at her white hair, and so she pulled the thin, bony body up, raising it to its knees.

Someone threw a stone. It struck the body between the breasts.

The Derwent and the cottages of Grange, 'a place she had always feared.'

Then the stout, red-faced man, shouting as though he were proclaiming some great news, called for order. Everything must be done properly. No one should say that they were out of justice. He strode forward, laughing. He caught the body in his arms, then dropped it again as he felt in his breeches pocket, from there brought faded green cord. He took the body again and roughly, as though he would tear one limb from the other, took the right foot and fastened it to the left hand, the left foot and fastened it to the right hand. So trussed, she lay motionless. Then suddenly raising her face, which now streamed with blood, she sent forth two screeches, wild, piercing, sounding far over the crowd out into the village, down the road. Then her head fell again.

Triumphantly he raised her in his arms, holding her, her head against her knees, as a woman might an infant. He danced her for a moment in his arms. Then he ran forward, the crowd shouting, yelling, laughing, and up the bridge some children ran that they might see better, singing and dancing: 'T'witch . . . t'witch . . . t'witch.'

He lifted his stout arms and flung her out, high into air. The little white body gleamed for a moment, then fell, like a stone, into the water.

Honister Pass, Borrowdale 'Titanic battles were fought above Stye Head and on Honister between rival bands of robbers, disputing their plunder, and it was true enough that many a time, walking up Honister, you would find a dead man there, by the roadside, his throat cut or a knife in his belly and often enough stripped naked . . .

'Over this country, when the giant Eagle flings the shadow of his wing, the land is darkened. So compact is it that the wing covers all its extent in one pause of the flight. The sea breaks on the pale line of the shore; to the Eagle's proud glance waves run in to the foot of the hills that are like rocks planted in green water.
  'From Whinlatter to Black Combe the clouds are never still. The Tarns like black unwinking eyes watch their chase, and the colours are laid out in patterns on the rocks and are continually changed. The Eagle can see the shadows rise from their knees at the base of Scafell and Gable, he can see the black precipitous flanks of the Screes washed with rain and the dark purple hummocks of Borrowdale crags flash suddenly with gold.
  'So small is the extent of this country that the sweep of the Eagle's wing caresses all of it, but there is no ground in the world more mysterious, no land at once so bare in its nakedness and so rich in its luxury, so warm with sun and so cold in pitiless rain, so gentle and pastoral, so wild and lonely; with sea and lake and river there is always the sound of running water, and its strong people have their feet in the soil and are independent of all men.'
  Rogue Herries *by Hugh Walpole*

Cockermouth
Town off the A66, 12m north west of Keswick.

The River Derwent flows past the house where William Wordsworth was born on April 7th, 1770. With the Derwent Wordsworth began his extraordinary relationship with nature that can be said to have restored faith in man's intuitive powers after centuries of their wasting away. In 'The Prelude', he describes in detail the imaginative process of development of his own mind through this relationship, how he was 'fashioned and built up even as a strain of music'. The poem carries the subtitle 'The Growth of a Poet's Mind'. It was begun in 1798/9 and completed in 1805.

> Was it for this
> That one, the fairest of all rivers, loved
> To blend his murmurs with my nurse's song,
> And, from his alder shades and rocky falls,
> And from his fords and shallows, sent a voice
> That flowed along my dreams? For this, didst thou,
> O Derwent! winding among grassy holms
> Where I was looking, a babe in arms,
> Make ceaseless music that composed my thoughts
> . . . giving me
> Amid the fretful dwellings of mankind
> A foretaste, a dim earnest, of the calm
> That Nature breathes among the hills and groves.

Hawkshead
Town north of Esthwaite Water.

His school at Hawkshead is open to the public at specific times.

On March 8th, 1778, Wordsworth's mother died; he was 7, nearly 8; his sister, Dorothy, was 20 months younger. She was sent to live with her mother's cousin in Halifax, he to Hugh and Anne Tyson at Hawkshead, where he would attend the Grammar School. At Hawkshead, suddenly cut off from his family and the life at Cockermouth he had so loved, William was

> . . . well pleased to recognise
> In nature and the language of the sense
> The anchor of my purest thoughts, the nurse,
> The guide, the guardian of my heart, and soul
> Of all my moral being . . .

Then, on December 30th, 1783, while he was at home for the school holidays, his father died. The loss, 'with all the sorrow that it brought, appeared a chastisement', and the boy turned to God for forgiveness. As it were in reply he received an image in memory of the place (the Kirkstone Pass) where he had been waiting for the horses to take him home for that fateful Christmas holiday:

Wordsworth used to go and sit on a stone bench east of the church – Church End, as it is known locally – for the view over the house tops of the village to Esthwaite Vale. But the place had more sombre meaning to him. A boy from his school died aged 12 and was buried there. Wordsworth would spend time musing over the grave. 'Nothing was more difficult for me in childhood,' he wrote, 'than the notion of death applicable to my own being . . .' Some sort of resolution to the problem occurred soon afterwards, when his father died, in one of those moments of revelation he called 'spots of time', invariably, as in this case, attached to place (see below).

> One Christmas-time,
> On the glad eve of its dear holidays,
> Feverish, and tired, and restless, I went forth
> Into the fields, impatient for the sight
> Of those led palfreys that should bear us home
> . . .'twas a day
> Tempestuous, dark, and wild, and on the grass
> I sate half-sheltered by a naked wall;
> Upon my right hand couched a single sheep,
> Upon my left a blasted hawthorn stood;
> With those companions at my side, I sate,
> Straining my eyes intensely, as the mist
> Gave intermitting prospect of the copse
> And plain beneath . . .
>
> And, afterwards, the wind and sleety rain,
> And all the business of the elements,
> The single sheep, and the one blasted tree,
> And the bleak music of that old stone wall,
> The noise of wood and water, and the mist
> That on the line of each of those two roads
> Advanced in such indisputable shapes;
> All these were kindred spectacles and sounds
> To which I oft repaired, and thence would drink,
> As at a fountain.

The image – an awakening – somehow heals the emotional wound. He does not explain how, but there is a bleak strain of realism, a sense of nature as harbinger of both life and death, 'tumult and peace, the darkness and the light . . . all like workings of one mind . . . symbols of Eternity'.

Grasmere
Town north of Grasmere lake, off the A591.

Wordsworth left Hawkshead for St John's College, Cambridge, in 1787, and did not return to the Lake District to live until December 20th, 1799, when he arrived with his sister at Dove Cottage in Grasmere. 'Home at Grasmere' is a celebration of this return.

Wordsworth's first view of Grasmere from Loughrigg terrace.

> . . . Who could look
> And not feel motions there? I thought of clouds
> That sail on winds; of breezes that delight
> To play on water, or in endless chase
> Pursue each other through the liquid depths
> Of grass or corn, over and through and through,
> In billow after billow evermore;
> Of sunbeams, shadows, butterflies, and birds,
> Angels, and winged creatures that are lords
> Without restraint of all which they behold.
> I sat, and stirred in spirit as I looked,
> I seemed to feel such liberty was mine,
> Such power and joy; but only for this end:
> To flit from field to rock, from rock to field,
> From shore to island, and from isle to shore,
> From open place to covert, from a bed
> Of meadow-flowers into a tuft of wood,
> From high to low, from low to high, yet still
> Within the bounds of this huge concave; here
> Should be my home, this valley be my world.

Stone Arthur, the 'eminence – of these our hills the last / That parleys with the setting sun', the fell that rises above the road by the side of Grasmere lake, and which Dorothy suggested should be named after her brother.

Airey Force in Gowbarrow Park by Ullswater – 'Not a breath of air / Ruffles the bosom of this leafy glen,' wrote Wordsworth in 'Airey-Force Valley'. Nearby, in the woods beyond Gowbarrow Park William and Dorothy saw the daffodils (below) immortalised in 'I Wandered Lonely as a Cloud', a poem which may have distracted many from his more searching work. Dorothy's description does however underline the significance of the moment.

Gowbarrow
Just north of Ullswater off the A5091.

Thursday 15th [April, 1802] When we were in the woods beyond Gowbarrow Park . . . I never saw daffodils so beautiful, they grew among the mossy stones about and about them, some rested their heads upon these stones as on a pillow for weariness and the rest tossed and peeled and danced and seemed as if they verily laughed with the wind that blew upon them over the lake, they looked so gay, ever glancing, ever changing.

Grasmere Journal (1800–3) by Dorothy Wordsworth

Martindale
East of Ullswater, via the B5320.

Over the fell road I walked, the sweet scent of earliest spring poignant in the soft air into which the snow was melting. Martindale vicarage, the most beautiful little white house imaginable, stood in its own field, with a great lime tree at the gate and a beck fringed with birch and alder bounding its little domain. It stood empty, as if waiting for me. . . .

At the end of the first year of the war, the poet Kathleen Raine (see also Bavington, Northumberland, and Sandaig, Scottish Highlands) came to live in the area where her beloved Aunt Peggy Black had taught, more than fifty years earlier.

I lived, then, during that summer when France fell, in a state and place where all was radiant with that interior light of which Traherne has written; and beyond the continuous interior illumination of moss and fern, of yellow welsh poppies and water flowing over stones reflecting the glitter of pure light, the warmth of the sun on the stone seat under the yew-tree, the scent of young birch-leaves and lime-blossom, the line of the fells ever changing in sun and shadow, certain moments there were of another kind of consciousness altogether. Such a state has been often enough described: Tennyson said he could enter it at will; Richard Jefferies and others have known it well. 'Nature mysticism' occupies, it may be, a relatively humble place on the ladder of perfection as compared with those states of consciousness attained by saints and sages; but as compared with normal consciousness the difference is as between the world and paradise, if indeed it be not precisely that. Descriptions of one state of consciousness in terms of another must, to those who have not themselves known the experience, always give the impression of being figurative or poetic; so it always must be when, in whatever field, ignorance passes judgement upon knowledge. But those who know are unanimous in reporting about such changes of consciousness are not of degree, but of kind; not some strong emotion or excitement but a clarity in which all is minutely perceived as if by finer sense.

I kept always on the table where I wrote my poems a bowl with different beautiful kinds of moss and lycopodium and long and deeply did I gaze at those forms, and into their luminous smaragdine green. There was also a hyacinth

growing in an amethyst glass; I was sitting alone, in an evening, at my table, the Aladdin lamp lit, the fire of logs burning in the hearth. All was stilled. I was looking at the hyacinth, and as I gazed at the form of its petals and the strength of their curve as they open and curl back to reveal the mysterious flower-centres with their anthers and eye-like hearts, abruptly I found that I was no longer looking *at* it, but *was* it; a distinct, indescribable, but in no way vague, still less emotional, shift of consciousness into the plant itself. Or rather I and the plant were one and indistinguishable; as if the plant were a part of my consciousness. I dared scarcely to breath, held in a kind of fine attention in which I could sense the very flow of life in the cells. I was not perceiving the flower but living it. I was aware of the life of the plant as a slow flow or circulation of a vital current of liquid light of the utmost purity. I could apprehend as a simple essence formal structure and dynamic process. This dynamic form was, as it seemed, of a spiritual not a material order; or of a finer matter, or of matter itself perceived as spirit. There was nothing emotional about this experience which was, on the contrary, ... almost mathe-matical ...

The Land Unknown by Kathleen Raine

Above, *Martindale, and* below, *the vicarage.*

Ullswater. 'I lived, then, during that summer when France fell, in a state and place where all was radiant with that interior light of which Traherne has written.' Kathleen Raine.

Time opens in a flower of bells
the mysteries of its hidden bed,
the altar of the ageless cells
whose generations never have been dead.

So flower angels from the holy head,
so on the wand of darkness bright worlds hang.
Love laid the elements at the vital root,
unhindered out of love these flowers spring.

The breath of life shapes darkness into leaves,
each new-born cell
drinks from the star-filled well
the dark milk of the sky's peace.

The hyacinth springs on a dark star –
I see eternity give place to love.
It is the world unfolding into flower
the rose of life, the lily and the dove.

'The Hyacinth' by Kathleen Raine

Coniston and the Ransome holiday home at High Nibthwaite.

High Nibthwaite
Village at the south-east end of Coniston Water, off the A5084.

Now, at last, the sun had set, Twilight was coming on. There was no wind, for the wind had gone with the sun as it so often does, and they were beginning to be afraid that the dark would come too soon for them . . .

   The mate rowed with slow, steady strokes. Her oars made no noise at all. They slipped in and out of the water without a splash. Swallow was in smooth water now, sheltered by the high ground of the promontory . . . They were in the Amazon River.

Swallows and Amazons by Arthur Ransome

Arthur Ransome's five best-loved childrens adventure stories owe their inspiration to the 'Lake in the North' – 'It had its beginning,' he wrote, 'long, long ago when, as children, my brother and sisters and I spent most of our holidays on a farm at the south end of Coniston . . . While away from it, as children and as grown-ups, we dreamt about it. No matter where I was, wandering about the world, I used at night to look for the North Star and, in my mind's eye could see the beloved skyline of great hills beneath it. *Swallows and Amazons* . . . I could not help writing it. It almost wrote itself.'

   The sense of preparation, of adventure, and of the very sanctity of the place, Ransome described in his *Autobiography* (1984):

Tea was always ready for our arrival, and after the long journey we were always made to get that meal over before doing anything else. Then 'May I get down?' and we were free in paradise, sniffing remembered smells as we ran about making

Coniston Old Man.

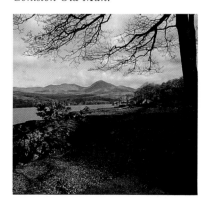

sure that familiar things were still in their places. I used first of all to race down to the lake, to the old stone harbour to which, before the Furness Railways built its branch line to Coniston village, boats used to bring their cargoes of copper-ore from the mines on the Old Man. The harbour was a rough stone-built dock, with an old shed or two, and beside it was a shallow cut, perhaps six feet across and twenty long, where the Swainson's boat, *our* boat, was pulled up half way out of the shallow, clear water which always seemed alive with minnows. I had a private rite to perform. Without letting the others know what I was doing, I had to dip my hand in the water, as a greeting to the beloved lake or as a proof to myself that I had indeed come home. In later years, even as an old man, I have laughed at myself, resolved not to do it, and every time have done it again. If I were able to go back there today, I should feel some discomfort until coming to the shore of the lake I had felt its coolness on my fingers.

Those holidays at Nibthwaite I owe to my father's passion for the lake country. They bred a similar passion in me that has lasted my life and been the mainspring of the books I have been happiest in writing. Always that country has been 'home', and smoky old Leeds, though well beloved, was never as real as Swainson's farm, Coniston lake and the valley of the Crake.   *Autobiography* by Arthur Ransome

Coniston. 'I had to dip my hand in the water, as a greeting to the beloved lake or as a proof to myself that I had indeed come home . . . If I were able to go back there today, I should feel some discomfort until coming to the shore of the lake I had felt its coolness on my fingers.' Arthur Ransome

Far Sawrey
Village between Esthwaite Water and Windermere, about 2m from Hawkshead.

The extraordinary mostly unnoticed feature of Beatrix Potter's little books is the reality of the settings. 'I can't invent,' she once wrote, 'I only copy.'

The farm in *Jemima Puddle-Duck*, the soft-headed duck who insisted on hatching her own eggs, *is* Hill Top Farm, Sawrey, and the view painted of the land behind the farm, where she is lured by the fox into his den to lay and is persuaded to bring her own stuffing, is faithful too. Even Beatrix's dog, Kep, the Collie, makes a guest appearance as Jemima's rescuer. In *The Tale of Tom Kitten*, we have the farmhouse itself, both its exterior (in colourful late spring, early summer) and its interior, exactly as you will find it preserved today. In *The Pie and the Patty Pan* it is the village that supplies the story background, it is even called Sawrey by name. In fact of the 13 books she wrote in her first 8 years living at Sawrey, from 1905, no fewer than 6 are set in the village, an effect of the extraordinary swell of feeling for the place that suffused this creative period.

Beatrix's lonely childhood in Kensington, London – she rarely went out or saw other children – was relieved only by family holidays, mostly to Dalguise (see Tayside, Scotland).

When she grew into a woman, her ageing parents became very demanding. But as her books began to sell she became financially independent. Independence from her unhappy past, to be herself, was what Sawrey meant to Beatrix, and what she had loved about Scotland, the realism of nature and life on a farm, she also found here. She could smell it, see it, feel it in a way that made dull Kensington pall. But at the start she was divided between the two, which made her longing more unbearable. When, finally, she settled in, the spirit of the place, which she helped create, suffused her books.

Ginger and Pickles was dedicated to Mr John Taylor, who ran the village shop and 'who thinks he might pass as a dormouse (three years in bed and never a grumble)'. Beatrix wrote to Louisa Ferguson that Taylor had died before publication:

. . . Poor old 'John Dormouse' is dead – just before the book was finished. I was so sorry I could not give him a copy before he died. He was such a funny old man: I thought he might be offended if I made fun of him, so I said I would only draw his shop and not him. And then he said I had drawn his son John [the village carpenter] in another book, with a saw and wagging his tail [John Joiner in The Roly-Poly Pudding], and old John felt jealous of young John. So I said how could I draw him if he would not get up? And he considered for several days, and then 'sent his respects, and thinks he might pass as a dormouse!' It is considered very like him. Also it is very much like our Timothy Baker, but he is not quite so well liked, so everybody is laughing.

Beatrix Potter's home at Sawrey. Sawrey, the village, delighted Beatrix Potter, and in return she delighted its inhabitants by including some of their ways and characteristics, and the place itself, in her books. This reciprocal swell of feeling became the spirit of Sawrey for a time, and today people flock to her house, which has been faithfully restored so that you will find many features and pieces of furniture that are also subjects of her paintings in the books.

NORTH YORKSHIRE

In If Only They Could Talk, *James Herriot, 'a city boy, brought up in Glasgow', introduces us to the spirit of the landscape and rural community of the Yorkshire Dales in a way that only an outsider thrown into the thick of it could. 'I was totally unprepared for the beauty . . . but their wildness and peace captivated me instantly,' he wrote. Darrowby is a composite label for Thirsk and Richmond, among other places. You will not find it on the map, but it is more real a recreation of the area in the late '30s and '40s than any that you will.*

Right: The pure waters of the Swale near Keld.

Thirsk.

Richmond.

Darrowby

A young vet, new to the Dales, is on his way by bus to an interview with a Mr Siegfried Farnon, MRCVS, where he is confronted by a cow with a blocked teat, property of an eager looking farmer by name of Sharpe.

The driver crashed his gears again as he went into another steep bend. We had been climbing steadily now for the last fifteen miles or so, moving closer to the distant blue swell of the Pennines, I had never been in Yorkshire before but the name had always raised a picture of a county as stodgy and unromantic as its pudding; I was prepared for solid worth, dullness and a total lack of charm. But as the bus groaned its way higher I began to wonder. The formless heights were resolving into high, grassy hills and wide valleys. In the valley bottoms, rivers twisted among the trees and solid greystone farmhouses lay among islands of cultivated land which pushed bright green promontories up the hillsides into the dark tide of heather which lapped from the summits.

I had seen the fences and hedges give way to dry stone walls which bordered the roads, enclosed the fields and climbed endlessly over the surrounding fells. The walls were everywhere, countless miles of them, tracing their patterns high on the green uplands.

But as I neared my destination the horror stories kept forcing their way into my mind; the tales brought back to college by veterans hardened and embittered by a few months of practice.

Mr Sharpe was waiting, still looking eager. He led us into the byre and Farnon gestured towards the cow. 'See what you can make of it.'

I squatted down and palpated the teat, feeling the mass of thickened tissue half-way up. It would have to be broken down by a Hudson's instrument and I began to work the thin metal spiral up the teat. One second later, I was sitting gasping in the dung channel with the neat imprint of a cloven hoof on my shirt front, just over the solar plexus.

It was embarrassing, but there was nothing I could do but sit there fighting for breath, my mouth opening and shutting like a stranded fish.

Mr Sharpe held his hand over his mouth, his innate politeness at war with his natural amusement at seeing the vet come to grief. 'I'm sorry, young man, but I owt to 'ave told you that this is a very friendly cow. She allus likes to shake hands.' Then, overcome by his own wit, he rested his forehead on the cow's back and went into a long paroxysm of silent mirth.

I took my time to recover, then rose with dignity from the channel. With Mr Sharpe holding the nose and Farnon lifting up the tail, I managed to get the instrument past the fibrous mass and by a few downward tugs I cleared the obstruction; but, though the precautions cramped the cow's style a little, she still got in several telling blows on my arms and legs.

When it was over, the farmer grasped the teat and sent a long white jet frothing on the floor. 'Capital! She's going on four cylinders now!'

The North Yorkshire Moors, taken by Frank Sutcliffe, a contemporary of Revd J C Atkinson, whose Forty Years in a Moorland Parish, *(1891), like Gilbert White's* Selborne, *anatomises the natural history of his homeland, as well as the superstitions of his parishioners.*

Malham: Goredale Scar

A gigantic collapsed cave system between frowning limestone cliffs, a mile or so east of Malham, off the A65, 5m north west of Skipton.

Goredale Scar has for centuries been an attraction for artists – James Ward, Turner, to name but two, but its greatest paean may be Thomas Gray's description in his Journal (1775), heralded as an exemplary evocation of the Sublime, one aspect of Edmund Burke's definition of aesthetic pleasure in 1757 (*A Philosophical Enquiry into the Sublime and the Beautiful*) and akin to Old Testament awe.

Oct. 13, to visit *Gordale-scar*. Wind N. E.: day gloomy and cold. It lay but six miles from Settle, but that way was directly over a fell, and it might rain, so I went round in a chaise the only way one could get near it in a carriage, which made it full thirteen miles; and half of it such a road! but I got safe over it, so there's an end; and came to Mallham (pronounce it Maum) a village in the bosom of the mountains seated in a wild and dreary valley: from thence I was to walk a mile over very rough ground. A torrent rattling along on the left hand. On the cliffs above hung a few goats; one of them danced and scratched an ear with its hind foot in a place where I would not have stood stock-still for all beneath the moon: As I advanced the crags seemed to close in, but discovered a narrow entrance turning to the left between them. I followed my guide a few paces, and lo, the hills opened again into no large space, and then all further way is barred by a stream, that at the height of above 50 feet gushes from a hole in the rock, and spreading in large sheets over its broken front, dashes from steep to steep, and then rattles away in a torrent down the valley. The rock on the left rises perpendicular with stubbed yew-trees and shrubs, staring from its side to the height of at least 300 feet; but those are not the things: it is that to the right under which you stand to see the fall, that forms the principal horror of the place. From its very base it begins to slope forwards over you in one block and solid mass without any crevice in its surface and overshadows half the area below with its dreadful canopy. When I stood at (I believe) full four yards distance from its foot, the drops which perpetually distil from its brow, fell on my head, and in one part of the top more exposed to the weather there are loose stones that hang in the air; and threaten visibly some idle spectator with instant destruction: It is safer to shelter yourself close to its bottom, and trust the mercy of that enormous mass, which both her novels – *Agnes Grey* and *The Tenant of Wildfell Hall*. Here is Ellen Nussey's account of Anne Brontë's last trip to Scarborough.

On the 25th we arrived at Scarborough; our dear invalid having, during the journey, directed our attention to every prospect worthy of note.

On the 26th she drove on the sands for an hour; and lest the poor donkey should be urged by its driver to a greater speed than her tender heart thought right, she took the reins, and drove herself. When joined by her friend, she was charging the boy-master of the donkey to treat the poor animal well. She was ever fond of dumb things and would give up her own comfort for them.

On Sunday, the 27th, she wished to go to church, and her eye brightened with the thought of once more worshipping her God amongst her fellow-creatures. We thought it prudent to dissuade her from the attempt, though it was evident her heart was longing to join in the public act of devotion and praise.

She walked a little in the afternoon, and meeting with a sheltered and comfortable seat near the beach, she begged we would leave her, and enjoy the various scenes near at hand, which were new to us, but familiar to her. She loved the place, and wished us to share her preference.

The evening closed in with the most glorious sunset ever witnessed. The castle on the cliff stood in proud glory gilded by the rays of the declining sun. The distant ships glittered like burnished gold; the little boats near the beach heaved on the ebbing tide, inviting occupants. The view was grand beyond description. Anne was drawn in her easy chair to the window, to enjoy the scene with us. Her face became illumined almost as much as the glorious scene she gazed upon. Little was said, for it was plain that her thoughts were driven by the imposing view before her to penetrate forwards to the regions of unfading glory. She again thought of public worship, and wished us to leave her, and join those who were assembled at the House of God. We declined gently urging the duty and pleasure of staying with her, who was now so dear and so feeble. On returning to her place near the fire, she conversed with her sister upon the propriety of returning to their home. She did not wish it for her own sake, she said; she was fearing others might suffer more if her decease occurred where she was. She probably thought the task of accompanying her lifeless remains on a long journey was more than her sister could bear – more than the bereaved father could bear, were she borne home another, and a third tenant of the family-vault in the short space of nine months.

Goredale Scar, for Thomas Gray the epitome of the Sublime.

nothing but an earthquake can stir: The gloomy uncomfortable day well suited the savage aspect of the place and made it still more formidable.

I stayed there (not without shuddering) a quarter of an hour, and thought my trouble richly paid, for the impression will last for life.

Scarborough
Seaside resort on the North Sea coast, 15m south east of Whitby on the A171.

The first time Charlotte Brontë caught sight of the sea at Bridlington, a coastal resort a few miles south of Scarborough, 'she could not speak till she had shed some tears.' But it was her sister Anne for whom the sea was an inspiration. She had worked as a governess at Scarborough and the spirit of the place affected

Scarborough Castle and 'proud waves dashing'.

The night was passed without any apparent accession of illness. She rose at seven o'clock, and performed most of her toilet herself, by her expressed wish. Her sister always yielded such points, believing it was the truest kindness not to press inability when it was not acknowledged. Nothing occurred to excite alarm till about 11 am. She then spoke of feeling a change. 'She belived she had not long to live. Could she reach home alive, if we prepared immediately for departure?' A physician was sent for, her address to him was made with perfect composure. She begged him to say 'How long he thought she might live; – not to fear speaking the truth, for she was not afraid to die.' The doctor reluctantly admitted that the angel of death was already arrived, and that life was ebbing fast. She thanked him for his truth-fulness, and he departed to come again very soon. She still occupied her easy chair, looking so serene, so reliant: there was no opening for grief as yet, though all knew the separation was at hand. She clasped her hands, and rever-ently invoked a blessing from on high; first upon her sister, then upon her friend, to whom she said, 'be a sister in my stead. Give Charlotte as much of your company as you can.' She then thanked each for her kindness and attention.

'Ere long the restlessness of approaching death appeared, and she was borne to the sofa; on being asked if she were easier, she looked gratefully at her questioner and said, 'It

is not *you* who can give me ease, but soon all will be well, through the merits of our Redeemer.' Shortly after this, seeing that her sister could hardly restrain her grief, she said, 'Take courage, Charlotte; take courage.' Her faith never failed, and her eye never dimmed till about two o'clock, when she calmly, and without a sign, passed from the temporal to the eternal.

My soul is awakened, my spirit is soaring
And carried aloft on the wings of the breeze;
For above and around me the wild wind is roaring,
Arousing to rapture the earth and the seas.

The long withered grass in the sunshine is glancing,
The bare trees are tossing their branches on high;
The dead leaves, beneath them, are merrily dancing,
The white clouds are scudding across the blue sky.

I wish I could see how the ocean is lashing
The foam of its billows to whirlwinds of spray;
I wish I could see how its proud waves are dashing,
And hear the wild roar of their thunder to-day!

From 'Lines Composed on a Windy Day' by Anne Brontë

St Mary's churchyard in Scarborough where Anne Brontë is buried.

Whitby
Old whaling port, 15m north west of Scarborough on the A171.

On the north-eastern shores of England there is a town called Monkshaven . . . a name not unknown in the history of England, and traditions of its having been the landing-

'The magnates of Whitby were those who had the largest number of ships engaged in the whaling trade.'

place of a throneless queen were current in the town. At that time there had been a fortified castle on the heights above it, the site of which was now occupied by a deserted manor-house; and at an even earlier date than the arrival of the queen, and coeval with the most ancient remains of the castle, a great monstery had stood on those cliffs, over-looking the vast ocean that blended with the distant sky. Monkshaven itself was built by the side of the Dee, just where the river falls into the German Ocean . . .

And who were the great people of this small town? Not the younger branches of the county families that held hereditary state in their manor-houses on the wild bleak moors, that shut in Monkshaven almost as effectually on the land side as ever the waters did on the sea-board. No; these old families kept aloof from the unsavoury yet adventurous trade which brought wealth to generation after generation of certain families in Monkshaven.

The magnates of Monkshaven were those who had the largest number of ships engaged in the whaling-trade.

Elizabeth Gaskell describes the whaling port of Whitby as Monkshaven in the opening pages of *Sylvia's Lovers*, a novel set in the period of the Napoleonic Wars. More than half a century later, Gerald du Maurier recommends the tiny fishing port to the lecturer and preacher Alfred Ainger, for the exciting spectacle of its forty or fifty strong herring fleet leaving harbour – 'with all the town, men, women and children, pushing the boats off'. By then there is no lingering sense of Gaskell's press ganged whalers and disenchanted lovers, though he does exhort Ainger's party to 'walk along the cliffs westward . . . through fields and over

The spirit of Whitby, the spirit of the Whitby fisherman.

stiles till they reach Sylvia Robson's cottage.'

What sustains continuity in the responses to 18th, 19th, and even 20th-century Whitby is the spirit of its people, the tight, insular, self-sufficient spirit of the Whitby fisherman and his family, hemmed in by the primitive landscapes of savage sea and wild moorland. In the 1960s Peter Terson wrote a play for television about them and when he returned to ask what they had thought of it, one responded by dislodging his front teeth.

Out of this self-same primitive landscape came the first inspirational poem in the Anglo-Saxon style, which, as C L Wrenn has written, 'set the whole tone and method of subsequent Anglo-Saxon poetry.' The story of its poetic inspiration in 670 in the imagination of a humble herdsman is described by Bede in his *History of the English Church and People* –

In this monastery of Whitby there lived a brother whom God's grace made remarkable. So skilful was he in composing religious and devotional songs, that he could quickly turn whatever passages of Scripture were explained to him into delightful and moving poetry in his own English tongue. These verses of his stirred the hearts of many folk to despise the world and aspire to heavenly things . . . [but] he had never learned anything about poetry: indeed, whenever all those present at a feast took it in turns to sing and entertain the company, he would get up from the table and go home directly he saw the harp approaching him.

On one such occasion he had left the house in which the entertainment was being held and went out to the stable, where it was his duty to look after the beasts that night. He lay down there at the appointed time and fell asleep, and in a dream he saw a man standing beside him who called him by name, 'Caedmon,' he said, 'sing me a song.'

'I don't know how to sing,' he replied. 'It is because I cannot sing that I left the feast and came here.'

The man who addressed him then said: 'But you shall sing to me.'

'What should I sing about?' he replied.

'Sing about the Creation of all things,' the other answered. And Caedmon immediately began to sing verses in praise of God the Creator that he had never heard before . . .

Now we must praise the Guardian of Heaven,
the might of the Lord and His purpose of mind,
the work of the Glorious Father; for He,
God Eternal, established each wonder,
He, Holy Creator, first fashioned
heaven as a roof for the sons of men.
Then the Guardian of Mankind adorned
this middle-earth below, the world for men,
Everlasting Lord Almighty King.

Gazing out from the Abbey over 'the vast ocean that blended with the distant sky', it is easy to accept this story of Caedmon's gift coming to fruit. Equally, when angrier moods are abroad in the elements which have, since the beginning, demanded irresistable tithes of Whitby's fisher folk, it is no less easy to accommodate the elaborately wrought extreme of Bram Stoker's 1897 idea of this part of the coast as the very Gate to Hell.

Cutting from the Dailygraph, 8 August (Pasted in Mina Murray's Journal)

From a Correspondent   *Whitby*
The day was unusually fine till the afternoon, when some of the gossips who frequent the East Cliff churchyard, and from that commanding eminence watch the wide sweep of sea visible to the north and east, called attention to a sudden show of 'mares'-tails' high in the sky to the north-west . . .

The approach of sunset was so very beautiful, so grand in its masses of splendidly-coloured clouds, that there was quite an assemblage on the walk along the cliff in the old church-

Whitby Abbey, near where Lucy falls foul of Dracula, 'the western sky marked by myriad clouds of every sunset colour.'

yard to enjoy the beauty. Before the sun dipped below the black mass of Kettleness, standing boldly athwart the western sky, its downward way was marked by myriad clouds of every sunset-colour – flame, purple, pink, green, violet, and all the tints of gold; with here and there masses not large, but of seemingly absolute blackness, in all sorts of shapes, as well outlined as colossal silhouettes . . .

Shortly before ten o'clock the stillness of the air grew quite oppressive, and the silence was so marked that the bleating of a sheep inland or the barking of a dog in the town was distinctly heard, and the band on the pier, with its lively French air, was like a discord in the great harmony of nature's silence. A little after midnight came a strange sound from over the sea, and high overhead the air began to carry a strange, faint, hollow booming.

Then without warning the tempest broke. With a rapidity which, at the time, seemed incredible, and even afterwards is impossible to realise, the whole aspect of nature at once became convulsed. The waves rose in growing fury, each overtopping its fellow, till in a very few minutes the lately glassy sea was like a roaring and devouring monster. White-crested waves beat madly on the level sands and rushed up the shelving cliffs; others broke over the piers, and with their spume swept the lanthorns of the lighthouses which rise from the end of either pier of Whitby Harbour. The wind roared like thunder, and blew with such force that . . . it was found necessary to clear the entire piers from the mass of onlookers . . . To add to the difficulties masses of sea-fog came drifting inland – white, wet clouds, which swept by in ghostly fashion, so dank and damp and cold that it needed but little effort of imagination to think that the spirits of those lost at sea were touching their living brethren with the clammy hands of death, and many a one shuddered as the wreaths of sea-mist swept by.

At times the mist cleared, and the sea for some distance could be seen in the glare of lightning . . . running mountains high, (it) threw skywards with each wave mighty masses of white foam, which the tempest seemed to snatch at and whirl away into space; here and there a fishing-boat, with a rag of sail, running madly for shelter before the blast; now and again the white wings of a storm-tossed sea-bird. On the summit of the East Cliff the new searchlight . . . discovered some distance away a schooner with all sails set, apparently the same vessel which had been noticed earlier in the evening. The wind had by this time backed to the east, and there was a shudder amongst the watchers on the cliff as they realised the terrible danger in which she now was . . . in the words of one old salt, 'she must fetch up somewhere, if it was only in hell' . . . The wind suddenly shifted to the

Reputed to be the storm-wrecked schooner Demeter *that inspired Bram Stoker to bring Dracula ashore in similar style at Whitby.*

north-east, and the remnant of the sea-fog melted in the blast; and then, *mirabile dicta*, between the piers, leaping from wave to wave as it rushed at headlong speed, with all sail set . . . A great awe came on all as they realised that the ship, as if by a miracle, had found the harbour, unsteered save by the hand of a dead man!

From *Dracula* by Bram Stoker, 1897

NORTHUMBRIA

Lindisfarne
Island off the North East coast of Northumberland, linked to the mainland by road at low tide. Also known as Holy Island.

Lindisfarne carries a sense of the early Christian spirit of the area long before the Industrial Revolution, a sense of ascetic purity, humility, piety, and companionship with nature associated with its most famous abbot, Cuthbert, the Patron Saint of Northumberland.

The dynamic force of Christianity – what is now known as the Golden Age – began here, after a shaky start, in the 7th Century when Irish missionaries came from Iona, a community founded by Columba in 565, and founded monasteries at Lindisfarne and Jarrow, and at Lastingham and Whitby in Yorkshire.

In 'Marmion', Walter Scott describes a visit to Cuthbert's Lindisfarne by nuns from Whitby Abbey, led by St Hilda, in what was a steady stream of pilgrims, which may have been why Cuthbert chose to live for a period on Farne Island in perfect solitude –

Then from the coast they bore away,
And reach'd the Holy island's bay.
The tide did now its flood-mark gain,
And girdled in the saint's domain:
For, with the flow and ebb, its style
Varies from continent to isle;
Dry shod, oe'er sands, twice every day
The pilgrims to the shrine find way;
Twice every day, the waves efface
Of staves and sandall'd feet the trace . . .

Durham
Cathedral City, 12m south of Newcastle, between the A167 and A1(M).

Lindisfarne was subject to many Viking raids – 'on the deep walls, the heathen Dane had pour'd his impious rage in vain' (Scott's 'Marmion'). When eventually 'the rude Dane burn'd their pile, The monks fled forth from Holy Isle', taking the body of St Cuthbert, who had died in 687, with them. After a long period of transporting his coffin from place to place, they laid their abbot to rest in Durham in a church built for the purpose, to be replaced in 1104 by the magnificent Cathedral. There, before forty-six witnesses, the coffin was opened and St Cuthbert's body found to be uncorrupt. The poem, 'Durham', was written soon afterwards, one of only two Old English topographical poems to have survived (the other is 'The Ruin', see Bath, Avon).

All Britain knows of this noble city,
its breathtaking site: buildings backed
by rocky slopes peer over a precipice.
Weirs hem and madden a headstrong river,
diverse fish dance in the foam.
A sprawling, tangled thicket has sprung up
there; those deep dales are the haunt
of many animals, countless wild beasts.
In that city, too, as men know,
lies the body of blessed Cuthbert,
and the head of Oswald, innocent king,

lion of the English; also Bishop Aidan
and Eadberch and Eadfrith, eminent men.
Æthelwold the Bishop sleeps beside them,
and the great scholar Bede, and Abbot Boisil
whose fortune it was first to teach the saint,
then still a boy; Cuthbert excelled
in his lessons. Innumerable relics are left
in the minster by the blessed man's tomb,
scene of many miracles, as documents say.
The man of God awaits Domesday.

Little Bavington
Village 15m north west of Newcastle, between the A68 and A696

Kathleen Raine was born in Ilford, Essex, in 1908, but fundamental to her childhood and later literary development (see Sandaig, Scottish Highlands, and Martindale, Cumbria) were her visits to her Aunt Peggy at Little Bavington.

Places have their identity as flowers or creatures have, their soul, or *genius loci*. A place, in nature, is, after all, only a larger and more complex organism, a symbiosis of many lives. . . .

I have written of my years in Northumberland as if they had preceded in time all that belonged to other phases of my life; but that is not so. Northumberland was anterior only in a symbolic sense: not only because from beyond the Border came my ancestors, but also because there I found, in the few short years I lived at the manse with my Aunty Peggy Black, my own image of a Paradise already lost long before my birth.

Farewell Happy Fields by Kathleen Raine

Pure I was before the world began,
I was the violence of wind and wave,
I was the bird before bird ever sang.

I was never still,
I turned upon the axis of my joy,
I was the lonely dancer on the hill,

The rain upon the mountainside,
The rising mist,
I was the sea's unrest.

From 'Northumbrian Sequence' by Kathleen Raine

'They were iron men, steel men; they talked of hardly anything else, for only by iron and steel could they eat. Once a man had worked in Palmer's [shipyard] for some years, he felt he would be no good for anything else; nor did he want to be.' Katie Mulholland *by Catherine Cookson*

South Shields

South and North Shields stand, one on each bank of the mouth of the Tyne. Tyne Dock, a dock on the Tyne river east of Newcastle, is connected with South Shields; to the west lies Jarrow.

The port of Newcastle-Upon-Tyne was still a major shipbuilding and engineering industrial centre when Catherine Cookson was born, in 1906. Number 5 Leam Lane, Tyne Dock, her birthplace, was one of a small group of houses within a few minutes walking distance – 'under five great slime-dropping arches' – of the actual dock gates. When she was five or six the family, which consisted of her grandparents, her mother Kate, and Catherine herself, moved a short distance away to a small terraced house in William Black Street in East Jarrow. Here her memories really begin. 'Everything that I have written since seems to have been bred in that kitchen. Other things have been bred in me – the niceties, if you like – but the rawness of life came from that kitchen.'

The 'rawness' was the stigma of her illegitimacy and the alienation even by her fellows which that involved, the drunkenness and being sent for the beer with 'the great jar', the poverty and the pawn. These years are well known to readers of her autobiography, *Our Kate*, or of *The Fifteen Streets*, in which little Katie shares some of the agonies of this period of Catherine Cookson's life. But the novels that sprang from this early time achieve their power not from the dreadful facts of her childhood, but from their being brewed in a mixture of love and hate. The hate drove Catherine Cookson to educate herself and get out at the earliest opportunity, the love brought her back from what she began to see as the vacuousness of her new life in Hastings, Sussex. What she had discovered was the strength of her roots in the North, and she wrote about it in *The Invisible Cord*. Trying to pull them up had led to a complete nervous breakdown, which lasted ten years. Only when she started writing, inspired by the spirit of the place, which was the spirit of its people, bad and good, did she recover fully.

The timber ponds at Jarrow Slake (or Slacks) by Tyne Dock, opposite which Catherine Cookson lived from 1911/2.

The spirit of the North is in its people; is, still, the spirit of its people. 'Basically, people from the north seem more fatally impregnated with their landscape than people who live in the south.' Alan Sillitoe in 'Mountains and Caverns'

The close-knit, deeply rooted, working-class family myth-of-the-North, which Catherine Cookson never knew at home, is described in *Tilly Trotter*. She gives it to the Drews, a mining family, who share it with Tilly who has come to tea one Sunday. The banter, the chatter, the stories, the whole interchange builds to a crescendo until Tilly bursts out in hysterical laughter in response to the depth of her need –

As Tilly watched Mrs Drew's head move slowly back and forward there was rising in her a swirl of merriment such as she had never felt in her life, and when Mrs Drew ended, 'Swing they will, the both of them, from the crossroads an' we'll all have a field day,' the laughter burst from her throat. It surprised not only herself but all those at the table, because they had never heard anyone laugh like it. It was a wavering sound that swelled and swelled until, holding her waist, she turned from the table and rocked herself. She laughed until she cried; she couldn't stop laughing, not even when Katie, herself doubled up with laughter, put her arm around her and begged, 'Give over. Give over.' Nor when Sim lifted her chin and, his own mouth wide, cried, 'That's good. That's good.' And he kept repeating this until he realised her face was crumpling and that the water running down it was no longer caused by merriment; and so, straightening up, he looked round the table and raised his hand, saying, 'Enough is enough.'

The noise in the room gradually subsided, and Tilly turned to the table again and, her head bowed, murmured, 'I'm sorry.'

'They take a light and go into the belly of Leviathan.' Coal fuelled the Industrial Revolution. Between 1850 and 1914 the North Eastern Coalfield provided the energy to urbanise and industrialise Western Europe.

Ferryhill
17m south of Newcastle between the A167 and A1(M).

D H Lawrence noticed among the miners of Eastwood, where he grew up, that the physical awareness among them made them 'deeply alive, instinctively. . . . They avoided really the rational aspect of life. They preferred to take life instinctively and intuitively. They didn't even care very profoundly about wages. It was the women, naturally, who nagged on this score . . . The collier went to the pub and drank in order to continue his intimacy with his mates. They talked endlessly but it was rather of wonders and marvels . . . than facts. It was hard facts in the shape of wife, money, and nagging home necessities, which the collier fled away from, out of the house to the pub, and out of the house to the pit . . . [or] he roved the countryside with his dog, prowling for a rabbit, for nests, for mushrooms, anything. He loved the countryside . . . And very often he had a genuine love of the beauty of flowers. . . . I've seen many a collier stand in his back garden looking down at a flower with that odd, remote sort of contemplation which shows an awareness of the presence of beauty.'

Sid Chaplin was a miner and lived at Ferryhill, where he wrote *The Thin Seam* which, with some of his other pieces, formed the basis of Alan Plater's play, *Close the Coalhouse Door*. *The Thin Seam* tells of a single night down the pit, climaxing in the pit's collapse and the death of a miner. His title has a double meaning however. Lawrence's sense of the miner's sensibility to beauty above ground is transferred to his unspoken intuition of the mystery that lies at the core.

He stared at me angrily, the impotent rebel in him struggling for expression. Then he turned abruptly on his heel and walked away. I watched him go. I noted the tired stoop of his shoulders, the drag of his heavy boots, the listless hang of his arms. But his hands were clenched. He was still fighting. The cross-grained spirit of him was still alert. And I saw him as a symbol of my own folk. Dour, hard as the very rock they tunnel, contradictory, and uncertain to understand, unless you know the way the cleat of their nature runs. But this is the way they are made: the way they have to be.

They take a little light and go into the belly of Leviathan. They take a lamp into the most terrifying darkness, and they are not afraid.

They take a little light because underground they know their poverty. Without light their arms are useless. In the strata they meet a darkness like a velvet pad pressed against the open eye, and this darkness, without a little light, is impenetrable and eager. At two hundred fathoms the sun takes no levy nor gives of his majesty. Only a memory of him, and an urge to return quickly. All is without form, and void. The bare rock is not tender, and returns blow for blow with sudden harshness. The Lord, only the Lord, broods over the depths, and men disturb His brooding, to pay in passion and the sweat and blood of their own bodies.

Men do this. My folk. They pierce the fabric of His temple; make an incision into the heart of His mystery. And at the same time, unknowingly, they tend the hem of His robe and make most glorious the thin seam of His garment.

The Thin Seam by Sid Chaplin

THE MIDLANDS AND THE NORTH

Alison Uttley's father ploughing at Castle Top Farm.

DERBYSHIRE

Cromford
Just of the A6, a mile or so south of Matlock.

Alison Uttley was born Alison Jane Taylor on December 17th 1884, at Castle Top Farm near Cromford. A lonely, imaginative child, she instinctively imbued every living thing with a spirit of its own. Trees in particular had always held 'a strange fascination' for her, 'ever since she had lain, an infant wrapped up in a shawl, in a clothes-basket in the orchard, babbling to the apple trees and listening to their talk. They are queer, half-human creatures, alive yet tied to the ground. Lucky they are tied, too, for rooted they are safe.'

Every day she had to walk on her own through dense woods from the farm to school in the hamlet of Holloway. It was two miles walk each way, and in winter she had to carry a lantern.

In the middle of Dark Wood the climbing path rose up a steep incline, too steep for Susan to hurry, with black shadows on either side. Then it skirted a field, a small, queer, haunted-looking field of ragwort and bracken, long given to the wild wood, which pressed in on every side. A high rudely-made wall surrounded it, through the chinks of which she was sure that eyes were watching. To pass this field was the culmination of agony, for she had to walk close to the wall in the semi-darkness of overhanging trees, and nothing could save her if a long arm and skinny hand shot out.

At the top of the field, which sloped up the wood, was a tumbledown building, which was the authentic House that Jack built, with rats and malt complete, but long ago it had been deserted and now Fear lived there. Once she saw a battered man creeping through the bracken towards the ruin, but he never saw the little shadow with a school bag on her back slip past the mossy gate of the field.

Beyond the ragwort field was a fair open stretch of wood, with cow-wheat and delicate fumitory growing by the path.

she was seven, a pair of eyes had looked at her from behind the tree, and once a dead white cow had lain there, swollen and stiff, brought to be buried in the wood.

A nut tree stood in her path, low, human, but it was friendly, and always she touched its branches with fluttering trembling fingers, receiving solace from the warm twigs, as she passed on to meet the oak. She held her head sideways, pretending to look up at the scrap of sky, but her eyes were peeping behind, like a scared rabbit's, and the tree seemed to turn its branches and look after her, whilst the thing, whatever it was, skipped round the trunk to the other side. She never turned to look behind her, but trusted to her sense of hearing, which had become very acute with the strain imposed upon it. She whispered a little prayer, a cry to God for help, as she left the tree behind.

Dove Valley
The Dove flows west of Ashbourne, A515, A52.

> Oh my beloved nymph! fair Dove;
> Princess of rivers, how I love
>   Upon thy flowery banks to lie;
>   And view thy silver stream,
> When gilded by a summer's beam,
> And in it all thy wanton fry
>   Playing at liberty,
> And with my angle upon them
>   The all of treachery
> I ever learnt, industriously to try.

From *The Compleat Angler* (1653)
by Izaak Walton and Charles Cotton

Dove Valley (*right*) is Eagle Valley in Adam Bede, by George Eliot (pseudonym for Mary Ann Evans), set in 1799 in the rural community of Hayslope in Loamshire, actually the village of Ellastone by the River Dove, the Staffordshire side of the border with Derbyshire (called Stonyshire in the book).

Adam Bede is a young carpenter who takes enormous pride and pleasure in his work and his part in the complex rural community of Hayslope, which is drawn with wit and vivid detail by Eliot.

The young squire, Arthur Donnithorpe, disturbs the balance of the community by seducing a pretty farm girl, Hetty Sorrel, with whom Adam is in love. Subsequently, Arthur deserts Hetty, who, broken-hearted, agrees to marry Adam. Then, before the marriage, Hetty discovers she is pregnant.

'Great boulders lay among the trees like primitive beasts.'

The trees were not so close together, and a glimpse of the blue sky came through in summer, or a star in the winter.

The child's heart ceased its heavy pounding and she took in deep breaths in readiness for the next ordeal, an immense rugged oak tree which waited at the cross-road, where her path cut across two others. One way led downhill to a cottage in the fields below the wood, a path no one used. The other went up the steep sides of the wood past great boulders which lay among the trees like primitive beasts crouching in the dark, until it faded away to nothing in the bracken.

But something was behind the oak tree, hidden, lurking, and the leaves all watched her approach. She threw back her head and stared boldly at it, but her feet were winged for flight as she slipped softly along. Once two years ago, when

Hetty runs away to find Arthur, fails to find him, and is arrested and convicted for the murder of her unwanted child, and only saved from the gallows at the last moment. The plot was suggested to Eliot by her Methodist aunt, Elizabeth Evans, to whom a girl had confessed a similar act of infanticide, and it is to Elizabeth's home town of Wirksworth (just south of Cromford on the A6) – Snowfield in the novel – that Hetty Sorrel sets out when first she discovers she is pregnant:

It was about ten o'clock when Hetty set off, and the slight hoar-frost that had whitened the hedges in the early morning had disappeared as the sun mounted the cloudless sky. Bright February days have a stronger charm of home about them than any other days in the year. One likes to pause in the mild rays of the sun, and look over the gates at the patient plough-horses turning at the end of the furrow, and think that the beautiful year is all before one. The birds seem to feel just the same: their notes are as clear as the clear air. There are no leaves on the trees and hedgerows, but how green all the grassy fields are! and the dark purplish brown of the ploughed earth and the bare branches, is beautiful too. What a glad world this looks like, as one drives or rides along the valleys and over the hills. I have often thought so when, in foreign countries, where the fields and woods have looked to me like our English Loamshire – the rich land tilled with just as much care, the woods rolling down the gentle slopes to the green meadows – I have come on something by the roadside which has reminded me that I am not in Loamshire: an image of a great agony – the agony of the Cross. It has stood perhaps by the clustering apple-blossoms, or in the broad sunshine by the cornfield, or at a turning by the wood where a clear brook was gurgling below; and surely, if there came a traveller to this world who knew nothing of the story of man's life upon it, this image of agony would seem to him strangely out of place in the midst of this joyous nature. He would not know that hidden behind the apple-blossoms, or among the golden corn, or under the shrouding boughs of the wood, there might be a human heart beating heavily with anguish: perhaps a young blooming girl, not knowing where to turn for refuge from swift-advancing shame; understanding no more of this life of ours than a foolish lost lamb wandering farther and farther in the nightfall on the lonely heath; yet tasting the bitterest of life's bitterness.

Such things are sometimes hidden among the sunny fields and behind the blossoming orchards; and the sound of the gurgling brook, if you came close to one spot behind a small bush, would be mingled for your ear with a despairing human sob. No wonder man's religion has much sorrow in it; no wonder he needs a Suffering God.

Adam Bede by George Eliot

NOTTINGHAMSHIRE

Eastwood
Off the A608 (J27 M1) or the A610 (J26), north west of Nottingham.

I was born nearly forty-four years ago, in Eastwood, a mining village of some three thousand souls, about eight miles from Nottingham, and one mile from the small stream, the Erewash, which divides Nottinghamshire from Derbyshire. It is hilly country, looking west to Crich and towards Matlock, sixteen miles away, and east and north-east towards Mansfield and the Sherwood Forest district. To me it seemed, and still seems, an extremely beautiful countryside, just between the red sandstone and the oak-trees of Nottingham, and the cold limestone, the ash-trees, the stone fences of Derbyshire. To me, as a child and a young man, it was still the old England of the forest and agricultural past; there were no motor-cars, the mines were, in a sense, an accident in the landscape, and Robin Hood and his merry men were not very far away.

We lived in the Breach, in a corner house. A field-path came down under a great hawthorn hedge. On the other side was the brook, with the old sheep-bridge going over into the meadows. The hawthorn hedge by the brook had grown tall as tall trees, and we used to bathe from there in the dipping-hole, where the sheep were dipped, just near the fall from the old mill-dam, where the water rushed. The mill only ceased grinding the local corn when I was a child. And my father, who always worked in Brinsley pit, and who always got up at five o'clock, if not at four, would set off in the dawn across the fields at Coney Grey, and hunt for mushrooms in the long grass, or perhaps pick up a skulking rabbit, which he would bring home at evening inside the lining of his pit-coat.

D H Lawrence

Alan Sillitoe begins his essay, 'Lawrence and District' with a quotation from one of Lawrence's novels:

'I have no allocated place in the world of things, I do not

The North

Map 2

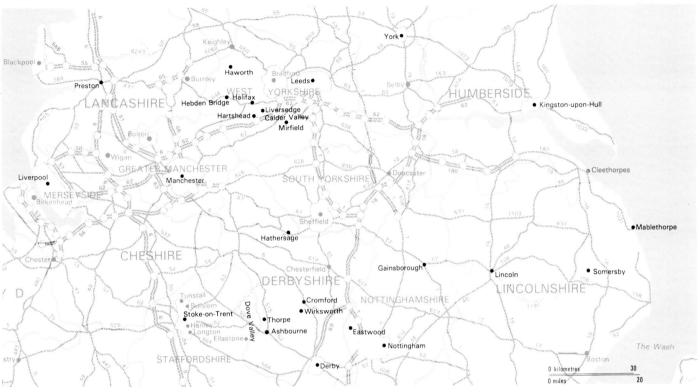

belong to Beldover (Eastwood) nor to Nottingham nor to England nor to this world, but they none of them exist, I am trammelled and entangled in them, but they are all unreal. I must break out of it, like a nut from its shell which is an unreality.'

This is what Lawrence might have directly said, words he gave instead to his great heroine Ursula Brangwen at the end of *The Rainbow*. And if one may put those thoughts on to him, and square them with his actions, as I think one can, then he did indeed break out of Eastwood and district, going far beyond that 'dry, brittle corruption spreading over the face of the land'.

Lawrence left Eastwood after his mother died of cancer in 1910, but the significance of the piece from *The Rainbow* is less that he found Eastwood claustrophobic or restricting, rather that he found reality and the world so. It was breaking out of this, getting back to 'the deep, black source from whence all these little contents of lives are drawn', and that was no escape, it was what distinguished his art.

'Landscape seems to be *meant* as a background to an intenser vision of life,' he wrote in an introduction to his paintings. He despaired that for the English 'it is a form of escape . . . ' and deplored equally people's possessiveness of nature, the way they 'love flowers as possessions . . . If they see a flower that arrests their attention, they must at once pick it, pluck it. Possession! A possession! Something added on to me! And most of this so-called love of flowers today is this reaching out of possession and egoism: something I've got: something that embellishes me.'

Round the wild, tussocky lawn at the back of the house was a thorn hedge, under which daffodils were craning forward from among their sheaves of grey-green blades. The cheeks of the flowers were greenish with cold. But still some had burst, and their gold ruffled and glowed. Miriam went on her knees before one cluster, took a wild-looking daffodil between her hands, turned up its face of gold to her, and bowed down, caressing it with her mouth and cheeks and brows. He stood aside, with his hands in his pockets watching her. One after another she turned up to him the faces of the yellow, bursten flowers appealingly, fondling them lavishly all the while.

'Aren't they magnificent?' she murmured.

'Magnificent! it's a bit thick – they're pretty!'

She bowed again to her flowers at his censure of her praise. He watched her crouching, sipping the flowers with fervid kisses.

'Why must you always be fondling things!' he said irritably.

'But I love to touch them,' she replied, hurt.

'Can you never like things without clutching them as if you wanted to pull the heart out of them? Why don't you have a bit more restraint, or reserve, or something?'

She looked up at him full of pain, then continued slowly to stroke her lips against a ruffled flower. Their scent, as she smelled it, was much kinder than he; it almost made her cry.

'You wheedle the soul out of things,' he said. 'I would never wheedle – at any rate, I'd go straight.'

He scarcely knew what he was saying. These things came from him mechanically. She looked at him. His body seemed one weapon, firm and hard against her.

'You're always begging for things to love you,' he said, 'as if you were a beggar for love. Even the flowers, you have to fawn on them – –'

Rhythmically, Miriam was swaying and stroking the flower with her mouth, inhaling the scent which ever after made her shudder as it came to her nostrils.

'You don't want to love – your eternal and abnormal craving is to be loved. You aren't positive, you're negative. You absorb, absorb, as if you must fill yourself up with love, because you've got a shortage somewhere.'

Sons and Lovers by D H Lawrence

The piece conveys Miriam's possessiveness from which Paul shrinks, but there is also a sense of the something she wants to possess, which Lawrence confronts in 'Fantasia and the Unconscious', while sitting with his back against the trunk of a tree:

I come so well to understand tree-worship. All the old Aryans worshipped the tree. My ancestors. The tree of life. The tree of knowledge . . . This marvellous vast individual without a face, without lips or eyes or heart . . . Here am I between his toes like a pea-bug, and him noiselessly over-reaching me, and I feel his great blood-jet surging. And he has no eyes. But he turns two ways: he thrusts himself tremendously down to the middle earth, where dead men sink in darkness, in the damp, dense undersoil; and he turns himself about in high air . . . A huge, plunging, tremendous soul. I would like to be a tree for a while. The great lust of roots. Root-lust. And no mind at all.

D H Lawrence's birthplace, Eastwood.

Like the schizophrenic, whose level of awareness / derangement breaks up the physical world into energies, intensities, drives, Paul Morel / D H Lawrence is shocked by the almost tangible forces released when (again, in *Sons and Lovers*) he and Clara make love in a field by the canal near the Morel home. The physical substance of the grass, of the peewits screaming in the field, even that of the two lovers themselves is stripped away, and the life-force in nature revealed.

All the while the peewits were screaming in the field. When he came to, he wondered what was near his eyes, curving and strong with life in the dark, and what voice it was speaking. Then he realized it was the grass, and the peewit was calling. The warmth was Clara's breathing heaving. He lifted his head, and looked into her eyes. They were dark and shining and strange, life wild at the source staring into his life, stranger to him, yet meeting him; and he put his face down on her throat, afraid. What was she? A strong, strange, wild life, that breathed with his in the darkness through this hour. It was all so much bigger than themselves that he was hushed. They had met, and included in their meeting the thrust of the manifold grass-stems, the cry of the peewit, the wheel of the stars.

When they stood up they saw other lovers stealing down the opposite hedge. It seemed natural they were there; the night contained them.

And after such an evening they both were very still, having known the immensity of passion. They felt small, half afraid, childish, and wondering, like Adam and Eve when they lost their innocence and realized the magnificence of the power which drove them out of Paradise and across the great night and the great day of humanity. It was for each of them an initiation and a satisfaction. To know their own nothingness, to know the tremendous living flood which carried them always, gave them rest within themselves. If so great a magnificent power could overwhelm them, identify them altogether with itself, so that they knew they were only grains in the tremendous heave that lifted every grass-blade its little height, and every tree, and living thing, then why fret about themselves? They could let themselves be carried by life, and they felt a sort of peace each in the other. There was a verification which they had had together. Nothing could nullify it, nothing could take it away; it was almost their belief in life.

Sons and Lovers by D H Lawrence

LINCOLNSHIRE

Somersby
Hamlet west of the A16, and 25m east of Lincoln.

The waters are out in Lincolnshire. An arch of the bridge in the park has been sapped and sopped away. The adjacent low-lying ground, for half a mile in breadth, is a stagnant river, with melancholy trees for islands in it, and a surface punctured all over, all day long, with falling rain. My Lady Dedlock's 'place' has been extremely dreary. The weather, for many a day and night, has been so wet that the trees seem wet through, and the soft loppings and prunings of the woodman's axe can make no crash or crackle as they fall . . . The view from my Lady Dedlock's own windows is alternately a lead-coloured view, and a view in Indian ink. The vases on the stone terrace in the foreground catch the rain all day; and the heavy drops fall, drip, drip, drip, upon the broad flagged pavement, called from time to time, the Ghost's Walk, all night. On Sundays, the little church in the park is mouldy; the oaken pulpit breaks out into a cold sweat; and there is a general smell and taste as of the ancient Dedlocks in their graves.

Can Lincolnshire be as depressing as Dickens paints it in *Bleak House* (1852), or can natives excuse his description as a device to reflect the bored mood of the haughty Lady Dedlock at Chesney Wold?

It seems bad for Lincolnshire when its greatest poet, Alfred Tennyson, born at Somersby in 1809, also reflects upon its 'dreary wind, dim shores, dense rains, and heavy-clouded sea!'. Only the memories of his young friend Arthur Hallam, a poet of great promise who died at 22, can make even his own homeland of Somersby sing. And 'In Memoriam' is, by its very nature, a sad song.

Somersby is a hamlet in the wolds, a relief in the flat farmlands of Lincolnshire, 'a range of hills reaching here and there a height of over 500 feet . . . dotted with copses and noble trees, amongst which lie tiny villages and square-towered churches,' Charles Tennyson

> I climb the hill: from end to end
>   Of all the landscape underneath,
>   I find no place that does not breathe
> Some gracious memory of my friend;
>
> No gray old grange, or lonely fold,
>   Or low morass and whispering reed,
>   Or simple stile from mead to mead
> Or sheepwalk up the windy wold;
>
> Nor hoary knoll of ash and haw
>   That hears the latest linnet trill,
>   Nor quarry trench'd along the hill
> And haunted by the wrangling daw;
>
> Nor runlet tinkling from the rock
>   Nor pastoral rivulet that swerves
>   To left and right thro' meadows curves,
> That feed the mothers of the flock;
>
> But each has pleased a kindred eye,
>   And each reflects a kindlier day;
>   And, leaving these, to pass away,
> I think once more he seems to die.
>
> From 'In Memoriam' by Alfred Tennyson

Main Street, Haworth. 'In the year that Jane Eyre *was published, with an open sewer running down Main Street and polluted water as the daily drink, life expectancy had been twenty-nine'. Stan Barstow in* A Brother's Tale.

WEST YORKSHIRE

Haworth
Village off the A629, south west of Keighley.

The house was one of a dozen on a short street only five minutes' walk from the centre of town. Brick. The front door was recessed, leaving a little square porch. A nonsensical strip of soil a couple of feet wide, and a low wall, separated the house from the pavement. Small entries gave access to the back yards. A narrow hallway, with a bend round the staircase, led to a scullery that was stuck on the back of the house like an afterthought . . .

In *Next of Kin*, Stan Barstow draws a picture of an ordinary terraced house as if you had never seen one before. The description is plain, unadorned, he doesn't pull any tricks on you, but it is a moment before you say, 'Wait a minute I recognise this;' maybe even, 'I live there.' Then you begin rediscovering it with him, agreeing or disagreeing with the odd judgement – 'Yes, the front garden IS nonsensical, I'd never thought;' and so on – looking at the ordinary, often for the first time. That is the way Stan Barstow manages to get you, every time.

And he is so unfashionable and yet so modern. Even the ordinariness of many of his characters is not fashionable any more, though it was twenty years ago. As a result of all of this, he gets you on his side, you trust him, and if you ever need a Yorkshireman to show you around Haworth, the home of Yorkshire's famous literary sisters, the odds are you might choose him, though there is no telling where you'll end up:

'Where would you like to go?'
'We needn't go very far. We could go to Haworth and come back over the moors, make a round trip. We haven't been to Haworth for a while.'
'Hmm.'
Eileen, brought up in the lush valleys of Somerset, had quite fallen in love with the West Riding, especially the north-west area where the country ran up from the textile towns into bleak moorland tops, and I had enjoyed showing her the parts she had not already found for herself, seeing it afresh through her foreign eyes and listening to her exclamations of pleasure. 'Oh, they don't know how beautiful and grand it is, and they won't believe you when you tell them.'
'Well, don't tell everybody or they might all want to come, and then there'll be no room for us.' . . .
We were driving towards the roofless outer wall of a nearly demolished mill. The sky could be seen through the window apertures and blocks of fallen stone lay piled in the foundations. It had been a proud building in its way, built to stand for centuries, its destruction after a mere eighty or ninety years another blow at the battered identity of these textile towns to which the coming of synthetic fibres and cheap imports had shrunk manufacturing space and reduced the numbers of hands needed to do the work. 'We shall have the ten-hour bill, yes we will, yes we will, men had chanted in these valleys. But their inheritance had become the transistor-radio production line and the anonymous prefabricated warehouses

Elizabeth Gaskell's portrait of Haworth. She wrote The Life of Charlotte Brontë *in 1857. The Parsonage is now a museum and headquarters of the Brontë Society.*

where monstrous container lorries brought and took away the convenience foods of supermarket shopping.

Well . . . in lonely Haworth in the year the ten-hour bill was passed, the year that *Jane Eyre* was published, with an open sewer running down Main Street and polluted water as the daily drink, life expectancy had been twenty-nine. Anne Brontë's term on earth matched that expectancy as though measured for it. She had seen her sister Emily die the year before, at thirty. Charlotte, who had watched them both enter the world, watched them leave it, and achieved thirty-nine.

At the bottom of Main Street I braked and stopped. Since we'd been here last, the traffic had been made one-way and a new bypass skirted the village on the low side. It also gave access to a large car park, offering more space for vehicles of both those who made long and deliberate pilgrimages and others, like ourselves, who had decided on a whim to 'have a run out' to the home of those famous young women who themselves thought nothing of walking four miles to Keighley station. One evening, Charlotte and Anne walked that road through a snow-storm and took the nightmail for London, where they confronted their astounded publisher with the news that Currer, Ellis and Acton Bell were indeed three different people and, moreover, unmarried sisters from a remote Yorkshire parsonage.

But I didn't want to go into the cramped rooms of the Parsonage today and look again at the touchingly tiny shoes, the unyielding sofa on which Emily had died, the minute script of the Gondal stories; nor gaze out at the weather-stained gravestones, rank on rank. What communicated itself to me today was not the achievements of the lives lived in that house, but the sombre brevity of their span. I thought that Eileen shared my mood, if I'd not, in fact, caught it from her. So we sauntered part of the way down Main Street, until the cutting wind slicing through the ginnels and courts drove us to seek shelter. We went into a bookshop where, attracted by handsome new paperback editions, I bought copies of the two major novels; then we crossed the square to the Black Bull.

A Brother's Tale by Stan Barstow

There is something fragile about Emily Brontë, which is certainly not her art – Heathcliff and the moors and Cathy's feelings are anything but fragile. She of course was physically fragile. As Barstow mentions, life expectancy was not high for anyone. But what seems to be fragile about Emily Brontë today is the connection we have with her genius which, in the context of this book, *The Spirit of Britain*, is probably the greatest of all geniuses. One novel and some poems, that is all. One masterpiece, and all her poems hopelessly true.

Nor do you have to go to Haworth or up to the moors to know how true, because the spirit that inspired Emily's work is there in us or in our unconscious ready to awaken. That is why there is scarcely any landscape description in Wuthering Heights. There did not need to be. Emily awakens the spirit in us, that it is also there in the desolate moors we can then plainly see.

Charlotte Brontë knew Emily was a genius and was worried.

Whether it be right or advisable to create things like Heathcliff, I do not know: I scarcely think it is. But this I know; the writer who possesses the creative gift owns something of which he is not always master – something that at times strangely wills and works for itself . . . To rules and principles it will perhaps for years lie in subjection; and then . . . it sets to work on statue-hewing.

Wuthering Heights was hewn in a wild workshop, with simple tools, out of homely materials. The statuary found a granite block on a solitary moor: gazing thereon, he saw how from the crag might be elicited the head, savage, swart, sinister; a form moulded with at least one element of grandeur – power. He wrought with a rude chisel, and from no model but the vision of his meditations. With time and labour, the crag took human shape; and there it stands colossal, dark, and frowning, half statue, half rock; in the former sense, terrible and goblin-like; in the latter, almost beautiful, for its colouring is of mellow grey, and moorland moss clothes it; and heath, with its blooming bells and balmy fragrance, grows faithfully close to the giant's foot.

The terrible spirit of which that 'nursling of the moors,' Emily, availed herself was not just part of Heathcliff, however, the name that copies two features of the primitive moors. Cathy was of the same spirit.

'My love for Linton is like the foliage in the woods. Time will change it, I'm well aware, as winter changes the trees. My love for Heathcliff resembles the eternal rocks beneath . . . Nelly I AM Heathcliff – he's always, always in my mind – not as a pleasure, any more than I am a pleasure to myself – but as my own being – so, don't talk of our separation again – it is impracticable.'

And for the same reason Heathcliff is Cathy too. We see that after her death.

'Be with me always – take any form – drive me mad! only do not leave me in this abyss, where I cannot find you! Oh God! it is unutterable! I cannot live without my life! I cannot live without my soul!'

The moorland path to Wuthering Heights.

Top Withens, likely inspiration for Wuthering Heights. 'Wuthering Heights is the name of Mr Heathcliff's dwelling. "Wuthering" being a significant provincial adjective, descriptive of the atmospheric tumult to which its station is exposed in stormy weather.' Lockwood in the novel.

The graveyard at Haworth by the Brontë's house. 'The place of interment . . . was dug on a green slope, in a corner of the kirkyard, where the wall is so low that heath and bilberry plants have climbed over it from the moor; and peat mould almost buries it . . . They have each a simple headstone above, and a plain grey block at their feet, to mark the graves.'

There is only one place where such a spirit will find rest.

Cold in the earth – and the deep snow piled above thee,
Far, far, removed, cold in the dreary grave!
Have I forgot, my only Love, to love thee,
Severed at last by Time's all-severing wave?

Now, when alone, do my thoughts no longer hover
Over the mountains, on that northern shore,
Resting their wings where heath and fern-leaves cover
Thy noble heart for ever, ever more?

Cold in the earth – and fifteen wild Decembers,
From those brown hills, have melted into spring:
Faithful, indeed, is the spirit that remembers
After such years of change and suffering!

Sweet Love of youth, forgive, if I forget thee,
While the world's tide is bearing me along;
Other desires and other hopes beset me,
Hopes which obscure, but cannot do thee wrong!

From 'Remembrance' by Emily Brontë

Leeds
Industrial city by the River Aire, at the end of the M1, where it meets the M62 (J27-29), 7m east of Bradford.

John Dyer wrote 'The Fleece' in 1757. It is a priceless view of the optimism felt at the very start of the Revolution that would, through the following century, transform the British landscape and the spirit of its people for all time, more so by far than the Technological Revolution that followed it.

Industrial Leeds and 'the winding Aire'.

... Wide around
Hillock and valley, farm and village, smile;
And ruddy roofs and chimney-tops appear
Of busy Leeds, up-wafting to the clouds
The incense of thanksgiving: all is joy;
And trade and bus'ness guide the living scene,
Roll the full cars, adown the winding Aire
Load the slow-sailing barges, pile the pack
On the long tinkling train of slow-pac'd steeds.
As when a sunny day invites abroad
The sedulous ants, they issue from their cells
In bands unnumber'd, eager for their work,
O'er high o'er low they lift, they draw, they haste
With warm affection to each other's aid,
Repeat their virtuous efforts, and succeed.
Thus all is here in motion, all is life.

The Calder Valley
Valley of the River Calder, south of Halifax.

'Miss Keeldar, just stand still now, and look down at Nunnely dale and wood.'

They both halted on the green brow of the Common: they looked down on the deep valley robed in May raiment; on varied meads, some pearled with daisies, and some golden with king-cups: to-day all this young verdure smiled clear in sunlight; transparent emerald and amber gleams played over it. On Nunnwood – the sole remnant of antique British forest in a region whose lowlands were once all sylvan chase, as its highlands were breast-deep heather – slept the shadow of a cloud; the distant hills were dappled, the horizon was shaded and tinted like mother-of-pearl; silvery blues, soft purples, evanescent greens and roseshades, all melting into fleeces of white cloud, pure as azury snow, allured the eye as with a remote glimpse of heaven's foundations. The air blowing on the brow was fresh, and sweet, and bracing.

'Our England is a bonnie island,' said Shirley, 'and Yorkshire is one of her bonniest nooks.'

'You are a Yorkshire girl too?'

I am – Yorkshire in blood and birth. Five generations of my race sleep under the aisles of Briarfield Church: I drew my first breath in the old black hall behind us.'

Hereupon Caroline presented her hand, which was accordingly taken and shaken.

'We are compatriots,' said she.

'Yes,' agreed Shirley, with a grave nod, 'And that,' asked Miss Keeldar, pointing to the forest – 'that is Nunnwood?'

'It is.'

Were you ever there?'

'Many a time.'

'In the heart of it?'

'Yes.'

'What is it like?'

'It is like an encampment of forest sons of Anak. The trees are huge and old. When you stand at their roots, the summits seem in another region: the trunks remain still and firm as pillars, while the boughs sway to every breeze. In the deepest calm their leaves are never quite hushed, and in high wind a flood rushes – a sea thunders above you.'

Shirley by Charlotte Brontë

Mention of the ancient forest sons of Anak reminds us that the Calder Valley is also the landscape of Ted Hughes' youth, the inspiration for 'Remains of Elmet' (1979), 'the last ditch of Elmet, the last British kingdom to fall to the Angles.'

The West Yorkshire mill country celebrated in Charlotte Brontë's novel, *Shirley*, lies on the northern slopes of the Calder Valley in the area of Liversedge and Mirfield, and the suggestion is that Shirley's roots

The Red House, Gomersall, home of the Taylor family, is Briar-maines in Shirley.

run deep here too. J J Stead, in 'The Shirley Country', an article for the Brontë Society in July, 1897, tells us that in January 1831, when Charlotte was nearly 15, she 'went as pupil to Roe Head [Mirfield], to Miss Wooler's School, and in 1835, she again entered the house as assistant, and there is no doubt that while here she accumulated the facts and literary landscape of her story.'

While at school, she became a friend of Mary Taylor, who described her first sight of Charlotte, 'coming out of a covered cart, in very old-fashioned clothes, and looking very cold and miserable . . . She looked a little old woman, so short-sighted that she always appeared to be seeking something . . . She was very nervous, and spoke with a strong Irish accent.'

Mary's father was a wool cloth manufacturer, and the family lived at the Red House, Gomersall – the Briarmaines of the novel. Charlotte wrote that 'the society of the Taylors ["brash, confident, articulate, frank, democratic, republican and nonconformist"] is one of the most rousing pleasures I have known.'

There can be little doubt that Charlotte's friends influenced the story, though her own father will have done so too, for the story turns on the real events of an attack by Luddites on Rawfolds Mill at Liversedge,

at a time (1812) when Patrick Brontë was 'perpetual curate' at nearby St Peter's, Hartshead.

New labour-saving machinery had led to mass unemployment in Nottingham, Leicester and Derbyshire. On the night of Sunday, April 12, 1812, 100 workers armed with muskets and hatchets attacked Rawfolds and were met with astonishing ferocity. Many were wounded, of the ringleaders some were executed and others transported for life. At about this time Patrick Bronte bought a pistol, fears were rife, and people took sides.

To begin with, the novel is concerned about what the Revolution is doing to the spirit of her people and to the landscape, and the indifference of outsiders (like Malone) to this –

The evening was pitch-dark: star and moon were quenched in grey rain-clouds – gray they would have been by day, by night they looked sable. Malone was not a man given to close observation of Nature; her changes passed, for the most part, unnoticed by him: he could walk miles on the most varying April day, and never see the beautiful dallying of earth and heaven; never mark when a sunbeam kissed the hill-tops, making them smile clear in green light, or when a shower wept over them, hiding their crests with the low-hanging, dishevelled tresses of a cloud. He did not, therefore, care to contrast the sky as it now appeared – a muffled, streaming vault, all black, save where, towards the east, the furnaces of Stilbro' ironworks threw a tremulous lurid shimmer on the horizon – with the same sky on an unclouded frosty night. He did not trouble himself to ask where the constellations and the planets were gone, or to regret the 'black-blue' serenity of the air-ocean which those white islets stud; and which another ocean, of heavier and denser element, now rolled below and concealed.

But in the end, like other writers of the Industrial Revolution (Gaskell, Eliot, Dickens), Charlotte declares herself in favour of change, and her story drifts off into romantic considerations, strangely unattached to her earlier themes and their declared deep roots.

For her novel *Jane Eyre*, Charlotte borrowed the house and grounds of another friend of hers from Roe Head School. Rydings, the Thornfield Hall of the novel, was Ellen Nussey's family home. Jane's world is built around it, and varied moods of nature are used to charge that world, which, like the Hall itself, she clearly feels benefits from having someone in control, 'A rill from the outer world was flowing through it. It

Ellen Nussey's house, Rydings, is Thornfield Hall in Jane Eyre.

had a master; for my part, I liked it better.'

Unlike her genius sister Emily, Charlotte, who had been so surprised by Wuthering Heights, does not allow nature sway. She uses nature, but emblematically, as a device. When Mrs Reed has denounced Jane's character to Mr Brocklehurst, and Jane is enraged (or would like to be) –

A ridge of lighted heath, alive, glancing, devouring, would have been a great emblem of my mind when I accused Mrs Reed; the same ridge, black and blasted after the flames are dead, would have represented as meetly my subsequent condition when half an hour's silence and reflection had shown me the dreariness of my hated and hating position.

On Midsummer Eve, Jane needs the garden of Thornfield Hall to express what she cannot.

A splendid Midsummer shone over England: skies so pure, suns so radiant as were then seen in long succession, seldom favour, even singly, our wave-girt land. It was as if a band of Italian days had come from the South, like a flock of glorious passenger birds, and lighted to rest them on the cliffs of Albion. The hay was all got in; the fields round Thornfield were green and shorn; the roads white and baked; the trees were in their dark prime; hedge and wood,

full-leaved and deeply tinted, contrasted well with the sunny hue of the cleared meadows between.

On Midsummer-eve, Adèle, weary with gathering wild strawberries in Hay Lane half the day, had gone to bed with the sun. I watched her drop asleep, and when I left her, I sought the garden.

It was now the sweetest hour of the twenty-four: 'day its fervid fires had wasted', and dew fell cool on panting plain and scorched summit. Where the sun had gone down in simple state – pure of the pomp of clouds – spread a solemn purple, burning with the light of red jewel and furnace flame at one point, on one hill-peak, and extending high and wide, soft and still softer, over half heaven. The east had its own charm of fine, deep blue, and its own modest gem, a rising and solitary star: soon it would boast the moon; but she was yet beneath the horizon.

I walked a while on the pavement; but a subtle, well-known scent – that of a cigar – stole from some window; I saw the library casement open a hand-breadth; I knew I might be watched thence; so I went apart into the orchard. No nook in the grounds more sheltered and more Eden-like; a very high wall shut it out from the court on one side; on the other a beech avenue screened it from the lawn. At the bottom was a sunk fence, its sole separation from lonely fields: a winding walk, bordered with laurels and terminating in a giant horse-chestnut, circled at the base by a seat, led down to the fence. Here one could wander unseen. While such honeydew fell, such silence reigned, such gloaming gathered, I felt as if I could haunt such shade for ever; but in treading the flower and fruit parterres at the upper part of the enclosure, enticed there by the light the now rising moon cast on this more open quarter, my step is stayed – not by sound, not by sight, but once more by a warning fragrance.

Sweet-brier and southernwood, jasmine, pink, and rose have long been yielding their evening sacrifice of incense; this new scent is neither of shrub nor flower; it is – I know it well – it is Mr Rochester's cigar. I look round and listen. I see trees laden with ripening fruit. I hear a nightingale warbling in a wood half a mile off: no moving form is visible, no coming step audible; but that perfume increases: I must flee. I make for the wicket leading to the shrubbery, and I see Mr Rochester entering. I step aside into the ivy recess; he will not stay long: he will soon return whence he came, and if I sit still he will never see me.

But no – eventide is as pleasant to him as to me, and this antique garden as attractive; and he strolls on, now lifting the gooseberry-tree branches to look at the fruit, large as plums, with which they are laden; now taking a ripe cherry from the wall; now stooping towards a knot of flowers, either to inhale their fragrance or to admire the dew-beads on their petals. A great moth goes humming by me; it alights on a plant at Mr Rochester's foot: he sees it, and bends to examine it.

'Now he has his back towards me,' thought I, 'and he is occupied too; perhaps, if I walk softly, I can slip away unnoticed.'

I trod on an edging of turf that the crackle of the pebbly gravel might not betray me: he was standing among the beds at a yard or two distant from where I had to pass; the moth apparently engaged him. 'I shall get by very well,' I meditated. As I crossed his shadow, thrown long over the garden by the moon, not yet risen high, he said quietly, without turning –

'Jane, come and look at this fellow.'

Later, after Rochester has asked Jane to marry him, Weather enters to articulate their fate:

But what had befallen the night? The moon was not yet set, and we were all in shadow: I could scarcely see my master's face, near as I was. And what ailed the chestnut tree? it writhed and groaned; while wind roared in the laurel walk, and came sweeping over us.

'We must go in,' said Mr Rochester: 'the weather changes. I could have sat with thee till morning, Jane.'

'And so,' thought I, 'could I with you.' I should have said so, perhaps, but a livid, vivid spark leapt out of a cloud at which I was looking, and there was a crack, a crash, and a close rattling peal; and I thought only of hiding my dazzled eyes against Mr Rochester's shoulder.

The rain rushed down. He hurried me up the walk, through the grounds, and into the house; but we were quite wet before we could pass the threshold. He was taking off my shawl in the hall, and shaking the water out of my loosened hair, when Mrs Fairfax emerged from her room. I did not observe her at first, nor did Mr Rochester. The lamp was lit. The clock was on the stroke of twelve.

'Hasten to take off your wet things,' said he; 'and before you go, good-night – good-night, my darling.'

He kissed me repeatedly. When I looked up, on leaving his arms, there stood the widow, pale, grave, and amazed. I only smiled at her, and ran upstairs. 'Explanation will do for another time,' thought I. Still, when I reached my chamber, I felt a pang at the idea she should even temporarily misconstrue what she had seen. But joy soon effaced every other feeling; and loud as the wind blew, near and deep as the thunder crashed, fierce and frequent as the lightning gleamed, cataract-like as the rain fell during a storm of two hours' duration, I experienced no fear and little awe. Mr Rochester came thrice to my door in the course of it, to ask if I was safe and tranquil: and that was comfort, that was strength for anything.

Before I left my bed in the morning, little Adèle came running in to tell me that the great horse-chestnut at the bottom of the orchard had been struck by lightning in the night, and half of it split away.

MERSEYSIDE

Liverpool
Britain's great seaport on the north bank of the Mersey, also fed by the M57 and M62.

'You've never said where you come from?',
'Manchester,' replied she.
'Eh, then, you've a power of things to see. Liverpool beats Manchester hollow, they say. A nasty, smoky hole, bean't it? Are you bound to live there?'
'Oh yes! it's my home.'
'Well, I don't think I could abide a home in the middle of smoke. Look there! now you see the river! That's something now you'd give a deal for in Manchester. Look!'
And Mary did look, and saw down an opening made in the forest of masts belonging to the vessels in dock, the glorious river, along which white-sailed ships were gliding with the ensigns of all nations not 'braving the battle,' but telling of the distant lands, spicy or frozen, that sent to that mighty mart for their comforts or their luxuries; she saw small boats passing to and fro on that glittering highway, but she also saw such puffs and clouds of smoke from the countless steamers that she wondered at Charley's intolerance of the smoke of Manchester. Across the swing-bridge, along the pier, – and they stood breathless by a magnificent dock, where hundreds of ships lay motionless during the process of loading and unloading. The cries of the sailors, the variety of languages used by the passers-by, and the entire novelty of the sight compared with anything which Mary had ever seen, made her feel most helpless and forlorn.

In *Mary Barton* (1848), Elizabeth Gaskell catches the spirit of Liverpool perfectly, and in some important ways it has not changed radically since then. As a port open to the world, it has never been too inward looking or taken itself overly seriously. The spirit of its people has been its saving grace. Even after the near collapse of the Docks earlier this century, the city's definitive entertaining sense of humour turned its working class (Dickens's Mercantile Jack) into heroes and made it the hub of a youth culture that spread worldwide.

When Daniel Defoe turned up in 1680 he was amused to be picked up by some Liverpudlian comedian and carried on his shoulders from the now famous ferry to the shore:

I entered Lancashire at the remotest western point of that county, having been at West-Chester upon a particular occasion, and from thence ferry'd over from the Cestrian Chersonesus, as I have already call'd it, to Liverpoole. This narrow slip of land, rich, fertile and full of inhabitants, tho' formerly, as authors say, a meer waste and desolate forest, is called Wirall, or by some Wirehall. Here is a ferry over the Mersee, which, at full sea, is more than two miles over. We land on the flat shore on the other side, and are contented to ride through the water for some length, not on horseback but on the shoulders of some honest Lancashire clown, who comes knee deep to the boat side, to truss you up, and then runs away with you, as nimbly as you desire to ride . . .

Liverpoole is one of the wonders of Britain, and that more, in my opinion, than any of the wonders of the Peak; the town was, at my first visiting it, about the year 1680, a large, handsome, well built and encreasing or thriving town; at my second visit, anno 1690, it was much bigger than at my first seeing it, and, by the report of the inhabitants, more than twice as big as it was twenty years before that; but, I think, I may safely say at this my third seeing it, for I was surpriz'd at the view, it was more than double what it was at the second; and, I am told, that it still visibly encreases both in wealth, people, business and buildings: What it may grow to in time, I know not.

Tour Through the Whole Island of Britain by Daniel Defoe

Nearly two centuries later, when Dickens arrived in the guise of the *Uncommercial Traveller* (1860), walking the dock-quays, 'keeping watch on poor Mercantile Jack', by which he meant the lowliest worst-treated sailor, he discovered a city that knew how to enjoy itself:

For miles and hours we explored a strange world, where nobody ever goes to bed, but everybody is eternally sitting up, waiting for Jack. This exploration was among a labyrinth of dismal courts and blind alleys, called Entries, kept in wonderful order by the police, and in much better order than by the corporation: the want of gaslight in the most

dangerous and infamous of these places being quite unworthy of so spirited a town. I need describe but two or three of the houses in which Jack was waited for as specimens of the rest. Many we attained by noisome passages so profoundly dark that we felt our way with our hands.

One hundred years after Dickens, the poetry of Henri, McGough, and Patten, given academic respectability as a 'school', The Liverpool Poets, joined the music of the Beatles, who matched these poets' humour and desire to entertain with serious messages not too far 'underground'.

The daughters of Albion
    arriving by underground at Central Station
    eating hot ecclescakes at the Pierhead
    writing 'Billy Blake is fab' on a wall in Mathew St

    taking off their navyblue schooldrawers and
    putting on nylon panties ready for the night

From 'Mrs Albion You've Got a Lovely Daughter' (1967)
by Adrian Henri

STAFFORDSHIRE

Stoke on Trent
From 1910 a borough incorporating Hanley, Burslem, Tinstall, Longton, Fenton, and Stoke, known as the Potteries.

Five contiguous towns – Turnhill, Bursley, Hanbridge, Knype, and Longshaw – united by a single winding thoroughfare some eight miles in length, have inundated the valley like a succession of great lakes. Of these five Bursley is the mother, but Hanbridge is the largest. They are mean and forbidding of aspect – sombre, hard-featured, uncouth; and the vaporous poison of their ovens and chimneys has soiled and shrivelled the surrounding country till there is no village lane within a league but what offers a gaunt and ludicrous travesty of rural charms. Nothing could be more prosaic than the huddled, red-brown streets; nothing more seemingly remote from romance. Yet be it said that romance is even here – the romance which, for those who have an eye to perceive it, ever dwells amid the seats of industrial manufacture, softening the coarseness, transfiguring the squalor, of these mighty alchemic operations.

Anne of the Five Towns by Arnold Bennett

Arnold Bennett, born 1867 near Hanley, left for London on March morning in 1889, and couldn't get away fast enough. To be fair to the potteries, it wasn't just the place he wanted to escape, he had been under some pressure from his father, a erstwhile potter and pawnshop owner, who had made good as a solicitor. At home, while his father had been articled, there had been 'an atmosphere of grim sticking to it, of never being beaten by circumstance.' When he qualified, he regarded himiself as a self-made man, and the pressure was on his son to be the same.

In fact Bennett never deserted his homeland in his heart. 'It is on record,' writes Alan Sillitoe, 'that during his life away from the Five Towns he could never resist – when out at dinner – lifting the plates to look at the Potteries trademark'. The Five Towns, were, of course, Henley, Burslem, Tinstall, Longton, and Stoke (Fenton was left out apparently because he preferred the sound of 5), and Bennett's act of faith was their wholesale promotion to the world. He pulls none of his punches in the Five Towns novels, but at the same time allows that the spirit of the industrial north could ignite the mind of a Clayhanger:

To the south of them, about a mile and a half off, in the wreathing mist of the Cauldon Bar Ironworks, there was a yellow gleam that even the capricious sunlight could not kill, and then two rivers of fire sprang from the gleam and ran in a thousand delicate and lovely hues down the side of a mountain of refuse. They were emptying a few tons of molten slag at the Cauldon Bar Ironworks. The two rivers hung slowly dying in the misks of smoke. They reddened and faded, and you thought they had vanished, and you could see them yet, and then they escaped the baffled eye, unless a cloud aided them for a moment against the sun; and their ephemeral but enchanting beauty had expired for ever.

'Now!' said Edwin sharply.

'One minute ten seconds,' said the Sunday, who had snatched out his watch, an inestimable contrivance with a centre-seconds hand. 'By Jove! That was a good 'un.'

In that head of his a flame burnt that was like an altar-fire, a miraculous and beautiful phenomenon, than which nothing is more miraculous nor more beautiful over the whole earth. Whence had it suddenly sprung, that flame? After years of muddy inefficiency, of contentedness with the second-rate and the dishonest, that flame astoundingly bursts forth, from a hidden, unheeded spark that none had

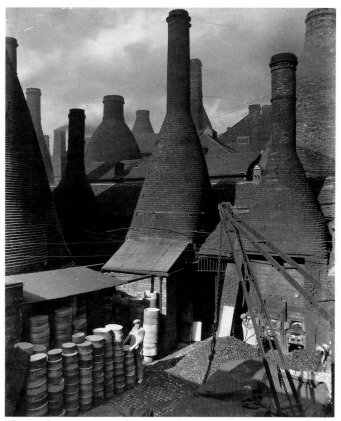

The landscape – 'an architecture of ovens and chimneys.'

ever thought to blow upon. It burst forth out of a damp jungle of careless habits and negligence that could not possibly have fed it. There is little to encourage it. The very architecture of the streets shows that environment has done naught for it: ragged brickwork, walls finished anyhow with saggars and slag; narrow uneven alleys leading to higgledy-piggledy workshops and kilns; cottages transformed into factories and factories into cottages, clumsily, hastily, because nothing matters so long as 'it will do'; everywhere something forced to fulfil, badly, the function of something else; in brief, the reign of the slovenly makeshift, shameless, filthy, and picturesque. Edwin himself seemed no tabernacle for that singular flame. He was not merely untidy and dirty – at his age such defects might have excited in a sane observer uneasiness by their absence; but his gestures and his gait were untidy. He did not mind how he walked. All his sprawling limbs were saying: 'What does it matter, so long as we get there?' The angle of the slatternly bag across his shoulders was an insult to the flame. And yet the flame burned with serene and terrible pureness.

Clayhanger by Arnold Bennett

MANCHESTER

Major commercial city, 35m east of Liverpool, 15m from J20 of the M6, 5m from J18 of the M62.

For several miles before they reached Milton, they saw a deep lead-coloured cloud hanging over the horizon in the direction in which it lay. It was all the darker from contrast with the pale grey-blue of the wintry sky; for in Heston there had been the earliest signs of frost. Nearer to the town the air had a faint taste and smell of smoke; perhaps, after all, more a loss of the fragrance of grass and herbage than any positive taste or smell. Quickly they were whirled over long, straight, hopeless streets of regularly-built houses, all small and of brick. Here and there a great oblong many-windowed factory stood up, like a hen among her chickens, puffing out black 'unparliamentary' smoke, and sufficiently accounting for the cloud which Margaret had taken to foretell rain.

North and South (1855) by Elizabeth Gaskell

Cotton wagon unloading. 'I would rather be a man toiling, suffering – nay, failing and successless – here, than lead a dull propserous life in the old worn grooves of . . . the South, with their slow days of careless ease.' North and South *by Elizabeth Gaskell*

Nature vs Man
It was a town of red brick, or a brick that would have been red if the smoke and ashes had allowed it; but as matters stood it was a town of unnatural red and black like the painted face of a savage. It was a town of machinery and tall chimneys, out of which interminable serpents of smoke trailed themselves for ever and ever, and never got uncoiled. It had a black canal in it, and a river that ran purple with ill-smelling dye, and vast piles of building full of windows where there was a rattling and a trembling all day long, and where the piston of the steam-engine worked monotonously up and down, like the head of an elephant in a state of melancholy madness. It contained several large streets all very like one another, and many small streets still more like one another, inhabited by people equally like one another, who all went in and out at the same hours, with the same sound upon the same pavements, to do the same work . . .

The fairy palaces burst into illumination . . . A clattering of clogs upon the pavement; a rapid ringing of bells; and all the melancholy mad elephants, polished and oiled up for the day's monotony, were at their heavy exercise again.

Stephen bent over his loom, quiet, watchful, and steady. A special contrast, as every man was in the forest of looms where Stephen worked, to the crashing, smashing, tearing piece of mechanism at which he laboured. Never fear, good people of an anxious turn of mind, that Art will consign Nature to oblivion. Set anywhere, side by side, the work of GOD and the work of man; and the former, even though it be a troop of Hands of very small account, will gain in dignity from the comparison.

Hard Times (1854) by Charles Dickens

There are many battles being fought in the Mancunian landscape of Mrs Gaskell's *North and South* – between the cultures of the North and the South, between the two classes in the North, between Nature and aspiring New-nature (industry), as well as between Catholics, Protestants and Dissenters.

Courtyard of Long Millgate, Manchester, 1875.

Dickens reduced it to a battle between Nature and Man, a 'civilising' process in which the former gained 'indignity' from the latter. His Coketown (actually a blend of Preston and Manchester) was 'a triumph of fact . . . it had no greater taint of fancy in it than Mrs Gradgrind herself.' But not all industrialists were as unimaginative as Gradgrind, and perhaps there are two sorts of 'natural': nature as absence of artifice, and new-nature when artifice has become so completely absorbed that it becomes natural; today, the culture of the industrial city is with us and can no longer be called un-natural; 'new-natural' has become 'natural'.

Michael Butor may be the only novelist to have conjured with the spirit of Manchester since the Industrial Revolution. *Passing Time* (1961) is a worrying picture of a deepening neurosis, a set of obsessive thought patterns rather than a town. It may now be time for someone else to fix the spirit of the city, thirty-four years on.

'I see men here going about in the streets who look ground down by some pinching sorrow or care – who are not only sufferers but haters.' North and South *by Elizabeth Gaskell*

. . . came at last to Oak Park, full of autumn crocuses amid the grass, where children were playing under their nurses' eye, Oak Park, which takes its name from a magnificent oak tree standing alone among elms and planes with tawny foliage like foxes' and bisons' pelts: I went up to have a closer look at it, while the sun dropped behind the chimneys of the cosy little houses and in the damp air everything took on a crimson haze; its bark seemed made of thick rust or acid-corroded stone, or concrete mingled with coal-dust and lead filings; like the crust that coats old buildings, it seemed to have been deposited by the air of the town.

What a sense of chill and desolation I felt when the keeper in his black, red-braided uniform blew his whistle at me, for I had lingered over-long by the pond, in its cement basin whose cracks were filled in with tar, watching the white, green-splashed ducks swimming about.

I had overstayed the legal hour of sunset, after which nobody may loiter in the parks.

Acknowledgements

Maps
John Flower, Edgeley Park, Guildford, GU5 9DW. Rob Shone (18, 19, 21), 6-8 Northampton Street, London N1 2HY.

Photography
Joe Cornish: Cover shots, 197. National Trust Photographic Library (London)/Joe Cornish: 9, 78b, 79, 89. Tim Hawkins: 7, 46, 52, 56, 57, 66. Derry Brabbs: 176a/b, 177, 178-9, 183a/b, 184a/b, 185a/b, 186. Charlie Waite: 181. Derek Widdicombe: 191. Nick Wright: 16a, 17b, 20, 95, 106. Jeremy Young: 108, 111, 113b, 126a/b, 127a/b, 129, 130a/b, 131, 132. Julian Bajzert: 137, 140, 141, 142a/b, 143. Simon MacBride: 16b, 36, 41, 53, 133, 153, 157, 162, 163, 208. Simon Warner: 149, 210, 213b. Rob Cousins: 40a/b, 44, 61. David Ward: 169, 193. Piers Dudgeon: 12, 26, 29a/b/c, 32, 33a/b, 45, 58, 59, 60a/b, 62a/b, 69, 70, 71a/b, 75, 77, 81a/b, 86a/b, 87a/b, 92a/b, 113a, 116a/b, 120, 121a/b/c, 124a/b, 125a/b, 134a/b, 165a/b, 180, 182, 187a/b/c, 188, 189, 194a/b, 204, 212. David Sillitoe: 103. Hermann Lea: 48, 55, 65. Daphne du Maurier Estate: 22, 23. National Trust Photographic Library (London)/David Norton: 25. National Trust Photographic Library (London)/Will Curwin: 205. Gavin Maxwell/James Watt/Campbell, Thomson & McLaughlin: 145, 146. Images Colour Library, London: 17a, 37, 85a/b, 88, 148, 172a, 173, 200. West Country Tourist Board: 22, 23. Birmingham Museums and Art Gallery: 49 ('The Village Philharmonic' by Stanhope Forbes). Wales Tourist Board: 72, 78a, 80, 84. Oxfordshire County Council Museum Services: 90, 94a/b, 95b, 117, 118a/b. Fitzwilliam Museum, Cambridge: 96 ('Primrose Hill' by John Linnell). The Guardian: 104. The Institute of Agricultural History and Museum of Rural Life, Reading: 115a/b, 54. The Brotherton Collection, Leeds: 128. The Still Moving Picture Company Ltd, Edinburgh: 156a/b, 160, 161, 172b. Glasgow City Library: 166, 167a/b. Southern English Tourist Board: 95a. The Sutcliffe Gallery, Whitby: 192, 195, 196, 198. John Rylands Museum, Manchester: 203. Haworth Parsonage Museum: 211, 215, 216. Yorkshire Tourist Board: 213a, 214. The Evening Sentinel, Stoke-on-Trent: 219. Northern Picture Library: 220, 221a/b. National Maritime Museum, London: 18, 105, 99. Beamish North of England Open Air Museum, Co Durham: 202. Dickens House Museum, London: cover (portrait Charles Dickens). National Portrait Gallery: cover (portrait Emily Bronte). Borough of Tyneside: 200a/b, BBC Hulton Picture Library: 201. Museum of London, 101. Greater London Record Office: 100. British Library: 91. Richmondshire Museums (Richmond, North Yorkshire): 190a/b. Jarrold & Co Ltd: 168. Welholme Galleries, Grimsby: 123a/b.

Text
Peter Ackroyd: *Hawksmoor*; Hamish Hamilton. Stan Barstow: *Next of Kin, A Brother's Tale*; Michael Joseph. Flora Thompson: *Lark Rise to Candelford*; Oxford University Press. Paul Gallico: *The Snow Goose*; Michael Joseph. James Herriot: *If Only They Could Talk*; A M Heath. Daphne du Maurier: *Jamaica Inn, Frenchman's Creek, The Rebecca Notebook, Rebecca*; Gollancz/ Curtis Brown/Daphne du Maurier Estate. Max Beerbohm: *Zuleika Dobson*; Max Beerbohm Estate, Sir Rupert Hart-Davis. Graham Swift: *Waterland*; Adam Thorpe: *Ulverton*; Secker & Warburg. Neil Powell: 'At Little Gidding'; Patricia Beer: 'A Visit to Little Gidding'; Hugh MacDiarmid: *Lucky Poet*, 'A Drunk Man Looks at a Thistle'; Carcanet. Kathleen Raine: Autobiographies (*The Lion's Mouth, The Land Unknown*); Scoob Books. Kathleen Raine: 'Kore', 'The Hyacinth', 'The Northumbrian Sequence'; Golgonooza Press. Arthur Ransome: *The Coot Club, Swallows and Amazons, Autobiography*; Jonathan Cape/The Arthur Ransome Estate. Adrian Henri: 'Mrs Albion You've Got a Lovely Daughter'; Rogers, Coleridge and White. John Fowles: *The French Lieutenant's Woman*; Jonathan Cape/Sheil Land Associates. Fiona Pitt-Kethley: 'Gala Day'; Sheil Land Associates. Catherine Cookson: *Tilly Trotter*; Sheil Land Associates. Sorley Maclean: 'The Island', 'Time, the Deer, is in the Wood at Hallaig'; Random Century. Laurie Lee: *Cider With Rosie*; Edmund Blunden: *The Hop Leaf*; Peters, Fraser & Dunlop. William MacIlvanney: *Laidlaw*; Hodder Headline. Frances Horovitz: 'Glastonbury Tor'; Bloodaxe Books. Iain Sinclair: 'Nicholas Hawksmoor, His Churches', *Downriver*; MBA. Robert Graves: *Goodbye To All That*, 'Rocky Acres'; A P Watt. Dylan Thomas: *Portrait of an Artist as a Young Dog*, 'Poem in October'; Dent. John Cowper Powys: *A Glastonbury Romance, Maiden Castle, Owen Glendower*; Llewellyn Powys, *Dorset Essays*; Laurence Pollinger. Gavin Maxwell: *Ring of Bright Water*; Penguin/The Gavin Maxwell Estate. Michael Butor: *Passing Time*; T S Eliot: 'The Waste Land', 'East Coker', 'Burnt Norton', 'Little Gidding'; Alison Uttley: *The Country Child*; David Jones: 'The Sleeping Lord'; Faber & Faber. John Betjeman: 'Sunday Afternoon Service in St Enodoc Church, Cornwall'; John Murray. Works by R S Thomas: Macmillan and Bloodaxe, by permission the author. Henry Williamson: *Tarka The Otter*; The Henry Williamson Estate/A M Heath.